Travel with Moon

*Dedicated with fond memories to
Robert (Clob) Kehoe.
1950–2000
Great friend and travelling companion.
Never forgotten.*

MOON

Travel with Moon

Overland to the back of beyond

First published in 2023 by Tony 'Moon' Flood
Co. Wicklow
Ireland

Paperback	ISBN: 978 1 78846 290 7
eBook	ISBN: 978 1 78846 291 4
Amazon paperback	ISBN: 978 1 78846 292 1

Produced by Kazoo Independent Publishing Services
222 Beech Park, Lucan, Co. Dublin
kazoopublishing.com

Kazoo Independent Publishing Services is not the publisher of this work. All rights and responsibilities pertaining to this work remain with Tony 'Moon' Flood.

Kazoo offers independent authors a full range of publishing services. For further details visit kazoopublishing.com

Cover design by Andrew Brown
Printed in the EU

1

"HEY MOON, I'M THINKING OF HEADING TO India," my friend
Clob announced one day.

"Right," I said, "I'm coming with you!"

This was Ireland in the early seventies and there was nothing
much happening. I hadn't a clue what was going on with my life at
the time, so I hopped on the idea. We were in our early twenties,
and keen to expand our horizons – and we were definitely up for
adventure.

We met up again a week later to decide what we needed to bring.
We had about £120 each, from bits of savings and selling a few bits
and pieces. We got a small bag each, a haversack and a small tent.
We headed into Dublin to catch the mailboat to Liverpool. In Lime
Street Station, over a cup of coffee, we checked out the train fares
to London, but we decided to hold on to our money and hitchhike
instead. It was easy getting a lift, and when we arrived in London
we only stayed a day, had a look around, and then headed out of
there to Dover. From Dover we got tickets for Calais, in France.
There was a large hovercraft operating on the channel route at that
time. It was a strange looking beast: huge, with four engines, very
noisy and very fast.

Once in France we headed to Paris by bus, walked around
Paris for a day or two, and then figured we'd head for Amsterdam.
We stopped in Belgium for a couple of days, in a town called De
Panne. Looking for somewhere to stay, we left the town centre
and wandered out to the outskirts where we came upon a lovely

old windmill, which would have been used for grinding corn in its working days. There were doors in the bottom of it, which were open, so we put our gear in there, just keeping our passports and money with us. When we got back into De Panne, we wandered around for a bit and met a few Belgian guys from the area. We got chatting with them and said we'd come back later on and meet them at the bandstand.

Around eight o'clock we arrived back into the square and, sure enough, there they were sitting up on the bandstand, playing guitars and singing. They had a few bottles of wine with them – quite big, more like five-litre jars. We had a couple of glasses of that, and we were all sitting around drinking and singing and playing music. It must've been about nine o'clock when I decided that I had to go and water the horse, so I went up the road to a small grassy area with bushes. I got back ten minutes later and there was no one on the bandstand. I was wondering what had happened, then somebody said the police had come in two vans and taken everyone away. "Oh, God!" I thought, panicking. "What am I going to do now? I don't know anyone; I don't speak the language!" I went back out to the windmill and sat down for a while trying not to freak out, then I came back in around eleven o'clock and they were all sitting back there on the bandstand, singing away and drinking the wine. "Great!" I thought, and I joined right back in.

But half an hour later there were flashing lights, more police vans arrived and they took us all away. They drove us to the police station, sat us down and said, "You Irish people, you can't drink the wine – you go crazy! We'll drink the wine!" They were messing, drinking the wine and shouting at us, "Long-haired people's not welcome around here, you know!" They put Clob sitting in a chair and they were threatening to get scissors and cut his hair, but eventually they just laughed at him and let him go. They told us we shouldn't be in their town, they loaded us back into the van and they drove us out of town, in the opposite direction to where the windmill was, and let us out. They were having fun with us: they put us in front of the van and shouted, "Run!" So we started running and they were beeping the horn and half chasing us, for three or four miles out of town, away from where we were staying.

We ended up having to walk all the way back in to town, and out the far side to the windmill. The Belgian lads were still with us so they ended up staying the night. You could have slept dozens in the bottom of that big windmill. We just sat in there, telling stories and drinking the last of the wine.

IN THE MORNING, WE GOT UP AND went into De Panne, stayed around for a while drinking coffee and chatting to the lads, then went our separate ways.

We got a lift handily enough and once in Amsterdam we headed straight to the main square, just up from the American Express office. It was absolute bedlam! Everyone from everywhere was there. All the heads from every part of America that had been at Woodstock seemed to be there, along with lots of Canadians and Germans, all sorts of nationalities! We stayed for a couple of days, walking around. We made our way to the outskirts again and found a site where they made large water pipes. We found a way to climb up at the back and we put our bags up into the top pipe, covered them up and went back into town. We weren't going to be paying for bed and breakfast or hotels; we hadn't got the money at that time – nobody had.

We had a good time, walking around, getting a beer here and there, and then we found out where the Heineken Brewery was, so we went to that nearly every second day. We'd go on the tour for the free beers, come out, get something to eat, go back to the square and meet all the people. The American Express office was like an international marketplace – you could buy or sell just about anything: vans, sleeping bags, tents … anything you wanted. The Magic Bus was up and running as well: cheap travel all the way to India – and possibly beyond – but we didn't take it up at that time.

We met a couple of Indonesian sailors, from a big ship. I said

The original Magic Bus

I was interested in ships so they brought us back to have a look around. They served up some fantastic food and we had a right time with them! They gave us a large bag of Indonesian ground coffee, which was great because we had an old stainless-steel jug that I had made a long time before, which we used to boil up now and then on an open fire. We hung around for another few days, then it was time to move on.

We headed across into West Germany. There was a delay at the border area so we had to wait around. I was lying on the grass when I suddenly jumped up with a terrible noise in my head. I didn't know what was happening, so I ran and asked one of the border guards for help. He phoned for an ambulance, which whisked me away to the nearest town that had a hospital. What had happened was that an insect had crawled into my ear and made itself at home! The doctor asked me where I was from and told me it could be expensive. I said, "I'm Irish and I haven't got much money." I lay down and there was a lot of noise and squirting and eventually he got the thing out of my ear.

"Ah," he said, "it's free for you! You're Irish, it's okay! No problem! Where do you want to go?"

"I'm going to have to make my way back to the border post: my friend is there waiting, but I don't know where I am."

He said, "Don't worry! The ambulance will bring you back." I thanked him and climbed back into the ambulance, whizzed back up the autobahn and got out at the border post.

We were still sitting around that evening, talking to the border guard. I asked, "Do you mind if we go across the field to that house over there to get boiling water? I want to make some coffee."

"Go ahead," he said. So off we went across the field, up to the house, knocked on the door and asked them if we could have hot water to make coffee.

"Oh no," they insisted, "keep your own coffee, we'll make the coffee." They not only filled our jug with coffee, but they gave us a big box of sandwiches as well.

The border guard was laughing when he saw this. "Now I know how you guys do it, how you travel around so freely!"

We found German people very, very easy to get on with. Hitchhiking was incredibly easy in Germany.

We got through the border and headed further into Germany. We were hitchhiking down past Cologne when two young German guys in an old Volkswagen pulled up beside us. We asked them where they were going and they told us they were going to a little log cabin up in the Alps, belonging to their grandfather. It wasn't that far: just a couple of hours' drive. I said, "We'll go with you, so." At the Austrian border, the guards just wanted to see our passports and how much money we had, and then they let us go on with the lads. Driving up through the Alps, the roads were winding up and up through spectacular scenery. I never thought I'd see anything like it in my life.

There was a river running by the cabin, with ice cold water straight from the top of the mountain. They were really good guys. We had a few beers that had been chilled in the icy water and we sat around chatting for a couple of hours. They told us they were in the military, doing their compulsory service, but they were

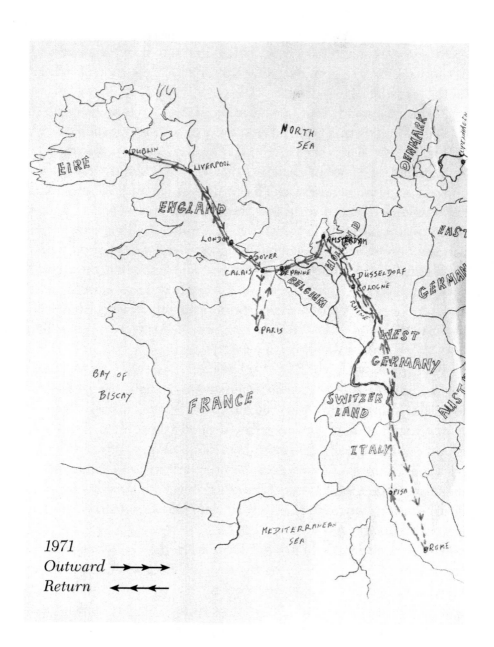

1971
Outward →→→
Return ←←←

on leave for a week or two. We didn't believe they were soldiers because they had long hair, but they said it was allowed, as long as they kept it tied up when they were in uniform. We had some more beers, then we had a lovely meal that evening.

After a great night's sleep, we got up in the morning and we said to the lads, "We're goin' to climb up a bit further and see what's there – do a bit of exploring."

"Okay," they said, "but be careful now, don't go too far up."

The ground wasn't covered in snow, just a bit lying when we got up higher. We were very close to the border between Austria and Switzerland. We couldn't believe what we saw when we got higher up the mountain. There was a large sign which had "Austria" and "Switzerland" printed on it, and there, embedded in the sign, was what looked like a bullet cut in half. Strange looking sign! That was the border. It was amazing being up there: we walked around for a couple of hours in the crisp clean air, and when we arrived back down to the cabin there was a nice little stove lighting. The lads produced a bottle of home-made schnapps, made from wild flowers. We'd never tasted anything like it! We spent four or five days there, then it was time to move on again.

We came down from there and headed back into Germany. We spent a good while there, but there wasn't much going on – no festivals or anything in most of the towns at the time – but some of the markets were amazing. You'd need transport to buy stuff though, and we were holding on to our money. We were living on a budget of about two pounds a day at the time. That wasn't including accommodation, because we never really stayed in any hostels or anything like that, just in the houses of people we met, if we were invited.

We were sitting in a bar near Dusseldorf, having a beer beside the Rhine, when a guy came over to us. He said his name was Hans, and that he was captain of a boat. We said, "Ah, good, good, good," but we didn't really have a word of German, and he had very little English. He bought us a beer and eventually, between the bartender and him and Clob and myself, we worked out that he was looking for two people to help out on the boat, doing a bit of cleaning and cooking. It sounded good to us, so we had a few beers with him, and we went with him back to his boat. It was a big barge full of goods he was bringing up the Rhine. He showed us a little cabin where we could bunk up, then he showed us where everything was. It was getting late, so we had a little bit to eat and some coffee, then he just showed me where the fridge was, what he usually had for meals, and where the coffee was. He liked good coffee.

It was my first job as a chef: he would give me his menu for the day each morning, how he wanted his eggs cooked, which sausage for lunch, and so on. Clob got the job of cleaning the galley and the wheelhouse, and cleaning all the windows. We didn't have to do too much, probably two or three hours' work a day, as we headed off up the Rhine. It was absolutely amazing chugging along there, past picturesque houses and little villages.

Every evening we pulled up, not always at a town, sometimes just at the riverbank. We'd get out and have a walk around, come back later and make dinner. We'd always have a glass of wine, then a few beers later on. When we pulled in at a big town we'd dock overnight, have dinner around eight or nine o'clock, then we'd all go into a bar, and we never once had to put our hand in our pockets when we were working on that barge. He would always buy us two or three beers each, and we'd sit around, doing our best to have a chat, mainly using sign language, but it was a fantastic experience. We continued all the way to the Austrian border – it must have taken about two weeks. We got off the boat there as we were heading for Italy. It was sad leaving Hans – such a nice man. I had an old bugle I used to carry around with me and, after we had shaken hands, I ended up giving the bugle to him. "That's for your wheelhouse," I told him. He couldn't believe it. He loved it! We said our farewells and took off for the border.

WE FELT LIKE MILLIONAIRES WHEN WE CHANGED our money
for lire; you got thousands for a fiver! Food was cheap so, although it
was tight, we had no problem surviving on what we had. Eventually
we got a lift. We got a good way down in to Italy when the driver
said he was turning off, so we decided to get out there and look for
a lift to Rome. We got picked up by a Fiat 500 – a lovely little car.
Clob got into the back and I sat in front. It was pretty hot so we
had shorts on. Your man could speak a little bit of English. "Oooh
you're Irish? I've been in Dublin." Then he started getting a bit
funny, going on about Irish boys, and I looked at Clob and Clob
looked at me.

We realised there was something weird going on. With that he
put his hand on my bare leg!

"Hey!" I yelled. "You don't touch either of us. Stop the car!"

He did stop the car, we got out and there was a bit of an
argument.

I said, "We're not getting back in there," so we took our bags
out.

He drove away and that was the end of it. Nothing like that had
ever happened to us before – it was really a bit frightening for a
pair of naïve Irish lads!

We got some food in a small village nearby and waited about
three hours until eventually a Renault pulled up and the driver
said he was going to Rome. A couple of hours later we pulled up
in Rome. It was late enough, so we stayed on the outskirts and

found a little place to camp, put up the tent then caught a bus into the centre. We got off near the Vatican, had a look round there, and then Clob says, "Come on, we'll go up the Spanish Steps." I was laughing about it; I didn't realise they were actually called the Spanish Steps. I didn't know much about Italy! So we went up the Spanish Steps and sat around. By God, it was hot at that time: it was June I think, maybe the beginning of July. We split a can of Coke between us and wandered around the ancient city. We went down to the Colosseum: what an amazing building! It was full of wild cats – the local people used to leave food out for them. We headed to the Circus Maximus, where they used to race chariots. You could still see what was left of the track, but there was a big motorway going through that part of the city. Across from there was a statue of a chariot and horses, up on top of a high walled building, and below that was a little back street full of small restaurants, so we decided we'd have a treat. We sat down in one of these little restaurants, and ordered spaghetti bolognese. They brought a nice big bowl of spaghetti bolognese over to each of us, and a basket of fantastic bread and we got a small carafe of wine. I think it worked out about 700 lire for the lot. If it was in today's euro it wouldn't have been any more than about fifty cent, but then it was more than forty years ago!

We went back and took down the tent and got a bus to a place outside Rome, called Fiumicino, near the airport. There were a lot of little wooden buildings in a row – like a little tourist area – but they were all empty, doors open, broken furniture in some of them, others had very little in them. They seemed abandoned so we decided to stay. We put our bags into one of them, closed the door and went to explore the area. There were a couple of shops and a harbour with a few big boats and yachts moored in it. We stayed there a couple of days, cooking on a little fire on the beach – mainly tins of beans and pots of stew, with Italian bread. Occasionally, we travelled in and out to Rome.

One day we were out walking and saw guys getting down off one of the big yachts. I said to Clob, "I think that looks like Paul McCartney and Ringo and them," and he said, "Are ya mad, or what?"

"No, no," says I, "you wouldn't know now – it could be."

It turned out that it was the Beatles that were on board. We never got to meet them, just found out more about it by going up closer. Later on we met one of the guys who was working on the yacht as a cook, and it turned out he was Irish but he'd been living in London for a long time. It's strange who you meet up with when you're travelling! We had a great time there. Rome was very interesting, and we stayed in Fiumicino for another four or five days, then it was time to move again. We hadn't realised everywhere is so far apart and so big. We'd done two and a half, maybe three thousand miles, since we'd left Ireland. It had been some experience anyhow. We headed out of Rome and said we'd go to Spain. We were joking that Bacardi in Spain would've been about a pound a bottle.

We hitchhiked to Pisa and that was something else: to see the old leaning tower, with the river and the beautiful church beside it. It was a nice little place, and very quiet at that time. We were there a day or two and planning to leave the next day when Clob says, "I think we'll go to mass in the morning before we head off."

This was strange, because we weren't fantastic Catholics. We had gone to mass every Sunday, growing up in Ireland, at least until we were fifteen or sixteen. But anyway, we went to mass in that strange, beautiful church, which has an almost solid gold ceiling, protected by armed police. After mass we sat under the leaning tower and we made a roll with cheese and tomato, which we had with a carton of milk for breakfast.

We were heading out of Pisa, walking down by the riverside on a narrow road with one or two archways on it, and Clob says, "Probably in about a day or two we'll be in Barcelona or somewhere."

With that there was a bang! All I could see was his body flying through the air, over my head and down a bank into the river.

The car hit him so fast that his haversack, which had been hanging on his shoulder, flew off and hit the ground. The round glasses he had been wearing landed on the road in front of me. I jumped over the little railings and crawled down the bank to the river, and all I could see was blood pumping out of the side of his head. He wasn't moving.

18

Terrified, I said, "Jaysus, don't die! You're the only one here speaks English. We're a million miles from nowhere – we could be on the moon! Don't die!"

I managed to haul him onto the riverbank.

By now one or two cars had stopped, but the car that hit him didn't stop for a good distance down the road. People were shouting, "Religion? Priest?"

I shouted, "No, get a doctor, get a doctor."

"Religion? Religion?"

I said, "He's all right. Catholic. Just get a doctor!"

Meanwhile, the driver of the car that hit him and the other fella who was with him came back. I was shouting at them to help me but they were screaming about their clean clothes, so I started flinging mud at them. "Jesus!" I said. "I can't believe this!"

Eventually we got him up onto the edge of the bank, just near where he went over and I could see then his ear was fairly hanging off and there was a hole in the side of his head. He was still unconscious.

At last the police and an ambulance came. The ambulance got him straight in and off to the hospital with me following in the police car, sirens blaring. When we got to the hospital he was taken straight into surgery and I was told to sit and wait. Sure, what else could I do? Eventually they came back with an interpreter who explained, "Your friend is quite seriously injured."

I said, "What am I supposed to do? What can I do?"

"You'll just have to stay here and wait now."

I had to show our passports to the police and they asked where we were from in Ireland, so I gave them our addresses. From what I learned afterwards, the interpreter contacted the British consulate who got in touch with the Irish authorities in Dublin, and the Gardaí went out to Bray and Greystones and explained what had happened to our families.

The police brought me to a youth hostel near the leaning tower, and the lady there said she'd take me in, that I could stay there as long as Clob was in hospital and that it would all be taken care of. She said she would give me a job in the hostel. They gave me a nice room upstairs, let me put my bag in and brought me down into their own dining room area, sat me down there and gave me a bowl of ravioli, bread and a glass of wine. They had a few words of English and I had a couple of words of Italian but we managed. They told me that I could work in the kitchen in the daytime, making up stuff for the evening meals.

She was a beautiful big Italian lady, her husband's name was Luigi and they had two sons. The older one must have been eighteen or twenty – I can't remember his name – but the younger one was called Francisco. He was eight or nine. They were really nice people, very kind to me. That evening I had a meal with them and when I went up to the room, they gave me a can of Coke to bring up and a little radio to keep me company. There wasn't much sleeping done for a day or two. I hadn't a clue what was going to happen. About two o'clock the next day, the police called again and brought me back to the hospital. By this time, Clob had had surgery on his ear and he'd come around. When I went in to see him, I was shocked to see the whole side of his face was black. He had a bandage all around the top of his head. He looked like he'd had the top taken off his head and sewn back on again. He just kept asking, "What happened?" and I'd say, "You'll be alright, you'll be alright," and he'd drift off to sleep. They said he'd be like that for a day or two.

Within a few days I found my own way between the hostel and the hospital and I got myself an old bicycle. I used to cycle around the area on it, getting to know where the shops were. Clob's parents got in touch from Ireland, wanting to know how things were, but other than that it was lonely, walking around, having no one to have a conversation with. There was a small train that used to go to Florence from Pisa. Some weekends I headed up to Florence. I used to spend the afternoon there, walking around. The centre of Florence is amazing: wonderful architecture, beautiful churches, beautiful things. What an amazing place! It was something different from hanging around in Pisa.

One day a couple of English girls arrived in the hostel. Most of the visitors were German, Austrian and Spanish, with a few Italians, so it was great to meet some people I could have a proper chat with. I went out with them that evening for pizza and coffee and the talk turned to what I was doing working in the hostel. I explained about the accident and that Clob was still in hospital. "He's going to be okay," I said, "but it was bad enough. He's lucky to be alive."

"Ah no! Where were you heading?" they asked.

"Barcelona this time," I explained. "Our plan was to travel around as much of Europe as we could. We did have plans for India but we put that on hold. I think you'd need more than a hundred pounds for that!"

Meanwhile, I was learning to cook: how to peel the big fresh plum tomatoes, chopping onions, making up the sauces, how to cook spaghetti properly. I learned a lot in that kitchen and it gave me a real taste for Italian food. She showed me how she made her own bread every day. As much as possible was made in house, very little was bought in. She used to borrow my stainless-steel jug to make coffee in, as her husband used to hide the espresso machine! She wasn't supposed to drink coffee or smoke, so I was also given the job of buying her Kent cigarettes and smuggling them in to her. I used to go to the shop down the street for eggs every second day – two big boxes at a time – and I would bring a trolley down every other day with four large bottles, which would be filled with wine from a barrel. We would have half a glass of wine topped up with water in the middle of the day. I thought it was strange but they said you should be doing that, because it's quite strong. I eventually got used to it.

After about fourteen days, Clob got out of the hospital and came to stay in the hostel. We were upstairs, laughing again. "How do I look?" he wanted to know. "They wouldn't give me a mirror."

"You look kind of strange," I said. "Eventually, when you get the bandages off, you'll see."

We both had beards at the time. When they shaved him, they shaved one side of his beard and the hair off one side of his head and left it long on the other side, and they didn't clip the beard at all.

"You look all right," I said. "A bit funny!"

Eventually he got hold of a mirror and, beJaysus, he freaked out! He didn't even know if he had two ears or one ear at the time. After another week or two, he got the bandages off. I could see a lot of marks round the ear and the side of his head. I was still amazed that he survived. I had definitely thought he wasn't going to live at the time. Another week passed and he was discharged completely, didn't have to attend the hospital any more. He just had to go to the doctor once or twice, to do with the insurance for the crash.

I remember the eldest son in the hostel had one of these new Fiat 500s, and we went with him one day to a little garage down the road. It was a motor shop: they sold big cylinder heads and large exhaust systems that you could put on to these tiny little cars. We may talk about boy racers today, but they had them in Italy back in the early seventies, flying around the place in these little cars. There were mopeds and scooters everywhere as well. We went to a few of the big motorbike shops and different places around looking at cars while we were there.

We must've been there six weeks or more altogether when we were eventually called into the solicitors. What they told us was unbelievable. We barely got the price of the medical bills and two tickets back to Ireland by train and I think there might have been about twenty pounds. Luckily we still had some of our own money.

Before Clob and I left Pisa, we used those train tickets. They were really only meant to be used on the mainline rail, but no one questioned them, so we hopped on the train to Florence and walked around admiring the wonderful architecture and beautiful artworks, walking across the goldsmith's bridge. It's absolutely fantastic, full of little shops, with the people working in them.

We got the train back to Pisa, stayed in the youth hostel that night, then the big event the next day: saying goodbye to all the family. The woman was like a mother to me the whole time I was there and they all treated us like we were family. We were sad to leave, but it was time.

Eventually we headed into Austria. Clob was in good form and we decided to go back to a couple of small villages, near where we had been with the Germans earlier in the year. We got a lift with a couple of long-haired English guys – a Woodstock crowd – in a van. They pulled up in a little town and they told us they were heading further on but we said we were just going to hang around there for a bit. We met a few people in the village, who told us that there was a rock concert on the following Saturday up in the Alps. It wasn't that far up, so on the Saturday we made our way to the concert.

We met the singer with a band called Green Mouse and he asked us, "Where are you from?" When we said, "Ireland," he shouted, "Oh, Irish people!"

They knew of Horslips and Thin Lizzy, and other bands from Ireland, including the Dubliners. He said, "Oh yeah, I know the music but we play mainly Rolling Stones stuff."

Clob said, "Well, Moon used to do a bit of go-go dancing in Ireland," and I said, "Jaysus, I'm not getting up anywhere this time!"

Meanwhile we made our way close to the stage and we each dropped half a tab of acid. An hour or so later, the television aerials started turning into little aeroplanes and flying around. Clob was painstakingly forming a cigarette into a complete circle. When a couple of people offered to light it for him he growled, "I'm not touching it! And neither is anyone else."

Then came the part we had forgotten about: "Moon, the famous go-go dancer from Ireland, come on up to the stage!"

So I giant-stepped my way up to the stage, which, in my acid-induced time warp, seemed to take hours. Willing hands shoved me up there. Well, the craic was mighty because the guys could sing a bit in English, but they weren't in tune and they were missing half the words of "Satisfaction". And I was trying to dance to it, while the crowd seemed to recede and return like waves in the ocean! I attempted to dance to a couple of songs and eventually I was lifted down off the stage, in absolute rag order.

Later that evening, still tripping, we walked back down the mountain. It was dark by now, so when we came to an orchard we laid out our sleeping bags under the trees.

Clob kept going on about vampire bats and Dracula, until an apple hit me on the head and I leapt up, totally freaked out, convinced I was being attacked by vampires! Clob just yawned and mumbled, "Go asleep, Moon! No vampires here."

Next day, back in the village, we met a couple of girls who

lived nearby and they said we could go back to their place. They lived with their mother and father on a small farm. We learned so much about the Austrian houses during our visit. The carts and the animals were underneath the house area; you went up a stairs to the first floor. That was a dining room and sitting room area. There was a big cooker, like a range, and they fried up eggs and gave them to us with bacon – weird bacon, very salty – and a load of bread and big coffees or tea if you wanted it. Talking and joking, I noticed that over the cooker area there were holes in the ceiling. Being inquisitive, I asked them what they were for. They said it was the main bedroom up there, so the heat from the cooker went up through the holes. In the morning they would fold back the rug and take the circles out. No one would walk there as it was in the corner. Then, in the evening, when they were going to bed they just dropped the circles back down, put the rug down and the room stayed warm most of the night. It seemed like a really good idea. I always remembered that, and used it many years later when building the sitting room/bedroom extension on to my own house back in Ireland.

We went back into the village and, as we were hanging around for a few days, we found a lean-to where we put our sleeping bags. The local policeman came along. "You've got twenty-four hours to leave town!" he announced and walked on. He must have been a John Wayne fan or something. Anyhow, he saw us there later and said nothing, so maybe that was all the English he had!

A few days later, we were hitchhiking at the edge of the town and weren't having any luck. There was a Franciscan monastery across the road. We saw the monks, with their brown robes, walking in and out and I went over and asked one if there were any buses out of there, or when would they run.

"Oh, you wouldn't get a bus today! Maybe early in the morning there's a bus leaves here."

It was like living in Kilmacanogue or Roundwood – just a bus now and again. But they asked us where we were from and when we said Ireland they said, "Oh you're refugees!"

"Oh, no, we're not refugees," I said.

"But the war?" They spoke a good bit of English.

"What war? No, no, it's just a kind of unrest, in the north of Ireland," and I tried to explain it, and that we lived in the Republic.

But he said, "Oh, come in anyway."

So we went in and we were sitting talking to them. We said we were trying to get into Germany, as we were heading for Ireland, and they said, "Get something to eat anyhow, first thing."

They were so convinced we were refugees, they gave us between five and eight pounds in Austrian schillings to help us on our way.

When the bus pulled up, we hopped on and said nothing. When we got to just before the German border, your man said, "Tickets please!" We handed them up and he examined them for a bit, looking puzzled. "Eh, they're train tickets," he says.

"Well, we're heading back to Ireland and those are our tickets anyhow."

He just said, "Don't be using them on buses," or something like that.

So, when we got into Germany we got on a train and headed across Germany into Holland. Eventually, we arrived back in Amsterdam. It was getting late in the year at this time, a bit chillier, so we stayed in a "sleep-in". Now sleep-ins, at that time, were brand new. They were like a lower grade youth hostel. You got a mattress on a floor, and if you had your own sleeping bag, well and good, that's what you slept in. We did have sleeping bags, so that was fine. In the morning they gave you a small yoghurt, a coffee, a croissant and a little pot of jam. It was about five shillings at the time, for the bed and breakfast.

We stayed there for two days then we set off for Ostend. From Ostend we took the boat over to Dover, hopped on a train to London, spent a few hours around London and got on another train back to Lime Street station in Liverpool. Back onto the passenger cattle boat, and back to Dublin.

We walked into the city, straight into O'Connell Street. "BeJaysus, some difference," I said. It had been a while since we'd heard people talking English all the time! We ended up in Bewley's on Westmoreland Street. We'd always liked Bewley's coffee shop – great atmosphere and a lovely cup of coffee there.

Afterwards we caught the number forty-five bus that went to

Bray. The conductor with the windey ticket machine came walking around.

"Tickets, please, tickets, please!"

We handed him these two fairly bent-up pieces of paper that were railway tickets from Pisa in Italy – one to Greystones and one to Bray.

He scratched his head in puzzlement. "They're train tickets," he said.

I said, "Well, CIE is CIE."

"You're right too! Stay where you are, you're all right!" he laughed. We looked a bit over the top, I suppose, with our long beards and hair, not to mention Clob's half shave!

When we got into Bray, I said to Clob, "I'll see you later." I walked up to where my mother lived, just outside Bray, near Ardmore Studios, and arrived at the house. I'd young sisters there at the time and younger brothers.

"Ahh, how yous doin'?" It was amazing – they went stone mad!

"Where were you and what's happening?"

"Ah, things are great. Just had a good time, that's what we had – except for the accident." And then it was into a bath, big hot dinner and into bed. I must've slept for two days.

I got a lend of the brother's car and I drove out to Greystones, to Clob's parents, to see how he was. Mr and Mrs Kehoe – they were lovely people! Mrs Kehoe thought I'd saved his life! I probably helped, but she told me I'd never have to pray again, that she'd pray for me for the rest of her life. But anyhow, we got on well. We went down to the Beach House bar in Greystones; we had a couple of pints and a good chat. So, we were back to the old way of life for now, but thinking about what was going to happen next.

4

AFTER TWO WEEKS AT HOME, THE ITCH for travel was returning. We hadn't seen what we wanted to see yet, so we started planning to hit the road again.

When Clob and myself were back in Ireland, we passed Christmas there and then we had a good chat. We were going to take a bit of time, get our money together and get our own transport together, so it would take a few months. I'd served my time as a coppersmith and sheet metal worker and I'd often sell copper pieces – bangles and different things – to a small boutique in Bray called Myrtle's. I made hearts out of silver spoons and stuff like that as well. I also had a small contract with a building company to repair the scaffolding that was cracked or broken, fixing their dumpers and bits and pieces. We always had a small workshop at home where we had welding plants and equipment, so I could use that. Clob's brother had a butcher's shop where he was able to get part-time work.

Eventually, Clob bought a high roof Transit and he'd do a vegetable run to the market for the shop three days a week, so he was making some money. I was making a good bit of money too, so we were planning to convert the van into a sort of camper.

The van was parked up at my mother's house while we were checking it out – figuring out what kind of layout we could put into it. We decided to put a large collapsible bunk bed that folded into a couch with a hinging mechanism on one side. I was organising getting the materials together. We'd pick up two smallish mattresses that wouldn't be too heavy, and then we'd have a storage area to go in on the other side, and we'd pick up a small two-ring cooker with a grill. We started getting all this together. I had a lot of stuff in the shed at the time. I would work on the frame of the fit-out in the evening time. We talked about the mechanical end of things too. It was a Ford Transit petrol, so I reckoned we'd get a decent sized toolbox and a workshop manual, a set of plugs, an oil filter, rotary arm, air filter, a couple of sets of points and stuff like that. We'd bring all of them with us because we mightn't find those parts too easily where we were going.

When the bunks were almost together, we picked up the cooker. It worked okay, but sometimes we had to fiddle with the jets on the grill. I cleaned it all up. We put in a table that hinged down as well – most of the stuff would hinge down out of the way. We had a rack built in at the front that would hold a stereo system. We had quite a few tapes, so we made a box to fit them into.

We had been working on it for almost six weeks and stuff was almost ready to go into the van. Next, we were going to build a large rack over the front of the cab with a ladder down the side and make brackets for a jerry can on one back door. There were two half back doors, and the top part of the roof – where it was high – opened outwards, which was good for ventilation. I reckoned we'd make the front rack area out of three-quarter box section and two-by-two-inch mesh, because we were going to put an extra fuel tank up there and two gas bottles would be built into one corner of it, with room for a large tarpaulin that we would take with us.

It was all coming together. Clob was very happy again; he was getting on well after the accident. This time we intended to make a big move. It would be great to get on to the Continent: totally different from what was happening in Ireland at the time. We were working away on the camper each evening when we had time. Our parents didn't mind. Clob's parents were not really upset, they knew that he was old enough to know what he wanted to do.

We put in the bottom bed area and it was bolted in place. It was fairly solid, with enough room underneath to put sliding boxes of clothes and shoes, tool kits and everything else we would need. We hung up a couple of bags each, like Christmas stockings, one for socks and one for underpants. Under the other end, where the presses went at the front, we were going to have boxes of food. We were going to take a couple of boxes of Heinz beans and peas, two or three boxes of Erin instant mash and two boxes of Irish stew. Water tanks were built into the roof area, beside the gas bottles. We had another water tank inside with a tap, which you could slide in and out, and a small basin for washing. There was no complete water system in it. We put two extra lights inside in the back and we had two batteries. We had an idea of what we were building but had only ever seen photos of them and didn't know much about campers. This one wouldn't have windows in the side, but the back opened up to let daylight in it, and the front was open. There was no bulkhead so you could walk through from the front seats – it was quite good that way. It had a sliding door on the side, which was another great benefit. It only needed another three or four weeks. The tyres were all perfect on it.

Clob was working in the shop at the time, three days a week; the vegetable run was finished with now. I was still doing a bit of welding and still selling a bit of copper jewellery. I had a big old British motorbike, a 350 Velocette, that I was going to sell as well. I reckoned we would need at least £300 each this time, and I knew that I could get a day's work here and there as we travelled. Clob was a tailor by trade, which made it harder to pick up casual work, but you could get welding work quite a few places. We planned to take off at the end of May 1972, directly into Liverpool.

With only a week left, everything was hotting up. The rack was finished, extra fuel tanks were in, gas bottles in position and water tank on the roof in position; music working properly, lights were all okay; full service done: new plugs and points, oil change. We reckoned that should get us about 6,000 miles without hassle. I had all the spare bits in boxes. Money was coming in: there was a guy buying the bike, supposed to come the next Saturday. I was hoping to get about £180 for it: it was quite a nice bike.

I got £175 for the bike in the end and I had another £150, so I was well on the way. In the end, I had £350 put away so I changed £150 into dollars and the rest into English pounds. It wasn't a great idea carrying the Irish pound onto the Continent – it wouldn't always be recognised. We didn't use traveller's cheques, we just used cash. Clob had roughly the same and reckoned he'd have another hundred by the weekend. We had everything we needed: we brought heavy clothes and light clothes, because we were going to be away for a while. Our passports were ready and we'd got our vaccination shots. It was a good idea to have that sort of thing if you were going to be hitting Morocco or even if you were going to Turkey or Iran.

5

ON THE SATURDAY MORNING WE WERE UP early, into Dublin and drove the van onto the boat. Our adventure was in full swing. Next morning the van comes off the boat and we're passing Lime Street station again. It was something else just hopping into our own van and driving: no more scrabbling together train fares or hitching on the side of the road.

We were heading for Dover again. We didn't bother with London this time round. We got the Ostend ferry and landed back in Belgium. We headed straight down to Amsterdam and this time we were going back to a place we knew a little bit about.

We arrived into the red-light area, close to the flea market. There was a decent bit of parking down there on the canal, so we pulled up there and locked up the van. We went down to the flea market and had a look around: there was a lot of good stuff in it. We went up the town then – up to the Dam, the centre. The American Express office was the same: big crowd around, a lot of people in the square, loads of Americans, some English, quite a few Germans; everything was still for sale in the American Express windows. We decided to stay in Amsterdam for three or four weeks. In the evening we went back to the van, on went the cooker, boiled up a few spuds, fried a few sausages and the like. We'd a load of food with us at the time, so it was much like sitting at home eating. In the evening, we'd go to the late night supermarkets, which we didn't have in Ireland then, where you could buy a box of beer. Once you had empty bottles to exchange, they were working out at less than ten pence; you got ten bottles for a pound. We'd have a few beers in the van then go for a walk around the town.

After a week we were getting to know the place: what supermarkets to buy in, what cheese to buy and what breads we liked. We could live cheaply because of the van. We'd buy milk, bread, potatoes – sometimes rice. Meat was quite dear so didn't eat that much; now and again we'd make a big pot of stew that lasted two days.

One day we got talking to a fella who was doing some welding. I said, "I'm a welder myself, but we're heading off for a while now – should be back in a few months."

"I'm often around in this place," says he. He gave me his name and his home number. "Get in touch if you ever want a day or two's work. There's plenty of work on the old barges."

By now we were ready to leave Amsterdam. We headed into Germany, towards Cologne. It was a lovely city, with a beautiful cathedral and lots of huge domes on the hotels and buildings. The autobahns were amazing in Germany. The police drove white Porsches, and they were nicknamed "the white mice": they'd sneak up anywhere. You couldn't get done for speeding, but reckless driving on an autobahn was a serious offence. There'd be a lot of fellas racing on it too. We met the German police quite a few times, but they were always nice to talk to.

We hung around in Germany for a week or two, then we headed down into Austria. We'd been there before, so we just wanted to have another look around. We went into one or two of the small villages up in the hills: nice and peaceful, and away from everybody. We hung around there for a week or two and then headed for France.

A couple of days later we arrived down in Montpelier. It was the grape harvesting season so we went into some of the vineyards looking for work. After a couple of attempts, we found a smallish place, and the man we spoke to told us to come in on Monday, that there'd be a week or two picking there. We were happy as Larry! Nice weather, nice area –we'd park up the van there no bother and take off into town anytime. Montpelier is a big place. Understanding French was an issue though. We could just about ask for a beer!

But we had a job on the Monday. I'd never picked grapes before, but soon got the hang of it. They gave us a basket and a secateurs;

we'd cut all the bunches off, carry them out to the edge and they got loaded into a big trailer. There must have been about fifteen people working there. We'd fill the trailer up in no time, it'd be taken in and come back ready for more.

Grape picking in Montpelier.

At first, lunch was always accompanied by a bottle of wine, but they soon discovered this was not such a good idea, leaving the Irish workers incapable of much activity for the afternoon, so the bottle of wine was moved to the end of the working day!

This went on for two weeks. We were happy enough: we did about six hours a day and made about forty pounds a week. It doesn't sound like much but it was quite a bit at the time – we lived on it no bother anyhow.

Just before we left Montpelier, we put a sign in the window of one of the little local cafes, saying that we were looking for anyone that wanted a lift to Barcelona. We found a Spanish couple, from the middle of Spain, so they took a lift with us and shared some of the petrol expenses. The Transit was quite a thirsty yoke – it did no more than twenty miles to the gallon if you took it easy.

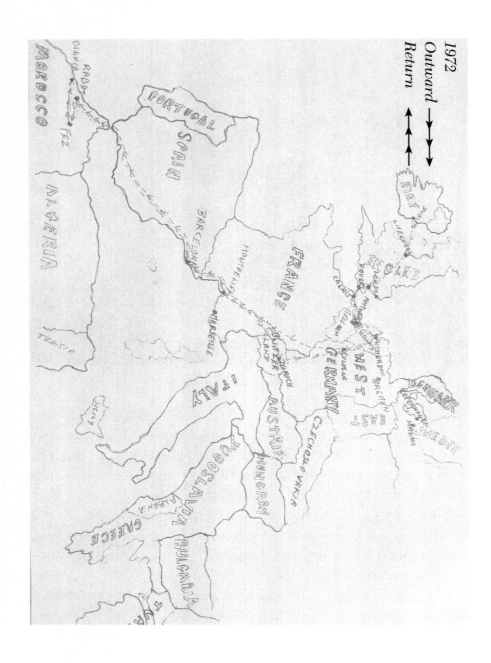

Fuel wasn't too expensive at the time though.

When we got to Barcelona, the American Express building was the first place to call, to see what was happening, what signs were up in the windows and people standing around. We slapped up a sign right away to say we were leaving Barcelona on Wednesday, heading for Morocco. So, on the Wednesday when we went back there, there were two or three people wanting a lift: two to the bottom of Spain and one going to Rabat in Morocco.

WE DROVE ACROSS THE MOUNTAINS FOR DAYS: a nice drive. Heading down through Spain, we saw nothing but orange groves all over the place, so we were eating oranges morning, noon and night! We got to the crossing point and onto the boat with no hassle. But when we got to Morocco, there was a big lecture, then, "Stand to one side! Leave the van! Your hair's too long!"

I couldn't believe this. We'd heard stories, but didn't know much about it. Clob cut about three inches off my hair and I cut three or four inches off his hair. We looked rough enough, but they let us in anyhow! There was a guy called Rikki with us as well who had to get the haircut, and another lad we nicknamed Santana, as he had a huge Afro hairstyle. He just got a jar of Vaseline and plastered the hair down to his scalp with that!

We got down into Rabat and were hanging around there for a while. We met some American soldiers. They were stationed in Germany, but they were down there in a van: one of these very cool looking Volkswagen camper vans. They asked if we wanted to trade anything; we gave them half a box of oranges and half a box of Spanish onions, and we got two boxes of muesli and a couple of large bars of dark chocolate off them. It was just a straight swap. We had a couple of big bags of flour and we'd often make pancakes. It doesn't take much to make a pancake – bit of flour, drop an egg in, little bit of salt, milk and whisk it up. You can make it sweet or you can make it savoury and you can use different things on them.

We often put a bit of ham in and rolled it up: lovely! You have to pick up ideas the whole time when you're travelling: what you can save and what you can't save. I used to wear a Bowie knife – a good one – on a belt. I was told it'd be a safety device in Morocco, so made sure I always wore it. Not that we expected trouble, but better to be safe.

After a while we went down to Fez, where we could see the French influence: a few nice little bakeries and the like. You'd get different-shaped loaves of nice bread there for little or nothing. We had a Moroccan lamb dish in a nice little place we found that was very cheap to eat in. We didn't do much cooking for the first week or two – it was so easy to walk out and just get your meal served to you. We went in to the leather markets, and saw lots of bags – quite nice sized ones, all sorts of different types. I'd say a lot of it was camel leather, and very reasonably priced. We were just looking around, not wanting to spend too much on stuff.

Eventually we got out of Fez and drove towards Ketama, up in the mountains. On the first night the fog came down and we were driving really slowly, on a very narrow rough road, looking for somewhere to park up for the night. There were two big rocks at the side of the road so I got out and moved them, so Clob could pull the van in off the road. He pulled in dead tight and climbed through into the back. We were sitting there having a smoke and a nice cup of coffee when we heard a giggling and tapping on the side of the van; this was very late at night. We had a window open a bit and someone said, "Try this, try this!" Next thing little lumps of hash kept popping in through the window. We gathered it up and put it into a box.

When we got up in the morning, Clob shouted, "Don't open the door!" We had parked right at the edge of a sheer drop! We got out on the other side – very carefully.

Back on the road, we drove on up into the mountains, and somewhere near the top we met a Moroccan farmer who said he lived in the valley just below us and that he owned a farm down there, and that there was a footpath going from where we were down into the valley. He had about thirty goats and two small fields of marijuana, hash plants. That was his main crop for the year. He invited us down to his house and we were sitting around talking with him and having a couple of cups of mint tea, with a block of cheese and some bread, when he went out to the shed, came back in, picked up his pipe and filled it up with "kif", as he called it. He handed around the pipe: it was like a peace pipe thing. There were three or four people in the house, and us – six of us altogether. So we smoked that and, by Jesus, it was powerful stuff: like having about four or five pints! It must've been around one o'clock in the morning when we said we'd better go back to the van and he gave us some to bring with us. I'll never know how we got back up the hill, but we crawled up to the van anyhow.

Next morning, we got up, went walking round the hills, came back, put on a big pot of coffee and had a chunk of nice fresh bread with cheese. The local cheese was good there, made with goats' milk. I didn't think we'd like it but it was quite nice. After breakfast we went back down to your man's farm. They'd started bringing in the goats for milking in the morning. The wife did most of the work, I think. They had a little donkey as well. It was quite a small little house, with about three rooms in it. The sheds had one end for the goats and one end for his grass plants where he used to package, shake it all down, make what they could.

We told him we'd be back anyhow because we were just going into town for a few days, so we headed down to Casablanca. It was a big place and I didn't like it as much as I thought I would. The markets were amazing. We went to one of the marketplaces: we weren't going to spend any money but we wanted to get some leather bags, because we knew we could sell them on the way back in Switzerland and places. We had some old folding bicycles we had picked up in Amsterdam, thinking they'd come in handy some time, so we traded them. I think we got ten or fifteen medium-sized bags, twenty smallish ones, and thirty of the watertight ones for passports and the like. We thought it was a good deal for the bicycles, so we stuck all the bags into the boxes in the van – it was getting a bit empty under the bed now as we were using up our supplies.

A couple of days later we were back up on your man's farm. Same old routine there: down to the house, make the tea, cheese and bread, out comes the pipe. We found by then it was kind of a nice thing, to smoke. We hadn't been drinking beer for nearly two months, so it was an alternative – it didn't mean we were going mad on it altogether!

After three or four weeks we left the hills again and went back to Fez. I got some semi-precious stones, and little rings and stuff like that in the market. I think I paid about ten pounds, but there was a good lot of stuff in it. I knew they'd be worth a lot more than that when I got into Zurich. I always liked wheeling and dealing!

When we left Fez we drove back to Rabat. We hung around the beaches, met a few people there, got some spices and learned a bit about how they cook the Moroccan lamb. They didn't use very hot spices, just nice flavours.

Another week passed by and it was getting late in the year so we said we'd head back across to Spain. The customs officer pulled the van to one side. "Passports!" We handed out the passports. "Oh, Irish people?"

"Yeah, we're from Ireland."

"Happy people!" he grinned, chalked an X on the windows and said "Go!" He didn't even look in the van. If he had, he would only have found leather goods in there.

We headed back into the mountains in Spain. We still had some of our own food left, so we took out the pots. We had two packets of instant mash – it was supposed to be "the business". Of course, it didn't taste as good as real potatoes, but we made that up and had a big tin of Irish stew. It still tasted great!

In the morning we had fresh bread and put a big pot of coffee on, before we headed out of the hills. It was a good drive from there back to Barcelona. We were empty at this time, nobody with us, and we still had a few bob. We got into Barcelona and put another sign in the window for anyone who wanted a lift to Montpelier or Zurich. We got an English fella and a Dutch fella. The Dutch fella said he was only going as far as Montpelier, the English fella said he didn't mind going as far as Zurich, so we shared the petrol expenses again. We made a few stops on the way – took our time, no panic!

We pulled into Montpelier, headed down to the usual little bar there, had a few beers, met a few people we knew and told them we were heading on to Switzerland. We got into Zurich late in the evening and pulled up in a big open car park. We parked up there, locked up the van and headed into town. We went to a few of the market places, brought a couple of the bags with us, and met a guy there who had a stall with bags. We showed him the bags and he was very interested and took about half of them. We more than trebled our money on them because the bikes that we had traded for them had cost very little. We also sold the half kilo of hash we had hidden under the petrol tank in the roof! We had more money then, so we went back to a bar and sat around there for the day. By then we were getting a bit into the idea of getting back to Amsterdam. I think it was into the middle of November at the time, getting quite cool again.

It wasn't far to the German border, where we got stopped and they asked us where we had been, and for our passports. "Oh, Morocco, Ketama, mountains, hash!"

We said, "Oh yeah, but we don't carry anything like that. What we have is two boxes of leather bags, which we're going to sell when we get into Amsterdam." I said, "We sold a few in Zurich, just helps with the petrol and keeps us going."

"No problem, on you go."

So we got back to Amsterdam and down to the old bar in the evening time. It was amazing: there was no smoking ban back then, but in half the bars in Amsterdam people were smoking joints, as well as cigarettes, and drinking beer. Sex shops were on every corner you turned, ladies in the windows displaying their wares – totally different from what we were used to! I remember walking up the town to get something for our dinner, and one of the women from the window area shouted at me. She said "Hey, honey, do ya want some funny?"

I said, "Sorry, honey, no money!"

She said, "No money, no funny!" The laughs!

We decided that we'd get rid of as much as we could of the rest of the bags – maybe keep a few for Ireland. A fella down in the flea market bought the rest and most of the little stones and the rings that I'd picked up. I'd only sold a handful of them in Switzerland.

Your man was always in the flea market so he'd know everything about what to buy, and what would sell. I learned a good bit about buying and selling at that time.

Clob was saying we should get back to Ireland for the middle of December. We were down to about fifty pounds. It was amazing how much we used on fuel, eating and drinking too. We headed up through Belgium and pulled into Antwerp. We knew one or two guys up there so we parked the van and went to see them.

It wasn't long till one of the guys said, "Did you bring anything back from Morocco?"

We said, "A few bags and a few rings, half a box of beads."

He said that the girl he was living with – Therese – did the markets, so we brought them around that evening to his place. First thing he did was hand us a joint on the way in – that's the way it was! So we sat down there with a good cup of coffee while the meal was being cooked, we talked about the bags, the rings and the stones.

"Ah," says I, "you can have the lot of them for ... let's see ... about the equivalent of eighteen ... twenty pounds for what's left."

She was delighted because she made her own armbands and necklaces out of stones; she knew what she was doing with them. She could make them with leather or with chains, she could do whatever she wanted with them. We got money for the bags we had left as well, so we'd have plenty of money going back towards England.

We hung around in Antwerp for about another week: lovely city – much nicer than Brussels and the people were more friendly. There were fantastic people in Amsterdam – every nationality on the planet – it was a packed-out city though, a lot of people for the size of it. I wouldn't be used to the cities, being from the mountains in Wicklow. You'd miss the mountains at times and the Irish way of going on, but still –nothing to learn. You learn a lot when you're travelling; it opens your eyes that the world is big: everything is new every day. It's a wonderful way of getting on.

WE LEFT ANTWERP TO GET THE FERRY from Ostend to Dover. We pulled in on the outskirts of London and parked up the van. I knew a few fellas living around London so we got the underground into the centre. The hair had grown back a bit after the haircut in Morocco and it was long again. The funny thing about Morocco was you could have a beard as long as you liked, but your hair had to be short. Mad!

In London we met our friend Dave, and we hung around with him for a few days. In Piccadilly we went for a burger and chips – we hadn't had that for a while – and we ended up in a bar that evening. We told Dave where the van was parked and he reassured us, "It'll be cool enough. If you want you can spend the night here, no need to go back out to it."

So we went back to his place that night, played a bit of music, had a few beers. There was a bloody big shower there, so we each had a good shower. We were up late in the morning and we left around twelve because he wasn't working at the time.

We headed back to the van, hung around London for another few days in various places, then we headed up the M1 towards Birmingham. Not one of my favourite cities, but we spent a full day there before carrying on to Liverpool. We hadn't booked any tickets, so we had to wait for nearly twelve hours before we could leave. We eventually got on the boat back to Dublin. We left the van in Liverpool, because we weren't going to stay in Ireland that long.

We got out as far as Bray and went up to my mother's. My brothers were all there. "BeJaysus, you're back!"

"Back for a while, anyhow," I said. "We'll hang around for a while, as long as it takes to get our heads right, then move on again." We got into the brother's car and I dropped Clob out to Greystones then went back to the house, sat down for a chat with the mother. My father was out at the time. My young sisters were there alright. I didn't see much of them growing up anyhow.

I hopped into the bath, got a change of clothes and left a load of washing there. I walked in to Bray that evening and I met one or two of the lads I knew there from Kilmacanogue. One fella lived up near the film studios close to where I lived, so we had a drink in the Ardmore Bar. Clob arrived into the Ardmore then so we sat there talking and people were asking us what we were doing. We told them we'd be at home for a little while. "Where were you, what was goin' on?"

"Ah," says I, "we were mostly around the centre of Europe and into Morocco and back."

"So, what are you doin' now?"

I said, "Well, we're home for the Christmas anyhow. We have the van in storage in Liverpool. I disconnected the battery, it's fully locked up – nothing in it that could do any harm to anything."

Christmas came round again. The wintertime's not great for travelling anyhow so we hopped around the place over Christmas. I went down to Clob's parents; I had Christmas dinner down there with them, then he had Stephen's Day dinner back in my place. We got on well with both sets of parents, and all the brothers and sisters. Clob could get a few days' work in his brother's shop when he wanted it. Myrtle's would take anything I had, but I hadn't brought anything back – that was the weird thing, I'd sold it all. But at the beginning of January I'd make some copper bangles up, a few silver hearts, bits and pieces like that. I'd also go and see that builder in January – might get a bit of work down there. I didn't want to move around in January or February anyhow; a month or two at home wouldn't kill us. We'd be taking off around March when the weather got a bit better.

That had been the plan – but Clob and I got talking and we both wanted to get back on the road, so we agreed we would head off now in the middle of January. We added up the money we had. We still had a lot of money left over from the previous trip, I had sold loads of bits of stuff that I'd made to Myrtle's and he'd got a few bob over Christmas, so we were heading off again!

Clob, Rikki and Moon in Morocco, 1972.

Moon and Clob, Avondale Park, 1972.

Greencamp, early morning, 1973.

Greencamp, our van in background, 1973.

Moon working in the shop, Greencamp, 1973.

Greencamp people, 1973.

Greencamp, 1973.

Tent 7, Greencamp, 1973.

WE GOT THE BOAT BACK TO LIVERPOOL and picked up the van. It hadn't cost anything to keep the van there because we knew the fella that owned the yard. We connected the battery and it started right away, so off we headed back to Dover, hopped on the ferry, got to Ostend, into Antwerp and around to our friend's place. He was very surprised to see us back so quickly.

"Ah," I said, "miserable cold weather, you know. You might as well get out of the place."

So we stayed with him for a few days, then headed down through France and into Spain, thinking if we got down to the south of Spain, it'd be warm down there. Things were looking up. We had a good bit of money, so we didn't bother with picking up people to share the fuel this time. It was too early in the year anyhow; no one was around. We headed back down to Morocco and back into Rabat. There were nice beaches there and it was quite a friendly area and cheap to stay in. It cost us nothing to stay there really, so we spent most of the winter down there. It was all very close: Rabat, Fez and Ketama, and easy for us to get around between them with the van.

It gets quite cold up in the mountains, so we mainly spent the time down in Rabat. There was no one around much at the time, although we did meet a few English people who were living in the area on and off. The evenings weren't too cold so we would go to a few of the little restaurants and coffee shops: we drank lots of mint tea! The van was running well, we had changed the oil in it recently, done the plugs and changed two tyres as well. The brakes were okay, though we'd have to get linings in another three or four months.

We drove up to see your man in Ketama and hung around for a few days. He gave us a bag of kif and we'd sit smoking one or two pipes in the evening time after dinner. It was very relaxing, with a pot of coffee. We still had two bags of coffee with us. There was a packet of Lyons tea still in the van from our first time away too.

We decided we'd bring more leather bags back to Amsterdam. We were planning to get back there around the middle of April. We were down in the big market again looking around. You could buy anything you wanted in the winter there. There weren't as many people buying stuff so everything was cheaper. Clob reckoned we should get a good few leather bags this time. The flea market in Amsterdam would take anything, so we spent as much as we could spend and kept the rest of our money for the journey back. Once we were back in Amsterdam, I could pick up a bit of work welding there if I wanted to. It was the middle of March then so in another week or two we'd be packing up again. Ah, it had been brilliant!

When April came, we were ready to leave. We had bought about sixty leather bags, so we headed back to Spain, up across France, into Belgium and up into Amsterdam. We had to park a couple of blocks down from our usual place as they were doing some work on the cobblestones, but we were still close to the flea market and the red-light district – very close to the city centre.

When we were leaving Wicklow, Clob had the idea to bring this weird little moped called a Raleigh Wisp – it had small wheels and a 50cc engine. He said we should bring it with us because we'd nothing else at that time. He threw it up on the roof rack. People wanted to buy it off us, but we didn't want to sell it because we found it very handy for getting around, up and down the little side streets. We were sleeping half the day, didn't get up until a bit late as there was no need to. We'd get up about eleven in the morning and make our way downtown. We had done a deal with the guy in the flea market: he took all the bags, gave us half the money then and said when he'd sold a few of them we could have the rest. The weather was still cold enough, so we bought big leather coats and picked up a pair each of knee-length Spanish leather boots as well. They had big hobnailed heels on them, but they were good and warm and comfortable.

For the first time in my life, I went into a sauna. There were big sauna rooms near the flea market, so we had to give it a go. You take all your clothes off and you walk in and sit on a towel. I was sitting there lookin across and I said to Clob, "Jaysus, I think we're in the wrong place!"

"Why?" he says. "What's wrong with you?"

Says I, "There's women on the far side with nothing on!"

Clob goes, "Ah sure, it's a mixed sauna."

I said, "Mixed? BeJaysus! It's kind of scary, y'know, we've never seen anything like that in Ireland!"

What an eye-opener! So we sat there trying not to blush; we must have been there for an hour or two. It was some experience anyhow!

A few days after we arrived I met the fella Jaak, that wanted the welding done on the barge, and asked if he had any work going. He said, "Maybe next week. Call over and I'll have something."

Cool! I thought, Clob's going to be cooking, I'll be the breadwinner.

Jaak was a very interesting fella. When I called I had a good look around. He had a very decent welding plant, good shield and gloves and a good chipping hammer and tools there and a set of burning bottles. The plate steel was about four or five millimetres thick. He wanted to put a sixteen-foot by twelve-foot section on the top, and it was a big enough job, but he had another guy there to work with me. We agreed I'd take on the job on a daily basis and he'd pay me in the evening, or at the weekend if I wanted it. I got down to work there on the Monday morning about nine o'clock. It was quite dry out, good weather for outside work, so I marked out the area he wanted the welding done on. He had most of the sections tacked into position, so the lifting and stuff like that was already done. I started welding that morning, welded all the way up till around one o'clock.

Now Clob was just down the road in the van, so he ended up coming up there around half one, brought up a couple of cheese

47

and tomato sandwiches and a flask of coffee, and we sat there talking for a while. He said he'd often thought about putting a barge together on the canal for himself. It's a nice way of living; there were quite a lot of people living on barges in around the Amsterdam area. This one had plenty of room in it already, but Jaak wanted the other sections opened up.

We welded up two sides in about three days. It was working out great and he was very happy. He asked me if I'd be any good with the acetylene torches for burning. I said, "No problem!" so he said he wanted the section marked and cut out for some windows that he was bringing over. There'd be a bit more work in it then, but I didn't really mind as we weren't that pushed about getting away for a week or two.

We soon got into the rhythm of working on the boat. Clob was doing most of the cooking now in the van. Sometimes we got on one another's wicks after being so long in the van, so there was no harm in having somewhere else to go to during the day, and to see a bit more of the area as well. I finished up early enough in the evenings to get around a bit. It was turning out very well.

By the end of the first week there I had most of the welding done: there were three windows on either side and two on the front. The doorway needed a frame welded into it too. It was a box section frame, just to hold the supports together. He was going to bolt on wood panelling all around the inside and then insulate it. I marked out the windows in the second week. I cut out the first one, which turned out perfect, so he was happy with that. He was particular about making sure that everything was fitting right. I had them all cut out within two days and all the edges cleaned. I got inside then and started working on the door frame.

I took a day off on the Thursday of the following week. Jaak didn't mind as I told him I mightn't be in one or two days as we wanted to go to a fair that was on outside the town: a bit of music playing and loads of stalls and different things going on. We had a good look around that day and talked to a few different people. There was a lot of different music for sale but we didn't buy any tapes, as we already had a good selection of music in the van. We had Crosby, Stills, Nash and Young; Bob Dylan; couple of Van

Morrison – it wasn't as if we were listening to the same stuff all the time. We'd be out in the evening time in the cafes and bars. We found the prices reasonable in the supermarkets, but we couldn't go near eating out as we didn't have that kind of money.

I went in on the Friday and finished off the door area, then Jaak wanted runners put in – angle runners, where the sections were divided up for filling in with the insulation – and then the timbers screwed on. The runners were very light gauge; I tacked a load of them along the inside. It was beginning to look well at that stage and I said I'd be coming back that way in the next year or so and would look in to see the finished job.

Clob and I went back up to the Dam Square the next day and sat around talking to a few people. It was damp but not too cold; the weather was getting a bit better. It was time we decided what we were going to do that year. We were using Amsterdam as a base to get around Europe; it's central for getting into Germany and France and anywhere you wanted to go. There were a lot of people in Amsterdam at that time of the year, people starting to move.

The middle of the following week, we had a good shower in one of those public shower places, cleaned all the clothes and got everything ready. We were just about out of gas in the bottles so I said to Clob, "I think we should go down to the flea market and see can we sell the old cooker and get a little paraffin stove. We can convert the top of it for cooking on, and there's no bother getting paraffin anywhere." The bottles of gas we had were oddball so we swapped the cooker for a stove heater called a Paul Warma – it was a globe-shaped yoke. It wasn't very good as it had only one top piece you could use as a cooking ring, but we got it working, though it was a bit smoky at times. But the gas was gone and we wouldn't have the hassle of finding those fancy bottles anymore.

Jaak had paid me a fair amount of money for my work on the barge. It worked out about eight to ten pounds a day, so we'd nearly an extra hundred quid leaving there. We tidied everywhere up; we never left any mess. We always had a little bag inside the door of the van and we were always conscious not to drop rubbish and to put any dirty water down the shores.

We were leaving the next morning when I said, "I think that tram goes out to the outskirts, heading for the German border – Arnhem way." Clob agreed and we decided that if we followed it we'd get straight out to the outskirts.

We had only gone about a quarter of a mile and we were following the tram through an intersection, next minute Bang! Bang! Bang! "Oh, Jesus! What's happenin'?"

I was driving, of course, and the van wouldn't go forward, wouldn't go back, wouldn't go anywhere. We were stuck on the tram tracks, because the tramline at that point went through a bushy area that didn't have a road: it was like a railway track and we were jammed on that! The tram behind was stuck, the one on the other side was stuck and we couldn't move!

Next thing the police arrived, then the chief of the tram company came and wanted to know what was going on. I said, "Em, we were following the tram and we got stuck on the line."

He says, "It's going to cost a lot of money to move that," and he goes, "Where are you from?"

"We're Irish."

He burst out laughing and said, "Oh, that's enough, anyhow! That just about explains it!"

Eventually, when we'd been there an hour or more, they brought over a small crane and lifted the van off the tracks. We were jammed in very tightly so it would have been no good trying to pull it out – it would've wrecked the van completely – so they lifted it off and put it back on to the road. There must've been four or five hundred people there by then, who had come to see what all the fuss was, and about six trams waiting behind us. I think the whole of Amsterdam was disturbed for about an hour that day. I was told we made headlines in the papers, but they didn't charge us, just gave us a big talking to about following trams. "Use the road signs and don't be following one of these things because it ends up causing a lot of confusion, a lot of hassle." There was more joking about it than anything; I'd say if it happened nowadays we'd be locked up!

At last we headed out to the German border. We got through the Dutch border post no problem and drove up to the German side. "Stop! Passports, documents, van papers." We handed all the van papers out. "Oh, you're Irish. Put that away. Passports, take them out." He got the passports and saw we'd been in Morocco three months before, so he goes, "Pull the van over to one of the sheds." Then he wanted to go through the van

We asked, "What are you looking for?"

"Drugs. Morocco hashish." He went through nearly every box in the van. One person had to stay in it because, as I said to him, "Legally you have to have someone in the room if you're searching it, because it's our home, as such," so I stayed around and he pulled out bits and pieces and he went through it all and then he found my Bowie knife.

"What's the big knife all about? What's this?"

I said, "I wear it when I'm in some places. I don't wear it all the time, and anyway we use it for cutting bread, meat, everything." He said no more about it and he put it back into its pouch.

"Now," he says, "I have to search each person."

Clob went into the van with him first and he tapped him all over and turned his pockets inside out, searched him up and down, checked his shoes, every bit of him, and said, "You're okay," and gave him back his passport. Then I got checked all over, then he came out and he said, "Hey! What's on the roof?"

"It's a spare fuel tank and a big canvas."

He said, "I want the canvas off, take that down," so I took down the canvas cover and they rolled it out and they went up to the fuel tank.

I said, "There's nothing in it; we hardly ever use it. Once or twice we filled it with petrol." I explained, "When you're going really long distances you're not sure about where you're going to get fuel. You could drive for half a day in Spain, and sometimes in Morocco for more than a day."

Eventually, after three or four hours, we were let go.

On we went into Germany, towards Bremen, and we pulled up in a little town nearby called Verden Aller. We bumped into a young German fella and an English girl who he was going with, Ann and Chris. He could speak a bit of English as he'd been living with this English girl for six months or so. He asked us where we were from and we said Ireland. He said, "Oh yeah, there's a war on there."

"Ah," we said, "not that much, not where we're from. You wouldn't call it a war."

They were staying in a big place at the corner of the street, that had extra rooms in it and a place to park the van, so he said, "You can stick around with us for a while, if you like."

We were happy to do so. It was a big house, alright. We moved a lot of the stuff out of the van into a fairly big room inside.

He worked in a bakery. As they were going out one evening, he asked, "Do you want to come with us? We're meeting a couple of friends, a German guy called Geoffrey and his girlfriend Susanna."

So we met in a bar. Geoffrey had four or five words of English, just like we had in German: *"Ein halber Liter Bier bitte."* But we hung round with them for a few days and Geoffrey invited us back to his place one evening. Little did we know, the whole of Europe seemed to be smoking dope. He sat down, took out his stuff, made a joint and put on some really weird but really good sounding music. It was the first time I'd heard a Dolby system and those sort of speakers. He was a painter and decorator and spent all his money on hi-fi systems. His girlfriend worked in a local supermarket and they had a little daughter as well.

It was a nice area and when we'd been there for a week or two Ann said, "If you want to hang around for a while, they're looking for some workers over at the English military barracks."

"Don't know about that," I said.

"Well," she said, "you can cook – you've been cooking in our house. They're looking for someone to cook, and a cleaner."

"Sure, why not?" we thought.

We arrived over at the barracks and one of the guys in charge came out and he says, "We're looking for two middle-aged women here, one for cleaning and one for cooking."

"Well," I said, "we're not middle-aged women and we're not middle-aged men, we're youngish fellas, but I've been cooking quite a bit. I'm very good at the main course dinners and stuff like that, wouldn't be great with a first class restaurant but cooking for this would be no problem."

Clob says, "I've no bother cleaning."

So they took us on and we started the next morning. I must've cooked five pounds of rashers and five pounds of sausages and about four dozen eggs and heaps of toast – breakfast time for the military guys. They gave me full marks anyhow. "Just like Mama used to make! Rashers and sausages well done, not half cooked!"

That evening they said there were only fifty or sixty coming in for their evening meal. They had huge steamer pots for potatoes that you could get two or three stone in at a time, a half a box of T-bone steaks and bunches of carrots. I cooked mushrooms and onions with the steak and we served it all up. Well, the English guys said it was the best steak they'd had since they moved out of England!

We were there for a few weeks and we got one day a week off. It paid okay and Ann and Chris didn't mind us staying in their place, because every other evening we were over in Geoffrey and Susanna's. The van was dark green and it used to get really hot inside, so Geoffrey said the thing to do was paint it white. He painted it white down as far as the extension on the roof part. It looked well and it did now deflect the sun. Dark green and black had made it like an oven, especially in the top bunk.

One Friday we arranged that we'd take everyone over to Bremen. There was a pub over there that had live music, so we all piled into the van: Geoffrey, Susanna, Ann and Chris, myself and Clob. It was a right sort of a bar! You could get a big boot of beer – it was the first time I had seen them. You drink out of them and share them around and get another one or two of them – you have to know the trick to it though when it gets near the end, or you end up getting a beer shower! There were bowls of peanuts on the counter and the band was pretty good. Afterwards we headed back to Verden Aller and were back working the next day.

Geoffrey said that we should organise a trip down to Amsterdam some weekend, we'd go down on the Saturday and come back Sunday as it was a couple of hours' drive. So Geoffrey, Clob, Chris and myself went down to Amsterdam. We pulled up, got a bit of food and then we went around to the little bar Clob and I used to go to. The first thing when you opened the door there was you were knocked over with the smoke coming out of it and I wouldn't say there'd be ten people out of a hundred smoking regular cigarettes. We hung around in there listening to music, had a couple of smokes and a few beers each. Geoffrey got what he wanted anyhow and we headed back on the Sunday afternoon.

We stopped at the border: "German? German? Yeah, yeah, okay. Irish? Irish? Passports? Okay." We told them we were living in Verden Aller. Geoffrey and Chris only needed their ID cards, they could move around there with ease like that.

When we had been working at the army base for about two months we noticed there was always a car tailing us. A couple of weeks later we were called into the office. This was the middle of 1973. They said, "It's getting too scary with you working here. The security we have to keep on you is unbelievable."

I think they thought we were an IRA cell or something. We went into Hamburg one day and when we came back to the van, it was surrounded by police. I walked over and I said, "What's happening?"

They said they wanted to check us out.

"Check us out?" I said. "We're living in Germany for the last couple of months; we're working in an English military base."

So they checked the van and our passports and they said everything was okay. Eventually, though, the military police said it was too expensive. The Baader-Meinhof gang was very active at that time in Germany, so there was all sorts of stuff going down, and they had to let us go. We didn't mind as we were getting ready to move on anyhow.

We stayed around for another week or two, with Geoffrey and Susanna and Ann and Chris, and had a few more parties. I'll never forget one of the nights before we left! We went to the pub down the road and we were well known there. I'd had a good few beers that night and coming back to the house, I wanted to get something for Susanna. I had seen a lot of flowers in a garden and it looked like they were just over a little tiny stone wall, so I hopped over the wall … I must've fallen down about six feet into the garden as it wasn't at the same level as the road! If I hadn't landed in the

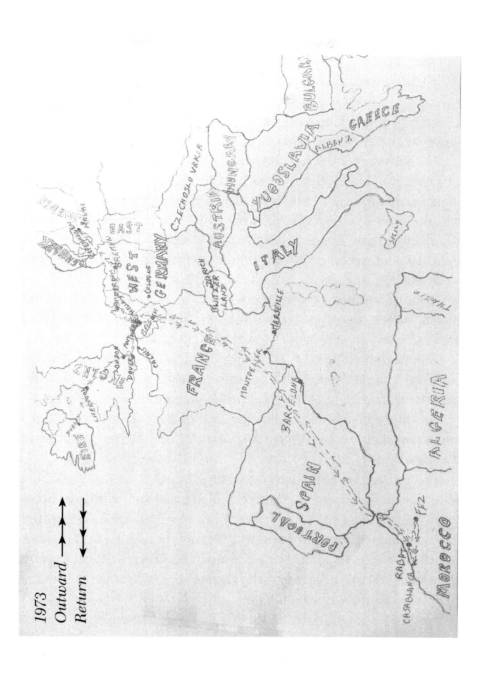

1973
Outward →
Return ↓

garden, I probably would've killed myself! I picked some flowers and I crawled out the gate and I gave them to Susanna and I said, "Get me home, I'm in bits!" BeJaysus, I was black and blue! The laughs of them all: they nearly had to carry me home!

We packed up the van and headed further north. Driving up the very north of Germany, Clob said to me, "Look at that, Moon! There's a sign there, says Copenhagen: I think it's 128 or 228 kilometres." Later on that evening, we went up to have a look at the ferry area.

We considered leaving the van behind while we checked out Copenhagen, but in the end decided to take it with us as it wasn't much more expensive than two walk-on fares on the ferry. With that we drove on to the ferry. We arrived in Copenhagen, drove into the main square, drove round in a circle and pulled up near Tivoli Gardens and we asked people where you would park a van if you were staying.

"Near the airport, there's a place: it's called Greencamp. It's full of army tents – everyone stays out there, y'know." That sounded cool so we decided to drive out that way and check it out .

Greencamp was so called because the tents were green! It was a sleep-in; you could stay in those places for the equivalent of about fifty or sixty cents a night at the time. It was like hostel accommodation, except in a tent. You got a breakfast with that: a carton of milk and a small bag of cornflakes, coffee and orange juice, slice of bread, stuff like that.

The guy in the hut where we went to check in said we wouldn't have to pay. We could park the van along the side, with two other vans. "If you want the breakfast you can buy it in the morning. You can use the place just as if you were staying here: just walk in, have a shower, whatever …" There were mixed showers: that was a weird thing too! You're walking into the shower and out comes two young ones with everything hanging out!

I said, "Fuck me! We're in the wrong shower again!"

"No, no, no, this is the way it goes here, y'know."

Everyone was going around half naked. Denmark definitely opened our eyes! Amazing: "Hello, how's it goin'?" and nothing on them! Sunny days though.

We were in Greencamp and getting to meet a lot of people. It was buzzing with people from America, all over Europe, even Iceland, Finland, some English, but we were the only two Irish there at the time.

The set-up was put together by the Danish government. This one had about fourteen large army tents with wooden floors in them, seven on each side. There was a shower block and a tuck shop where you could buy low-alcohol beers, lemonade, packets of crisps, nuts and the like. It was laid out very well. There was a hut at the gate where you checked in and paid for however many nights you wanted to stay. It was a great idea because it was about quarter the price of a youth hostel. There was a large area in the middle where they sometimes had a bonfire lighting in the evening. They were a new idea. A guy called Claus from Amsterdam had worked in the first ones in Holland and introduced them to Denmark. There was another one about two miles across the city called City Camp. The name came from the idea that half of the campsite had rooms and the other side had tents. It had the same layout, with the shower units and toilets and the like.

When we had been there a few days, I took the little Raleigh Wisp down off the van to get it going. I took out the plug and cleaned it up and put a bit of oil and petrol mix into it. It had a tiny little round tank and a miniature engine. It was a mad lookin yoke with very small wheels! There was no suspension – it was just like a bicycle with an engine hanging in it. It was quite slow – it'd go fifteen or twenty miles an hour, but I cleaned it all up and got it going. It sounded like a wasp buzzing when you started it up!

I followed the number thirty-nine bus, riding along the cycle lane all the way into town. There were plenty of places to put bicycles and everyone was riding bicycles. I locked it up and walked into the main square. The Town Hall is there, the city council's headquarters, and right outside that is a statue of Hans Christian Andersen. One of Copenhagen's tallest towers is on one side and there's a big pedestrian street. I walked along there past lots of big shops, down to the courthouse at the end. There's a big fountain at that end. I spent about two hours walking around the area and, when I was near Tivoli Gardens, I saw a lot of big Clydesdale horses with a wagon. It was an old Tuborg wagon full of wooden beer barrels. It looked amazing, with brass shining all over. The other big brewery in Copenhagen was the Carlsberg brewery.

One of the fellas had told me, "When you get into the centre, get yourself a Danish hot dog!" I went over to the hot dog stand and I explained what I wanted. One of the first things I learned was how to ask for a fried hot dog, with a little bit of mustard and a little bit of ketchup and some fried onions: *Ristet hot dog, lille sennep, lille ketchup, ristet løg* – and it's out in two seconds in front of you! It was the most amazing hot dog I ever ate! They were very famous – Copenhagen hot dogs. Eventually I got up on the bike again and headed back towards Greencamp.

That evening Clob and I were sitting around with a few people having a chat. There was a nice fella called Gypsy, from Iceland, then there was an English fella called Big Ian: he was built like a rugby player. I think his father was a doctor, from around Birmingham. I made our dinner in the van and got a few light beers. Light beer there is not the low-calorie stuff we call light beer. Danish light beer means it's only a half percent alcohol; you could drink them all night and you wouldn't get drunk on them. They taste okay and it's not a completely non-alcoholic beer, just a weak beer. We mainly drank the Carlsberg one but Tuborg and a few other breweries made them as well. They had many different types of beer there in Denmark, brewed in different parts of the country.

After dinner we hopped on a bus with four or five other lads into the city centre for the evening. The bus ticket was good for an hour and you could go on any bus within that hour. When you were getting off, if you weren't going to use it, you could give it to someone getting on and you'd say, "There you go – that one's good for half an hour," and it was acceptable to transfer the tickets like that. At some of the bus stations you'd see them clipped to the timetable board. You didn't need a watch because those buses were always on time. It was an amazing bus service, and they had a half-underground, half-overground Metro train service as well.

When we got into the centre we went to the main student bar, Huset. There was an information centre in it, live music and a cinema that showed arthouse films. We didn't drink too much beer in the bars there as it was bloody expensive, but in the off licence it cost next to nothing. Every corner you turned had an off licence. They were often just a wide doorway and a corridor filled with crates of beer for sale. The supermarkets were full of beer too – it was everywhere. This was the summer of 1973. Copenhagen was the cleanest city I'd ever been in in my life – you could let anything fall and pick it up and eat it! If you dropped paper on the street the person behind you would ask you to pick it up. Even if you lit your cigarette and dropped a match, they'd tell you to pick it up. They were very clean and really, really nice people.

I don't remember the names of all the people we met. There

Huset office, Copenhagen.

were fourteen conscientious objectors that didn't want to do military service, so they got to work in Greencamp instead. They had four different shifts in the day and their uniform was a grey jacket, like a little shop coat down to their waist, and a pair of grey trousers. They also worked in old folks' homes and those kind of places. You didn't have to go in the army if you didn't want to but men had to do some kind of National Service.

We met a German guy called Reinhardt who was quite shy and a bit of a loner. I went up to talk to him by the fire one evening. He could barely say, "How you doing?" in English. He had taken off from the German army and he ended up in Copenhagen because he could travel with his ID cards. We got to talk to him anyhow and he hung around the camp for a couple of weeks. There was a German girl there as well, Sabine; she got a job there because she had been living in Denmark for a while. She also had a friend from Finland, Päivi. I worked as a volunteer in the kiosk the odd day myself. I didn't mind doing it as we had a few bob and we weren't spending that much.

By the time the camp was closing for winter I had sold three or four hundred postcards. I used to sell postcards, cigarette papers, bits and pieces of anything that people wanted to buy. They could swap rolls of film, sell rolls of film, buy rolls of film. I did a good bit of photography myself. I'd a nice camera – a Brownie thirty-five millimetre. I still have a heap of photos.

We must've been there a couple of weeks when I met a German girl called Vanessa. The day after I met her we were joking about different things – I was cooking a bit of a meal and she said something about small onions, *kleine zwiebel* in German, and I thought it sounded really funny, so I called her kleine zwiebel from that day on. *Meine kleine zwiebel, liebling, ich liebe dich* – that sort of thing! But anyhow we got on really well.

9

THAT WAS AN AMAZING HOT SUMMER, AND really bright. I never experienced anything in my life like it: I had just found something totally different. I'm not lazy: I don't mind working. I just wanted to find out what the rest of the world was about and what was happening in the rest of Europe. Denmark opened my eyes – such a liberal country. They don't take any nonsense but as long as you keep the rule of law it's okay, you can do your own thing. Around the fire at night-time and in the camp area there'd probably be 150 people, and not a bad word between them. Everyone saying hello, *hej* was the word you learned. "Hej," was like, "How're you doing?" In the morning it's *"god morgen"*. It was really nice: everyone having a laugh and a chat. A lot of people smoked cigarettes and a bit of hash.

I found out another thing when I was there – and actually it was Vanessa, Kleine Zwiebel, who told me – that you couldn't buy cigarette papers in the shops as it was so expensive. They were about four times dearer than they would be in Holland or Germany. There were two Dutch guys who arrived and they brought boxes of cigarette papers up, so we'd sell them in the kiosk. I think they were around two or three pence a packet in Amsterdam; you'd pay around thirty or forty pence a packet in Copenhagen. Cigarettes and tobacco were quite dear, but the idea of the cigarette papers was incredible so there was a great opening for anyone to sell them. I don't know whether you could call it smuggling papers, but that's the way it was!

One day, when we were sitting round the bonfire in the middle of the camp, we met an Irish guy from Kilkenny. He was one of a few people playing guitars and he was pretty good. He actually stayed in Berlin for a good bit of the year but was visiting Copenhagen. He was a very good guitarist, he played in Huset a few nights – Bob Dylan stuff, a bit of Johnny Cash, anything like that.

Myself and Vanessa were getting on like a house on fire: it was sort of my first big love scene! We headed off into the city on the bus, went around, got an ice cream and sat in the pedestrian area. It was like moving pictures, there were so many different nationalities. You could sit there for hours, people watching – different nationalities, different people, carrying bags, looking at maps of where they were. When you arrived in Greencamp they'd give you a little map with Greencamp marked on it so you wouldn't get lost; the numbers of the buses and so on were marked. People did walk into the city – it was probably about an hour's walk into the centre – but the buses were so frequent you'd hardly bother.

One night there was a party, or some sort of national celebration in Denmark, so there was a bigger fire put up at the very top end of the camp. There was seating around it and we all had shorts on as it was a warm evening, late in the summertime. I was sitting at the fire there with meine kleine zwiebel, and there were a lot of other people with guitars, music started playing and the party was getting going when suddenly I felt this stinging on my legs, and I realised it couldn't be the fire. I didn't know about mosquitoes before! The place was full of mosquitoes – they just bit you and you got itchy. But if you're sitting round a fire with a pair of shorts on, you're in trouble because they're attracted to the light. I wasn't long about pulling a pair of long trousers on and trying to keep my arms and my face covered a bit too!

I was getting on great at the time, and Clob was staying between a house and Greencamp. There were lots of things happening, then we heard about a place called Christiania.

Christiania was a big piece of wasteground with a river running through it, and a big old military barracks on it. It covered a large piece of the part of Copenhagen over the bridge. It had been opened up about a year before by a group of young people, including Claus and a guy called Erik. One night there were a few wooden panels taken down and it was said that, within twenty-four hours, fifty or sixty people had moved into different parts of it, and by the end of a few weeks there were hundreds in there, so the main entrance area was opened up. It was the most amazing place inside. You'd walk in and there were roadways through it. You'd walk down one of the roadways and there was a big building with a wooden fronted area, called Fælleskøkken. It was a big restaurant that did very, very cheap meals and they had live bands in it. Across the way there was a place called Electric Ladyland, that was a nightclub. People moved into Christiania and built lots of strange little houses, and there were apartments and workshops set up there. There was a fella fixing old *kakkleovns*, which are a tall Danish stove. They were re-building them and putting new lining on the insides and selling them on. There was a candle shop, knitwear shops and there were a lot of little places there.

There were a lot of foreign people but quite a few Danish there too. Myself and the girlfriend spent a day walking around, amazed at it all. There was a guy with a brown bear and the bear used to drink bottles of beer, holding them in his two paws. That was some sight! There was another place that had parrots outside: they used to be singing and dancing and talking, outside the shop. We went over to the fella who was doing up all the old bicycles. He used to sell bikes but he had a welding plant and he used to make tall bikes, you'd nearly need a ladder to get up onto them. When you rode the bicycle you were about four or five feet up in the air. They were mad things with long handlebars on them! They looked unstable but most of the lads could ride them around alright. You'd fellas on unicycles too. Ah, such an amazing place! Another fella had an art studio. There was never much trouble there. You'd go in there for a bit of a party, for the late evening music, and Electric Ladyland would probably have a good band playing or they'd be playing good music.

Later that evening we headed back to Greencamp, into the old van. We had a couple of cups of coffee and sat there talking and smoked a pipe with Clob. He had a girlfriend as well, so he was staying in town most of the time and I was living in the van.

Clob suggested that the four of us should take a weekend out – just mark the spot where the van was, to keep our parking space. The girls were all on for it. Clob's girlfriend was French, but she spoke a good bit of English. Vanessa was German and she'd a fair amount of English. She'd learned a bit in school and got used to it from travelling around.

Anyhow, we got the van together. We had to give it a major overhaul as there were a lot of miles on it. Fortunately, there was a guy in Greencamp who had friends in a Ford garage and we got all the parts at fairly good prices. I knew a good bit about cars because I used to do stock car racing in Ireland, and it was no bother once we had the proper tool kit.

After a day or two we were ready to go. We packed up the van and headed up to Helsingør ("Elsinore" in English), where Hamlet's castle is! There was a short ferry ride to Helsingborg in Sweden, so we headed across. In Sweden we headed for Stockholm. A Swedish mile is completely different from an Irish or an English mile. We saw signposts where ten miles felt like about forty or fifty miles, driving forever! We later found out that one Swedish *mil* is ten kilometres.

In Stockholm we parked the van up and were walking around the place and we noticed a lot of police vans. They were green and white Volvo station wagons and quite a few of them had a dog pen in the back. We saw four guys, half hippie type, looking at us, as if to say, "What are they doin' here?" I walked over to them and I asked, "Where would we get a beer or a drink?"

"No chance," they replied, "most of the clubs are closed at this time."

It was about ten o'clock in the evening. There were no bars, so we didn't hang around in Stockholm that long. You couldn't get alcohol in Sweden except in private clubs – they all used to go to Copenhagen to get locked! I heard an old song about the Swedes coming to Copenhagen to get mad drunk all the time. There used to be a lot of them around on the weekends. That must've been the reason.

We drove back down out of there and went to a small island. There was very little on the island, just one or two small shops and a few houses, but the centre part of the island had a small wooded area with what appeared to be a lake, but it was actually a big inlet of the sea. We parked up the van about half a mile from the shops. It was a secluded area with just a few trees and a nice little bit of a beach. There was an old rowing boat parked up and nothing much else – very quiet. There was a lot of wood lying around so we put four poles in the ground and two across the top and we took down the tarpaulin and made a shelter. We had a few old fold-up chairs in the van, so we took them out; we got a small fire lighting and we cooked on the fire that night. We fried up a few pork chops and onions and wrapped the potatoes in silver foil and threw them into the fire. The girls were amazed at the way we cooked the potatoes. Back in Ireland as kids we used to work on the farms up around Kilmacanogue and see the farmer throw the spuds in the fire and kick them out afterwards and burst them open. The tin foil kept them from burning up. We had a nice dinner that evening.

It was a lovely evening and the sunset was amazing so we hopped into the rowing boat. We didn't know much about them, but we started rowing up and down a bit, and we noticed when you lifted the oars out of the water, you had phosphorescence, like little lights coming out of the water. It was bloody amazing! We were rowing around there having a great laugh; we could hear the music from the van as we'd left the side door open and had a tape going. I knew I was falling in love that summer. Amazing! I didn't want to let her go: we were made for one another, just fell for one another! We were out walking the next morning around the little island searching out the wild flowers and whatever else there was to see.

We went down to the shop later that day, got milk, and a twisty brown bread – bit bigger than a Vienna roll, only nicer. We got some cooking oil and I picked up quite a large chicken, and I brought it back. The first thing Clob says is, "What the fuck did you waste money on that for? How are we going to cook it? What's going to happen with that?"

"Don't worry about it, don't worry about it, we'll end up cooking it!"

We had cheese and tomato sandwiches and a lovely mug of coffee each, sitting back listening to music, holding on to one another. Kissin' and huggin' and the time of the year! Fantastic time! I think we could've stayed on the island forever!

That evening I said, "Right, here we go, Clob!" I went into the wood and found a big stake with a V in it, like an old slingshot. I bored a bit of a hole in the ground, tapped this into the ground about two foot away from the fire and about two foot high, and I found a nice round pole, cleaned it all up, rammed it up the chicken's arse, and they were all laughing. I got a bit of butter with garlic and crushed it up, rubbed it all over the chicken and hung it onto the fire. There were a few logs burning away and I gave it an odd twist. BeJesus, after a while you could smell this thing cooking away. It didn't take that long: I'd check it out now and again, pour a bit more oil onto it, get a bit of flame shooting out. It was getting quite brown and crispy – a few bits of black on the wings, but you wouldn't mind that. Well, with a load of the potatoes baking away in the fire, a couple of big tins of peas, a bit of salad on a dish – it was like a banquet! The fold-up table was out, the chairs around it, knives and forks whatever shape we could find. Off comes the chicken into a bowl: the wings just fell off and the legs fell off and we carved most of the breast. It was tender all over – beautiful! It was better than any chicken done in an oven. It was the first barbecued chicken we ever had like that. We spent half the night eating. I can tell you, the bones were like fossils, they were so clean after we finished with them! We tidied them all up that evening into a bag, any papers near the area –even if they weren't our own – we picked everything up. We sat round the bonfire, had a few little joints of hash – smoking away there, good craic, good music, sitting back, love of your life with you in your hand! Ah, beautiful!

We rambled around for another bit of a walk and we took the boat out again that evening. Well, I'll tell you, we could have stayed out the whole night in it, just letting it float around there, tipping the water with the oars, little luminous phosphorescence flying through the water – amazing! The place was full of jellyfish. I didn't do that much swimming; I was no good at it and don't even know whether Clob could swim either. I wasn't into it anyhow – a shower or a bath's enough water! These jellyfish, Jesus they were huge – about a foot in diameter! We actually found out later they were Portuguese Men o' War, so it was just as well we didn't go swimming! We heard afterwards that there were a lot of them around that year.

That night, I thought there couldn't be anything better in the world: holding someone like that and being in love. It made life into something else. You felt responsibility for one another. So we hugged and kissed and went to sleep. The next morning we didn't make it up till around ten. There was no rush, the world was there, we weren't running out of money – we didn't waste anything. We cleaned up the whole area, lit a fire, boiled a few eggs, put the toast on a toasting fork. Everything was wonderful!

When we had cleaned up the area, we took out the old fire grate we had brought with us; we used to throw it onto the ground, that way you could have a fire underneath and then you could put sticks on top or underneath, depending on what you were doing. Pots would fit on it too. I didn't go to the sea scouts for years for nothing – I remembered everything! This was a beautiful experience, away with the one I loved. We were laughing at the songs too: "if you can't be with the one you love, love the one you're with!" Maybe it was like that, but that wasn't the truth, it was my first big falling in love.

We headed back towards Denmark, to the border. We'd to change money back to Danish kroner – bloody Danish kroner and Swedish kroner, totally different currencies! The van was full of every kind of money – you wouldn't know what you were taking out of it: Irish, English, Belgian, Italian, Spanish, Moroccan! Jesus, every time we'd have to spend half an hour looking for change. It was like a bureau de change, everywhere we went we changed money.

We headed back into Copenhagen and straight back towards Greencamp. It was like we'd never left. We found our little spot where the van was parked: we could see the mark at the grassy edge and parked up there tight.

There was an old French van – one of those weird square Citroen things – parked behind us. There were still a good few around in the camp but we didn't feel up to doing too much, so we sat around the fire, had a couple of beers each, had an evening pipe, as they call it. Kleine zwiebel didn't drink that much anyhow, just the odd beer.

Some people were smoking a lot of hash. I only ever had a little blast in the afternoon and maybe one going to bed. I never got into the idea of waking up with a joint in the morning like people do with cigarettes. Some people in the camp just smoked away, but I never bothered. I used to get up, go for a walk round the area and down to the beach. It was a nice area we were in, in Copenhagen.

Later on, we'd go down to the centre, take a walk around, look at all the sex shops and red-light district. Even though prostitution was technically illegal in Denmark, it was very open; there were porno movie houses all over the place. They even had a *Snow White and the Seven Dwarves* porno movie! It was a bit weird but that's the way it was!

There were quite a few drunks on the streets there too. Even the Danes would be sitting outside the off licences with a crate of beer between maybe two or three lads; they'd drink it up, hand back in the crate with the empty bottles and take out a full one. It worked out ten pence a bottle. It was nothing once you had your empties and your crate, otherwise you paid a good bit more. An empty bottle was nearly the same price as the beer so you never saw empties thrown around – they were all used and re-used. We ended up getting a couple of the old timber Carlsberg crates. We'd four of them in the van: they were great for storage. They slid under the bed and under the press area.

We stripped the van out one day, myself and my little onion, and cleaned it all. We took out what we could unscrew fairly easily, we cleaned all around inside, the roof area, and we painted the inside top of the roof white again – brightened it up quite a bit. We took down the lights and washed the plastic bits on them. We had to get a battery too – we'd had to jump start it about a hundred times. We'd run it down with playing music most of the time. It had probably been in the van a year or two before Clob got it, so I picked up a battery from the same fella with the mates in the Ford garage. The gear stick came out one day and we couldn't fix that. The laughs of your man at us! He said, "Yeah, I think there's something wrong alright!" when I handed him the gearstick. At least it didn't cost that much. The AA cover was gone – we had that the first year. We'd loads of things the first year but the only thing left on it was the insurance – we wouldn't drive without that. We hadn't had tax for over two years, but nobody asked us about it.

Myself and the girlfriend went for a walk down the beach one nice evening. Looking straight across you could see Malmö, in Sweden. There was a very big shipyard over there and, on a clear day, you could actually see the people and you could see the shape of the ships they were building. If you looked to the left of where we were sitting looking at Malmö, there was a huge shipyard in Copenhagen called Burmeister and Wain. You'd see the big ships being built there too; there were thousands of workers in that place. Fyn is the island in the middle of Denmark and they had a big shipyard there, in Odense. There was quite a lot of shipbuilding in Denmark. Likewise in Holland and Germany. A fella was telling me they were building oil tankers in the big shipyard in Odense. They were building bulk carriers and liners in Burmeister and Wain.

It's such an easy-going country, Denmark! You could be out one day walking in the park and see Queen Margrethe out cycling with her two children. There would be no fuss; it wasn't an unusual thing to see. There were a lot of parks; Fælledpark was the big one – the people's park. Everyone used to go to it. We used to go out there some days: bring a few sandwiches, one or two beers and sit in the park. But when you were in love like that it didn't matter where you were. I thought I was going to live forever, and things were going to go on forever as well. Beautiful feeling!

There was a young German guy – I think he was about seventeen – and he was in the camp for about a week or two. He'd shout out, "Hey, Moon, it's fucking great to be alive!" He only spoke a few words of English but he had these mad sayings! There was a French guy who used to hang around there, he was mad as a hatter. When he was saying goodbye, he'd say, "hallo, I'm coming" … backwards! Mad characters. I was getting too fond of Danish pastries as well when I could get them: beautiful thing – Danish pastry and coffee!

We used to walk into Christiania, and on the way in there were stalls set up with people selling candles and oils and incense, and then there was a bench where you could buy sebsi pipes, chebangs, chillums, as well as all the different types of hash: Moroccan, Red Lebanese, Black Afghan, Sitrali – all up on the stall for sale. They had a little weighing scales up there. "You wanna see this? You wanna try that? You wanna have that?" It was unbelievable to see, but Christiania was a state within a state: it was like a young people's city within a city. The odd time you would see a police car in there, but not too often. To tell the truth, it was mainly foreigners that caused any hassle, rarely the Danes – or any of the Scandinavians. There were quite a lot of lads from Finland: beJaysus they were some men to drink! They were stone mad. Like they say about the Nordic countries: it's too dark and too cold for too long. It was a most amazing set-up, Christiania. I often went there; it was a weird place but kind of wonderful, with the people who lived in it, the restaurants and the dance halls. It wasn't mad expensive – you could get a meal there for around twenty-five pence. The beer there was sold at about five pence more than the off licences. There was a bakery in it too, where you could buy your Danish pastries and your bread.

I got used to the Danish dark bread. It was called *rugbrød* and you'd get six or eight small prawns on a slice; you'd hardly see the bread. Even the liver paste on a slice was about half an inch thick! I got fond of the meatballs too: *frikadeller*. I've got a recipe for them but we used to buy them in packets. They're made from pork and beef. You just roll them in a pan in a little bit of oil and get them nicely done: bloody nice! They're lighter too than just beef, with a little bit of onion in them. We got fond of them, so myself and the little onion often had them in the evening time.

There was a cafe we used to go to, called Truck Stop, down near Tivoli. That place was deadly! It was run by an American guy. The sign outside had two yellow lights with a bumper off a lorry. You'd go in there and you'd get a big American meatball. I wasn't mad about those or their burgers: they cooked them rare, but you could get them to burn them for you! They did lovely baked potatoes in their jackets and chicken now and again. We wouldn't go out to dinner that often but that sort of place was okay now and then. It was a good bit dearer than the places in Christiania.

The lads in Christiania weren't there to make big profits. It was aimed at young people who wanted an alternative lifestyle, and who didn't have a lot of money. You could go in there and go to a second-hand stall and get a pair of good jeans for a pound – almost brand new Levis. You'd buy a pair of trousers for ten shillings, a pair of sandals, brand new in a box, cost about the same. They'd be seconds with some minor thing wrong. There were always weird looking clothes. Reinhardt would often have a box of T-shirts: green ones, yellow ones – rare for him to have black. I don't know where he used to come up with them but you could buy two T-shirts for thirty pence.

Greencamp would be closing in a fortnight; the long summer was coming to an end. My little onion was going back to Germany the following week. That'd be something else. Around the first week in September, it was all winding down. There weren't as many people coming in and out. All the usual crowd were still there. In the last week, some of the lads we'd been hanging around with, Alex and Sabine and her partner Bengt, were all wondering what they were going to do – especially Sabine, now she had a baby about four months old. Sabine was going to stay in Denmark anyhow. I didn't know what I was up to myself yet. But anyhow, we'd hang on to one another for another week.

Myself and Vanessa headed into town, to see a film. We were looking around to see what we were going to go to; war films didn't appeal that much so we went to an old Robin Hood film. Vanessa didn't know much about Robin Hood, so we went into that – *The Sword of Sherwood Forest*. I think it was one of the first they made, starring Richard Greene. It was made in Ireland, in Ardmore Studios – not far from where I lived. It was probably made around 1960. It was pretty weird watching it in English with Danish sub-titles. After the film we hung around the city for a while, went into Huset, had a look around the bar to see if anyone we knew was there. We sat around with a few people chatting. There were a couple of people we knew there. You'd never see that many Norwegians or Finns, the odd Swede. There used to be a joke with some of the Danish about Sweden – "nothing wrong with Sweden, if you get rid of the

Swedes!" I found them alright – it was like the jokes between the English and the Irish, I suppose.

We arrived back at the camp, had a beer in the van, playing a bit of music, bit of a smoke before we went to bed. It was a really lovely feeling lying there. Beautiful! Ah, I think I loved Vanessa alright. We made mad love – unbelievable! That summer was something else.

Greencamp had been closed to new arrivals on the Wednesday, although there were still a good few there who were due to leave within the week. So the following Saturday was the day they were going to have the biggest party. There was a Carlsberg truck coming to take away a lot of empties but he was going to leave a lot of full ones, and the organisers said that they were going to have a "special" – it wouldn't be light beer for the party. So, there were four or five crates of decent beer laid on by Greencamp.

On Saturday in the afternoon, they were getting ready for party time, making something called "electric chocolate milk" and I was wondering, what is this going to be?

My little onion says, "What's electric chocolate milk about? I'm not really sure, but we're going to find out anyhow!"

And we did find out! It was a big water boiler filled up with hot water and they powdered up the chocolate and put it into it, but they also powdered up a load of moroccan hash and poured it in with the chocolate milk. "Not too much," they said, "stir it up a bit; keep it stirred." You got a little beaker, like you'd drink coffee out of, and everyone got about a quarter or a half a cup – about a hundred people at the party. "One cup and that's it! You don't come back for any more, don't do that!"

I took a tiny little mouthful. "Oh, Jesus, no, I'm not havin' that!" Sabine, of all people, drank about a quarter of a cup. Loads of people drank it. Well, the panic that night, man! There were people round the fire, lying on the ground and up the walls! Everyone looking like they were after drinking two gallons of beer: they were all stoned out of their brains. Clob and myself and my little onion didn't drink it – just a mouthful, we wouldn't chance any more. But, oh, some greedy fuckers drank two cups!

We went to bed later on that night, got up the next morning and there were still loads of people lying in the tents: some Canadians and Americans, someone else crying, "There's somethin' wrong with Ole!"

"There's somethin' wrong with Jack! He's awake but he won't get up. He says he can't get up, he can't walk."

"They'll be alright. Leave them alone for another day or a half day."

By Tuesday morning, some people were going. "I'm leaving today, I've to get a plane at half four."

"Are you?"

"Yeah, the plane's leavin' on Sunday at half four."

"Well," I said, "this is Tuesday! Yous are all fuckin' spaced out for the last two days."

It took about two days for most of them to come to. Sabine went home sick and she wasn't seen for a day or two. That was quite a party!

Anyhow, Vanessa was leaving in the morning, so that was the end of the story for that. Kiss and cry. "You have my address, I have your address, we hope to meet again. You live very near Hanover so not a big deal."

I left her down to the train station. It was the most amazing thing, the railway system over there. Straight down to the boat, on to the boat, off the boat, onto another train. You didn't have to wait two hours at either end, didn't have to wait five hours for the next one. Anyhow, kiss and goodbye, big hug and say farewell. That's one summer I won't forget.

Greencamp was finishing up. Most of the Americans and Canadians had left, albeit some of them two days later than they planned after that mad party, but we had about two weeks to take the place down.

There was Big Erik, Ole, Bengt, Clob and Mike around to start taking the place down. The trucks would come in in a few days, so we started dismantling the army tents, stacking up the wooden floors. It was heavy enough work, but we got a few beers during the day. It was just wind-down time, and in the evening time I would hop on the moped and fly into the centre, meet a few of the guys down at Huset. We'd still hit Christiania sometimes – down to Fælleskøkken, get a bit of food there. I knew most of the cooks down there and you'd always get a good meal, stews with rice and lentils and things like that. I was eating a lot of stuff like that now, just getting into it myself, only had potatoes now and again.

There were about four or five other guys in Greencamp, they all hung around Fælleskøkken and were talking about getting the remaining group and calling it Greencamp Family and moving into one of the houses. I wasn't interested in that myself. I wasn't interested in being linked up like that, I preferred to be free and easy.

Most of the tents were down, everything was getting packed. The wagons with the bathroom blocks and shop would be moved next – those units were all on wheels. It was good to get use out of the military tents and stuff for the summer season.

There were a lot of people moving into Christiania then. I think there were three or four hundred in it. There were new shops starting up – lots of little places. It was an amazing place to go through, with the big shipyard at the far end of it.

I had been over in Big Erik's house a few times. He lived in a little wooden structure, but it was quite a nice place, just on the outskirts of Copenhagen with a nice garden. He'd bought it a few years before – don't know what he paid for it. I was with Big Erik a couple of nights later and I met his wife, Birgitte – lovely lady – and I met a girl, a friend of theirs called Kate. I had a good chat with her, and she told me she lived down in the centre near the main station. She worked for the Copenhagen post. I had a good chat with her, said we'd meet up some time and go out, for a walk or whatever.

The van was moved out of Greencamp too. I was staying in a Danish fella's place: Ole. He said I could stay there for a week or two anyhow. He had a nice apartment. There were plenty of low rental places in Copenhagen. I was getting used to being in Copenhagen now. It was quite an interesting place. There are no hills or mountains in Denmark; it's fairly flat and you can easily ride a bicycle around most of it.

There was a big party in the town hall in Copenhagen a couple of weeks later, given by the Lord Mayor for all the people who had worked and helped out in City Camp and Greencamp. I hadn't been in the town hall before, so I was looking forward to it. We all arrived to the party, all beards and hair – a strange looking crowd coming to it! I think there were about eighty or ninety people there. We all went in and sat down and the Lord Mayor gave a little speech: "All you hairy people" and "good summer you had here" and "good work you did" and "everyone has their own way of going on", and so on like that.

Then the food came out: there was all sorts of little starter dishes with prawns and salmon and catfish and meatballs. Then they served what they call flæskesteg, it's roast pork belly. It was roast pork with potatoes and some vegetables and large bowls of salad. There was loads of food, too much to eat really! Then there were slices of cream cakes and cheesecakes and all that kind of stuff for the dessert. Coffee, tea, whatever you wanted – it went on for hours and hours. A few fellas were talking about where they were going to go to next and what they were going to do. Most of the guys, the conscientious objectors, they had to do something else for another few months.

The day after the party I met a guy called American Mike. He lived over beside a place called Brumleby, and they'd a bit of a party going on in the house. We didn't go to the pubs that much – we'd drink in a garden area or at someone's session in a house, bring a few beers with us. I met a few more Americans there, there was American Morton – to differentiate him from Danish Morton – and there was Butch, who was living in Brumleby. Brumleby was a small complex of houses, with the toilets across the yard from the house. They were divided into two flats, top and bottom ones. It was cheap accommodation from the council, but a very sought-after place, with a nice green area in the middle.

Most of the American guys I knew skipped America because they didn't want to go to Vietnam. Many of them ended up in Sweden and made their way to Denmark and quite a few of them stayed on there as they couldn't go back to the States at that time. It was only then that I realised why, and that it was all about getting put in the army at eighteen, to go to Vietnam and get your head blown off. And they weren't allowed have a beer until they were twenty-one! I could understand the lads. They didn't know where Vietnam was or what it was about other than being told to go out there and "fight for your country!" Jesus, it was one of the most stupid things I'd ever heard of. Butch and the lads were bloody sound people.

I had started going out with Kate by now and was planning to move down to her place. She lived in Dannebrogsgade, very close to the Central Station. There was a big supermarket in the station, so it was handy to get stuff when we were out. I was getting used to speaking a little bit of Danish now, making myself understood with the local people.

I still had a few bob but there were a few stainless steel factories over there so I decided to do a bit of work in them for a while. Now that we were in the EEC, we could work in Denmark. Before that it hadn't been so easy. Once Ireland joined the EEC it became just a formality: you walked in, got your job, got your personal identification number and your ID card. When I got mine, I got the metro to the factory area, walked around a good bit of it, and found one place where there was an English foreman – he'd stayed there after the war. He was a nice fella – showed me round the place and told me what they did. The boss asked me what I could do so I told him. He shook hands with me and said, "Come up on Monday." I said I had papers, but he said, "Ah just come up and make a few things for us and see how you get on." When I went up on the Monday, I got two stainless-steel handrails to make up. It was only cutting pipes, welding bends together, and putting on the mounting plates. I put them together in a couple of hours, cleaned them all down and polished them up. He was well surprised that I could do the polishing; a lot of people there just did welding and then left the rest to someone else. "Very good job," he said, and that I could start straight away.

I was working away there, getting on well in the job and getting on great with Kate. It was easy living with someone – makes it nice in the city. She was earning money, I was earning money, so we could go out on the weekend, go down to the town, to the Truck Stop Cafe. There was a big festival coming up in Copenhagen – a kind of dance party on the street. There was a big concert on in Fælledpark as well, with a Danish band called Burnin' Red Ivanhoe, so we headed off to that; there were hundreds of people at it. It had been a long hot summer, but it was getting near the end of it now. Butch and all the lads lived near the park, so they were all there. They were all trying to do different things. Clob had moved over near Christiania with the Greencamp family and a couple of English guys still hanging around with them. There was one guy from Iceland and Santana from Argentina was hanging around with them – the same guy with the big Afro who had been to Morocco with us.

Most weekends we'd all meet up. I was getting used to doing a good bit of cooking in the flat, which was nice enough. Kate had two cats, I didn't mind them but you'd smell them alright! We were on the third floor and you had to go all the way down to the yard to clean out their litter. I was enjoying the job, getting on well with the lads there. There was a fairly good canteen in the factory and you could get quite a bit of stuff in it. I only took sandwiches now and again, if we had stuff made, or leftovers to make up sandwiches. I still felt like moving on but I was going to stay most of the winter there. I was thinking of going over to Odense, taking a few trips in Denmark.

Clob was talking about heading to India – I wasn't sure when – but I didn't want to head off at that time. Kate and I were getting on very well, so it was the Summer of Love for me!

You could head to Sweden on the jet foil. They pulled into Copenhagen and took about thirty-five minutes to cross the Sound. I was on it once or twice; it was like a passenger speedboat. When they take off, they go up on two jet foils, like little legs, and sail along on the water. There was nothing much in Malmo back then – a bit of a centre, a shipyard, a lot of houses, but not really anything happening because they didn't have the bars they had in Copenhagen or Denmark. Denmark was very liberal compared to Sweden. Denmark is probably the most liberal country in Scandinavia. You'd get influxes of Norwegians, Swedes and Finns on the weekends. There was some beer drunk in Copenhagen on the weekends!

Kate looked well in the uniform when she was going to work. It was a yellow uniform with a little hat and a badge like a little brass bugle that reminded me of the Canadian Mounties. The postal service used an old motorbike, called a Nimbus. They were ancient; they'd been designed in Denmark and been in production from 1919 to 1960. They had a flat bar frame with a four-cylinder engine. The postal service ones had a sidecar on them. Ole had one and it was quite a strange looking machine with a big fishtail exhaust. I'm into old bikes and I eventually managed to find one in the UK, years later. It's a lovely machine: nice to drive.

It was getting close to Christmas and we were all going to meet up, have a bit of a do in our own place and then meet up with other people later on. It wouldn't be celebrated as much as in Ireland. I've been in a few places at Christmas and Ireland seems to have the biggest celebrations; it's more of a family thing. In Copenhagen we had a few beers with the lads I worked with. We met up with Butch and Morton, and Clob was still around. He hadn't moved on yet and I didn't think he'd move for a while. He was using the van sometimes. I could use it if I wanted to but I wasn't using it much at that time. There were four or five of us talking about going down to Bremen but I wasn't really interested. Kate and I were getting on too well. Second love of the summer.

It was good to be with someone in the winter, and I was still enjoying work. We went over to Christiania one day and there was a fella building a house out of bottles. He had about one and a half walls up and it looked amazing. Another fella had a boat, and he'd cut it and joined it together with beams. There was a doorway in it and two rooms – one bottom room with a kitchen in it and then a little bedroom with a small ladder up into it. There were all sorts of houses being built in the place, including the first octagon house, which was strange looking. There were two new restaurants as well – one was going to do Indian food. There were new repair shops and it was getting bigger and bigger by the month. Kate was offered a new apartment, which was a three room with two bedrooms. They wouldn't rent it to one person, but she asked if I would sign up to rent with her, which meant my name would go down as a person who was registered to live there, so we both had to sign the papers from the council. We went to look at it and it was a big place alright. Where we were living was quite small, so we moved about a week before Christmas. It was a nice spot, in a nicer area too. It was the first time I had my name on a door over there: Kate Andersen and Anthony Flood. There were nicer views out the windows and it was brighter and more open, and there was a park very close by.

I was beginning to think about what was going to happen in the new year. I was thinking about planning a trip east, to go as far as I could. I had enough money now to take a good trip and I was planning to leave in the middle of February. I talked to Kate and she didn't mind. We still got on very well together, but nothing is forever and you don't live forever!

I told the boss I'd be leaving in three weeks. He said he'd be sorry to see me go, and if I was ever back to just call up, that there could be work there. I started thinking about where I was going. I planned to go down to Amsterdam and from there to head for Istanbul. I was talking to all the lads. Butch and Morton said, "Ah, you'll be back!"

I said, "I should be, y'know. Copenhagen is more of a base now than Ireland. It's easier to get in and out of. I can get work very easily here. There's not much in Ireland still."

Clob hadn't taken off yet, but he said he was definitely going to India.

10

I DECIDED I WAS NOT GOING TO hitch this time so, on the twentieth of February, I took a train straight to Amsterdam. It was still the same: everyone met outside the American Express. You could get a ride from there to anywhere. I saw that the Magic Bus was leaving in two days. That one went all the way to India, but I wasn't into that. I got a ticket for one going down as far as Athens, one of the big old-style converted Mercedes vans. There'd be ten or twelve people heading down that way anyhow. It was strange to be on the road again.

We headed down across Germany and after two days we were in Athens. Most of the people were going all the way to Greece, although a few got off along the way. The following day I was hanging around Athens train station. There were a few steam trains still around at that time; there was one going to Istanbul in the afternoon. There was lots of hustle and bustle in the station. I got on the train and it was a long trip, but eventually we arrived on the European side of Istanbul. We hadn't crossed the Bosphorus yet. I got off the train. It was mental there! The oldest taxis and cars you've ever seen in your life – it was mad! There were hundreds of people running around the place, shops and markets – all the roaring and shouting in the markets. I saw a fella carrying furniture on his back, more than you'd put onto a small truck; he was bent over walking up the town with it on his back.

There were donkeys carrying all sorts of things – it really was something else! I was sitting around, trying to take it all in. There were men shouting, "chai, chai!" They were selling tea in little glasses; you'd get a sweet to put in your mouth and you sip the tea through it. I said I'd try it out. It was quite good. You filter everything through your teeth there – the coffee's the same, little bits in it all the time. That evening I went out to try some Turkish food in a little restaurant called The Pudding Shop. It was famous as a meeting place for Beats and hippies back in the sixties, and as far as I know it's still there! They

Istanbul furniture delivery.

make all these stewed lamb and chicken dishes with red sauces and yellow sauces and beautiful little potatoes chopped up in them. I got a lamb one – really tasty – with a nice bit of fresh bread that they bake in the round ovens. I was sitting there and I saw that they had Tuborg, so I got a pint. I didn't think they'd sell beer there, but they did. It was brewed there: there was a brewery in Ankara. Then I had a semolina pudding. I hadn't had one since I was eight or nine years of age, when my mother used to make them. It still tasted good. I stayed around there for a while and met one or two people, but I couldn't understand a word of the language.

I decided I was going to stay in Istanbul for a few days before I moved on. There was a small hotel up the road with three or four beds to a room. The beds were no more than four or five wooden poles, tied together with a few laths of what looked like weaving and a rush base. I reckoned I'd be better off if I used the sleeping bag to sleep in. It was dry and you were out of the way and that was about it, but it wasn't far from the little restaurant. I think it worked out at ten or fifteen pence a night.

I went walking round the markets the next day, to see all the semi-precious stones and Turkish wedding rings. They're like a puzzle ring, you can take them apart. The idea was, you put it on to your wife's finger – you can have a five piece one I think. If she takes it off and it comes apart, she definitely won't be able to put it back together, so you'll know if she's been unfaithful, or else why'd she take the ring off? One of the lads in the market was trying to sell me a box of them. I said, "I don't want anything at the moment, I'm not staying around, I'm heading on."

I went down to the bridge over the Bosphorus. I was walking along the bridge in the afternoon, and the weather was nice – it hadn't go that hot yet. I spotted a guy with a few little catguts hanging over the bridge, tied in a little rope. He had a little fire going with a hotplate on it and bread and stuff like that. He pulled up one of his lines and there were three or four medium sardines on it, and he asked did I want to buy a sandwich. I did, as I had never eaten one like that. He put three of them on the hotplate, they were turned over three or four times – done in a few minutes, and he stuck them in one of the flatbreads. That was it – nothing else in it. It was delicious! I had a cup of the tea with it. He said he'd been on that part of the bridge for three or four years; his customers were the people crossing. It was only a couple of pence for what I had.

You could see the military college on the far side, an absolutely huge building – the biggest building that I could see on the Asian side.

So I crossed to the Asian side for a while, to hang around there. I met two of the soldiers from the college there. We were just chatting and they said that there were good bars on that side too. There was one place they recommended – a club called Moby Dick's with the shape of a whale outside it – so I hung around that night and went to Moby Dick's. There were just beers, and food being served in the restaurant. The night club wasn't on at that time. It was a bloody big building though. Looking back across, the European side was a lot more impoverished looking than the Asian side. This side seemed a lot wealthier. That was not what I expected but I only stayed the one night on the Asian side. I was planning on just staying another few days. There's a big mosque there, the Blue Mosque, built in 1616. I went up to the mosque and took off my shoes and went in and looked at the rest of the people that were in there; they were all praying. You'd hear the muezzin calling out in the morning and in the evening time for prayer call. It was similar to the Angelus, except it goes off at dawn – I think it goes five times a day there, we only get two out of it!

They're nice people, but there was a lot of hassling: "You wanna

buy this? You wanna buy that?" I spotted some big, long forties and fifties Yankee cars going round. They had black and white stripes round the edge, just under the window lines. They were taxis but I didn't understand what the stripe meant. I was talking to one of the guys and he explained the ordinary taxi doesn't have the stripes on it. The ones with the

Dolmus taxi, Istanbul.

stripe were called Dolmus; it meant that you could share a ride with someone else to split the fare so the driver could stop and pick up more people on the way to where it was going.

The other one was just non-stop; it would just take you to where you were going. It seemed like a good idea. If it was stopping on the way and you split your fare it wasn't going to cost you a whole lot. They had a fibreglass car too: it was built on a Ford chassis and engine – I think it was called an Anadol. The whole body was fibreglass. There were quite a few of them around.

I went down to the bus station and there were buses going everywhere. I wanted to get a bus as far as Ankara, or a little further if I could. They said to get down there about eight o'clock in the morning.

It was Bedlam when I got down there, crowds everywhere. But I hopped on the bus, headed off, and about fifty miles outside of Istanbul the whole world changed. The poverty of the villages and towns I went through was unbelievable. The houses were tiny. It was a good old drive to Ankara.

Ankara's a very big city, again, millions of people. I wasn't going to stay there: I was looking to get a bus that went to within a hundred and fifty miles of the Iranian border. But there had been storms and flooding in some of the hill country. We'd pull up at some of the places to get something to eat and you'd be standing nearly up to your knees in mud, from the melting snow and rain. I got a bit to eat in a few places along the way, but I always took a couple of boiled eggs with an onion and bread. I had to be very careful with the water now, I'd drink the tea all the time, anywhere I could get it. I even had a bottle I used to put two of the teas into. It wouldn't matter if it was cold, at least it was made up with boiled water. I stayed off the regular water completely.

We were heading up into the hilly country. It was vast and very poor. You'd see people, donkeys and carts, and herds and herds of goats. What they ate there was mainly goat rather than lamb. It didn't matter anyhow, it tasted good: all the kebabs and the stews were good. The safest thing when you're not used to it is boiled eggs; you can't go wrong. I had a little bit of salt in my pocket all the time. Now and again, you'd get a few nice tomatoes, if you got to the right place. Tomatoes and eggs, fresh bread was what I lived on. They have a big dome with the fire in the bottom, and they pat out the bread in their hands, throw it in to the side of the oven; it sticks and when it's cooked it falls down into the fire area. They take it out and beat off the bits of ashes. You'd always have a fine sand in it, because I think that's what the lining part of the oven is. You'd feel it on your teeth but it didn't do any harm – you'd get used to it. There were some lovely people but it was like going back to the twenties or the thirties in Ireland: children with no shoes on half of them and little shirts and jackets on them. It'd make you wonder about what the rest of the world is like.

I got off the bus in a biggish town and there was going to be nothing moving for a week. There'd been bad flooding and some of the roads were covered in so much landslide material that nothing much could move. They didn't have much heavy machinery out there. I was talking to one of the guys, who'd come through the day before it all happened, and he said there were houses washed down and the place was completely wrecked in some areas.

I got a little hotel room to stay in again. It was weird, some of the rooms had full windows, some of them didn't, they just had a curtain across a hole in the wall. It mustn't have been used that much or maybe it was only in summertime. The room I was in had no heating. In the lobby area where you sat downstairs, there was a big log-burning stove – well, they burned anything they could get their hands on. The lobby and the restaurant were all in one. There were a few little shops, but nothing much in that area. I didn't mind so long as I got a dry bed.

I got cleaned up; my old boots were nearly destroyed – soaking – so I dried them off. The only other pair of shoes I had weren't worth putting on: little runners that'd be ruined. I'd a fair amount of gear with me. I always kept a few changes of clothes. It was a bit like Ireland – you'd want a pair of wellies out there, but I didn't have any. That would look a bit weird anyhow. I went back down to the little restaurant, had a cup of chai and got a chocolate blancmange pudding. We used to have blancmange puddings when we were kids. Puddings were a big thing out there!

The people were all quite friendly, you'd even get the odd one who spoke a bit of English. There was quite a lot of German influence there, as we all know the story of *The Guns of Navarone*. There are quite a lot of Turks live in Germany as well – I suppose it'd be like the many Irish living in England.

That night I was talking to a nice fella called Hosam. He'd never been out of Turkey. He had a certain amount of English and he spoke a bit of German. There wouldn't have been that many tourists in Turkey – not in that part anyway – back then. He had three or four acres of land that he grew vegetables on. He said if you grow your own and sell the rest off, to buy in food that you don't grow and feed your couple of donkeys, you can just about get by. He had two very young sons as well. But he'd been doing nothing for the winter. A lot of the land out there was reasonable – when it got warm you got good crops, but it wouldn't be getting close to that for a few months.

I had another two or three days there before the roads would be opened again. The minute those roads were open I was taking a bus to the Iranian border. That'd be a hoo-ha and a half! I'd need money for visas. I had changed most of the money I had brought with me into American dollars and English pounds – the only currency that spoke in those countries. I had changed just enough Turkish Lire to live in Turkey, but I didn't know what they called the Iranian currency yet. Iran was supposed to be a little bit hostile towards anyone from a 'Republic' but I would just have to see how it went.

You'd find different things out about countries when you're travelling. The Turks were very friendly but they'd a very strange attitude to the women. Most of the men were hard on the women. The women did most of the farm work, most of the housekeeping, most of the cooking, getting the timber to keep the fire going, kept the house going. You could see it in places you'd stop in: the men would be all sitting down with their water pipes, blowing away there. They'd have a big pipe with a glass bowl and the neck coming up would have four or five smoke tails coming out of it, and they'd all be sucking away on the big top on the pipe. It would be sweet tobacco and it could have strawberry or mint flavour, and they'd be just relaxing. They all had their little beads that they played with in their hands as they sat there in the doorways outside the little shops, pushing the beads through their fingers one at a time; they were like a half-sized rosary beads, but I think they called them worry beads. They'd sit there most of the day playing with these things. There'd be a few dogs around, but you didn't see pigs of course. There'd be a few horsemen around the hillsides and some little rotovator carts as well, but not much machinery at all.

The bus depot said the buses would be leaving in a day, so

we were all getting ready to move. You'd get a bit weary hanging around for a few days, though I never sat in the one place; I always mingled a bit, got talking to find out what was happening in each place. You'd make good contacts for stopping on the way back; you could save money. Like that fella I was talking to with the little farm place: I could've gone to his place if I'd wanted to. You'd get home cooking and a bed in exchange for a bit of work. You'd stay there for thirty or forty pence a night and they'd give you your dinner and your bed.

I had a passport wallet around my neck and I had that reinforced with a heavier leather cord. It had three compartments in it, the passport was tucked into one, some American money and some English in another part. I never carried very much money in my pockets or anywhere else, but this used to go down inside my vest and almost hang to my balls and I never let it out of my sight or let anyone touch it. I wouldn't carry anything loose like that out. You wouldn't mind losing your clothes, but if your passport and money were gone out there you'd be in trouble.

You find out the strangest things as you move around, for instance, I was told that when you got to Tehran it would be like landing in some part of America: the Shah was there at that time. The Americans had a lot to do with that: they've a lot to do with everywhere!

We were on the bus now, ready to leave. To get to the border area, we had to go through some desert – thousands of miles of it. We headed out but the bus was barely moving: I'd say it was doing about ten to twenty miles an hour. That bus must've been about fifty years old. It had a petrol engine anyhow – you could hear it! Some of the windows didn't close, some of them didn't open; some of the seats, you could just about sit on! Everything was fairly clapped out. It was a long way up into the hills to the border area. We were supposed to be there within a day, but it was looking more like it would be the following day. We'd have to have another stopover somewhere. You could see far-off mountains that were completely white.

That night we stopped pretty late. The driver said he was going to leave at first light, whatever time that'd be. By now I hadn't a

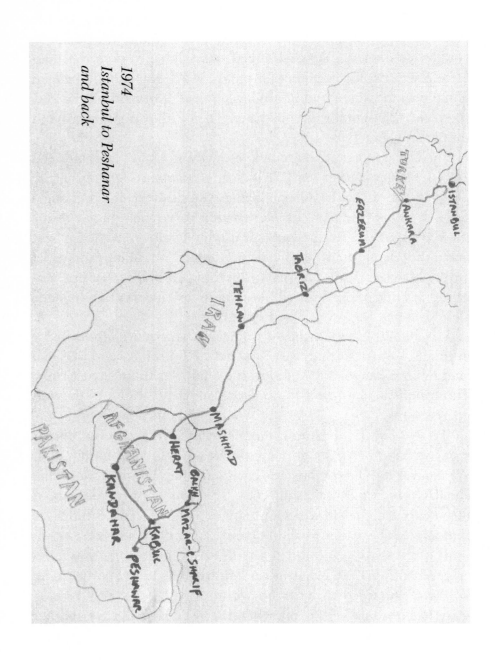

clue what day it was, I never knew the time – the only time you knew was when you were getting hungry. I ate the last boiled egg and half an onion and a bit of bread. Anyhow, first thing in the morning, the bus was blowing the horn and people were panicking outside, shoving things on. Someone got on there with two goats and a box of chickens. The noise of the goats bleating, chickens squawking – anything goes on those buses! Anyhow, we headed on, got to the border and that was it. The bus stopped there at the frontier.

UP WE GOT OUT OF TURKEY AND walked across a little bit of no-man's-land to the Iranian border. At passport control, I handed in the passport. "Oh, Irish? Revolutionary, oh, guns! You want guns?"

"No, no," I said, "I'm just travelling."

"You must fill in this, fill in that. Big papers – name address, where you came from, where you're going … fill in what you can. Give it back." Jaysus, I think I paid nearly four dollars for that visa. It took up two pages of the passport when they stamped it – stamps all in a row, and then they stamped over them. I was getting rid of a week's money in five seconds.

Anyhow, I was allowed in, so I got a short distance bus from the border – another rattly yoke through the sand and dust now! I started wearing a turban-type thing, tied around my mouth, otherwise you'd be choked with half the windows open the whole time.

One thing I had noticed just before we got off that bus was that there were smashed-up cars on big concrete plinths. There was one on each side of the road and I asked one of the people there who spoke a bit of English about it. He said it was to notify you that if you were speeding and you didn't have control of your car you'd end up being killed in a car crash, so they were put there as a warning. It was their policy for road safety, which I thought was pretty advanced at the time, but they do it in a few places now.

We came down to a town that had rail links, so I said to myself I definitely didn't want to stay on a bus for another forty-eight hours.

Everything moved slowly there; there was no panic – life there was like that. Some of the people in Iran wore beautiful clothes, but then others had very little. There were a lot of Nomadic tribes there as well, herding goats and camels: lots of camels and different breeds of goats. The Nomads moved from one area to another for grazing and water.

I got on a steam train, and we headed off across that vast country – there wasn't much greenery in the countryside we passed through. I got a few tomatoes and four or five boiled eggs and some bread. The bread was quite hard, so it didn't go off too quickly.

Between the smoke from the train, and dust and sand from the deserts blowin', it wasn't much different from when Laurence of Arabia was around, I think.

You could half-sleep on the train alright but you wouldn't get much room. There was no food wagon, but we'd pull in at the stations and people would come and hand you food in through the windows. The little stews and dishes like that were usually alright there – nicely spiced. They were selling tea, yoghurt, bread, eggs – anything you wanted, along the side of the train. You needed some kind of container to put a stew into. I always had a little pot with me that I could put anything into. There were always a lot of people running around the station areas.

It must have been about five in the morning when we got into Tehran. There wasn't much happening at that hour, but, by Jaysus, within three hours when I got into the centre, it was crazy! Big American cars, American flags – it was true alright what they'd said. The Shah was there. At the prayer calls that went from the towers in the morning, everything stopped. Even the train stopped once or twice and most of them got off to pray.

Tehran was a big city – a crazy place! I made sure to hold on to my bag and hold onto everything now. Walking around near the centre, I just happened to be going through my paperwork and I noticed that I had about three or four weeks until my smallpox vaccination was out, so I went down to the local hospital. They said there would be no one there for a few hours, so I sat and waited. Eventually I was called in and this fella gave me the vaccination, then he stamped the card to say that I had got it done. He said,

"You're heading towards Afghanistan? Afghanistan is full of smallpox!"

I hung round Tehran for a few days. I had found the Turks better craic – they had more going on than a big city like Tehran. There were lots of veils there, lots of women covered up, and lots of black clothing. The food was okay, but it was nearly all camel and goat, and whatever else you can find. They'd eat a bit of lamb there – there were quite a lot of flocks of sheep being herded around and you'd see them in the distance when you were on the train – but hundreds and hundreds and hundreds of goats.

I was still staying off the water as much as I could. Sugar cane juice was the safest: they had these little mangles set up, with little grinders on each side. They'd shove in two canes at a time and turn it by hand. The amount of juice that came out of them! It went into a plastic container and they served it in small glasses. It was very sweet but you weren't going to get anything nasty off it. Water was bloody dynamite unless it was served well boiled.

I was walking around some of the streets there and there were loads of little antique shops, selling old-style swords and guns and pipes and glassware. I was offered some turquoise a few times and I decided I'd have to find out more about it. There's a nice bright blue, and a greeny-blue – you have to really know which ones to go for. There were really nice pieces and you could get someone to set some of the pieces into a necklace or rings. There were stalls selling old coins, but you wouldn't know what you were looking at half the time.

After a few days I decided to head up towards the Afghan border. The small towns were nicer – a bit more relaxing.

I got a taxi to the bus station but before we got there, I realised something terrible – I had left my passport under my pillow in the hotel! I started banging the taxi driver's back, shouting, "Turn around! Turn around! Get me back to the hotel!" I had taken the passport out because they wanted to look at it and then I stuck it under my pillow when I went to bed, and forgot to put it back in the pouch. Disaster! I jumped out of the taxi and raced into the hotel, up the stairs to my room, and got there just as the cleaners were about to go in. I ran in, grabbed the passport and shoved it back into my pouch. Back to the bus station in the taxi but the bus had already left … what was I going to do?

So, I was walking around and came across a truck yard; there were about six trucks parked up, and I went around and asked each driver where they were heading for. I didn't want to wait around there for another bus. I got up to one truck – very colourful, full of paintwork and very old. I'd say it must have been from about 1958 and it had a big petrol engine in it. I got talking to the owner, Al. He was delivering goats, but he said he was going back to his home in the countryside. He would be going directly there but it'd be a good long drive, and he would be glad of the company. He was sitting with a few other guys who didn't have two words of English, but he introduced me and told them I was a young Irish fella, touring and heading further out east, planning to hit Afghanistan in a week or two and that I was going back with him. He was a decent fella, didn't drink beer at all, but they were all sitting around on the pipe. Mostly what they were smoking was a caramel tobacco stuff – the smell was so sweet it was like Scots Clan gone wrong! They did smoke grass, but most of them, when they were outside these little tearoom places, were smoking pipes full of flavoured tobacco – you could smell them when they'd light up.

From chatting away to him there, I found out he'd about a hundred and fifty goats, counting kids. He'd been keeping goats for the last ten years – they were hardy animals. He was talking about the nomadic tribespeople, and how when they moved, they usually moved around thirty camels, maybe up to a thousand goats, two or three families, and there could be another fifty donkeys, but they would bring all their tents on the back of the camels. They did a lot of walking. He said they had a special breed of a dog that's supposed to kill a wolf. He said the wolves had been known to take babies. He knew a lot of nomads – he did a lot of dealing with them for goats.

Before we left I had something to eat and then, with a full belly, met Al and got into his truck. It was unbelievable inside – all painted and there were beads hanging out of everywhere, colours all over the windscreen, little fancy curtains hanging halfway down the doors, like an old Bedouin thing: fancied up to the last. We headed off with a whining gearbox and whining back axles. We were travelling for about an hour or two, and he was always fussing about the truck, watching gauges, banging them to see if they were working right. The temperature gauge wasn't up to much, it was just a little dot thing that must've been an attachment. It was a noisy ride – not too comfortable, but it was okay, none of the trucks were comfortable out there!

The roads weren't great and it was very hilly country. There were a lot of different animals being herded about: a lot of camels, millions and millions of goats, lots of donkeys. There were lots of children and women too. He was telling me he had spent a good bit of time in London when he was very young, but he said he'd rather be back home. He seemed to be getting on well where he was now, on his small farm, with his wife and children, farming goats and breeding donkeys – interesting fella. After about four hours driving, we pulled over for the night. Al usually slept in the cab, so I just rolled out the sleeping bag on the back area. There was a big canvas cover on the back of the truck. We pulled over onto a kind of lay-by, nothing but desert all around – unbelievable, sand everywhere. You'd taste it in your mouth and I'd a fairly longish beard – it was always getting full of sand too.

I got into the sleeping bag and it must have been about eleven o'clock at night – I hadn't a clue what time the sun went down or when it got dark there. I didn't carry a watch. If I needed the time I'd ask somebody or look at a clock in a station or a town. It was very quiet. Not a murmur of anything. Nothing, not a light, nothing whatsoever! Black. Dead silence.

I woke in the morning when he started banging on the back. He said he was going to be moving in half an hour, at six o'clock. We headed off again, met a few other trucks – blew the horn and waved, more camel herds. Nothing only goats and camels, a lot of people on donkeys, a lot of small carts as well. There were very few engines, I suppose it was so far out of the city they didn't bother. One thing you had to do was carry fuel, Al had a couple of extra tanks on the back.

We headed back up into the hills. It was very warm but a nice drive anyhow – no radio or anything like that, we were just talking, Al pointing out different places and different things on the way. It was very hard to understand the names of places, easier to remember what they were. There were some very old buildings that had been unoccupied for a long time in a few places. The wind was full of sand belting off the bonnet, going into every crack and every little loose door frame – keeping it out of the eyes was the most important thing. Then we were higher up in the mountains, spectacular views, one or two trucks in front of us now, more camels – you nearly had to stop sometimes there'd be so many crossing. There was very little green – some of the higher hill areas had green pastures and decent water. He lived in a high area.

A couple of hours in, we were going to get something to eat. It was about half ten. We pulled into a small village with a few small houses. There was one of those ovens on the side of the road where they baked bread and they were doing kebabs, so I got a couple. Goat kebabs are quite delicious, they flavour them up with spices and stuff. Young goat is very like lamb really. I got a pot of chai tea: it's made with milk, tea leaves, cinnamon and a few things like that in it – it's nice. Then there was fresh yoghurt, like a big lump – throw a little bit of sugar cane juice over the top – tastes absolutely delicious. It's floating in a big tank, and they cut out pieces. Sitting outside at a little table there, I got talking to a lady who spoke a little bit of English. She said it would be another ten to twelve hours to the Afghan border, so I wasn't too pushed. I wasn't in a mad panic to get there. It was quite a friendly little town.

I bought a piece of fresh bread, very heavy cheese – it was goats' cheese but I'd have to get used to the taste of it anyhow – and a boiled egg and put it all in a bag for later. It was only a couple of pence. I walked around to a few of the places. Everyone just sits on the side of the road there. The fellas were sitting there with their worry beads out. The weather was quite nice – the temperature had gone up a good bit. I picked up a light green shirt, and a very light pair of trousers with just a tie band on the waist and a pair of sandals. I think it was about one pound fifty for the whole lot. They were looking to buy my jeans, but I said I might need them on the way back. I had to get out of those clothes, though – it was baking!

It was normally around twenty-five degrees but at that time the sun was coming down fairly strong. They said it was going to get hotter.

Al lived about an hour's drive further on and he didn't mind if I wanted to stay with him for a while. He didn't speak English much at home, but there was a little bunk room he said I could stay in. We got back into the truck and I couldn't wait to see what his place was like. We were heading right off the marked roads. If there was grass it would have been in the middle but there was no grass. It was an unusual drive, soft in places, lots of sand and very few houses out that way. You could drive for an hour and you wouldn't see anything – maybe a few camels and goats and people. After an hour or so we arrived into his town. There wasn't any mains electricity in it; there were one or two generators. The one they were on ran about four houses, fairly economically. They didn't know when they were going to get power up there – there were quite a lot of places without power. Fuel wasn't expensive. They only ran it for a couple of hours in the morning and a couple of hours in the evening. It was mainly for fridges and a few lights on in the morning and in the evening, but they had a lot of oil lamps. It was scented oil – nice when they had them going. They just had radio, no television or anything like that.

He stopped the truck and we went into his house. Right away he was met by the wife and the two children. They were very friendly and invited me in. First thing she did was get a meal ready, a nice spicy stew. It was goat, potatoes, carrots and there was a big loaf cut up on the table. There was some kind of juice to drink – it tasted quite good. They made it themselves: it was crushed berries – not apple, but there was a bit of an appley taste off it – maybe pomegranate or something. It was a nice meal – not too hot, just a few spices. I wasn't shown around outside that night, as it was getting a bit late. We sat around there and he took out a pipe; I wasn't surprised by that at this stage. There was a lovely open fire where they burned a lot of sods of manure. They mixed the manure with straw, made it into a round loaf shape, added a little water to it to stick them together and they stuck them on the side of the out-buildings. It was strange to see rows of these on the wall. Once they dried, they'd fall off the wall. There was very little timber around so that's what they used. The fire was blazing away. It was rather like burning turf at home, except that they were round instead of long rectangular pieces. If you put a few of them on the fire, there was massive heat out of them.

There was a big open fire and a bit of a chimney. They were small rooms with no windows as such – just square openings with a small curtain pulled down. They'd open them in the evening time, to let the cooler night air circulate. It was probably a bit like it had been a hundred or a hundred and fifty years ago in Ireland. We were sitting there talking and he asked me if I wanted to try the pipe. "Ah I'll take little bit," I said. I hadn't smoked for months, I just had a few tokes out of his pipe. It was nice with a refreshing cup of chai, talking about the time he was in England. He was going to study to be a lawyer or a doctor but he had had enough of it after a couple of years. It wasn't his own idea at the time. I think his father had said he'd better get some sort of education, that things would change. He said they weren't changing that quick, so when his father died he went back home. I think his mother and father were both dead at that time. He had one brother living in Tehran and didn't see anyone else from his family.

In the morning when we were up, I wanted to see this goat farm. Up we went to the back – it was about a hundred yards from where the house was, through little passageways. There were three or four fields up the back and there were quite a few donkeys around. It was quite open, but he let a few roars and all the goats came flying over – seemed like hundreds, I think it was about a hundred and fifty. They milked a lot of them; there was a small milking parlour and the milk was sold locally. They made a fair amount of cheese and yoghurt. It was all made in one little shed, and it was the same kind of yoghurt you'd get everywhere out there – a solid block. The cheese was quite nice – they made the soft white one and then they made the heavy brown type. The soft white one you'd have to eat within a day or two, but the other one you could hang on to. He told me they were going to kill one of the goats in a day or two. They lived mainly on goat, and they had a vegetable garden as well. They used money very little – that little farming area seemed to have a really good barter system in place. They didn't talk about money as such. I didn't see anyone with a schoolbag while I was there. I think some of the kids were taught at home. It was a nice little area, very quiet – in the evening it was just blue sky and stars.

I spent my days helping him get the goats in and out, Jesus it was amazing. The baby donkeys were beautiful – he had about fifteen of them. He said there was always a market for them, that he might put three or four in the back of the truck and head off with them. He'd always sell them – at any of the markets you went to, donkeys were nearly always the first thing sold. They're a fantastic animal: they'd carry you around all day if you want them to. You'd see them carrying bundles of sticks – little small sticks that people picked up all over the place, you wouldn't see many trees. They had baskets like you'd see in the west of Ireland with sods of turf in them. They'd go out around the fields and they'd pick up all of the manure, all the droppings from camels, and they could end up making twenty or thirty of those briquettes with the straw – any kind of straw and grass would hold them together. It was the same idea with the walls: timber frames and then plaster them with straw and mud.

I was getting used to the little town there, thinking I wouldn't mind staying for a while with him. We were going to go to the market on the following Saturday and that'd be an interesting trip. He didn't want any money from me, so I was happy to help out where I could. I got on well with the two little kids. They were fairly shy at first – they'd shout, "Hallo Mister!" then laugh and run away. They didn't get many foreigners up there. I was the foreigner now.

He'd picked out a goat one evening: it was going to be the dinner over the weekend. He'd cut its throat, hang it and bleed it out in two seconds – hardly even a baaaa. He'd open the belly and clean it out, cut around the head and the feet and – Jesus, I couldn't believe it – it was like taking a jacket off, the way he pulled the skin off it! It was still warm. Everything was done quickly: liver and kidneys all separated, blood put into a little bucket. There was no waste. It's not a black pudding they make, but it's something like that: they chop the kidneys, and the liver is kept separate, and they have a kind of crumb and spices that go into the blood. They stir it up, it gets a bit thick, they leave it to set a bit and when it's set they take large pieces out by hand and roll it in a big ball. It stays together and they're put into stewpots. They come out still in a ball – I think it's all the crumb they put in. It tastes similar to black pudding, though not quite the same texture and it wouldn't have the fatty bits in it. It was really nice. We had that the next day.

I couldn't wait till the Saturday, heading off to the market. There'd be a celebration when we got back. He was bringing six small donkeys and selling a few goats as well – a couple of them were in kid. He expected to get the equivalent of between five and seven pounds for a goat, and eight to ten for the donkeys. It seemed like a lot of money but he said the donkey has a good long working life, which meant you could keep a donkey for years, and these were only six months old.

We headed into the market town. I think there was one car in the village where we were, and about three trucks – everyone else used donkeys, and a few carts or camels, and there were a few horses around too. When we were heading along the road we'd see the nomadic tribes: they used quite a few horses as well. The market was unbelievable. People were riding in with camels, horses, donkey carts and trucks. There were stalls around the edges and animals in the middle. It's hard enough to understand a market when they're speaking in English, never mind bidding on anything there. There were fifteen batches of donkeys and about twenty batches of goats, a couple of camels, horses, foals and boxes and boxes and boxes of chickens everywhere.

Al's goats were selling anyhow – he got enough for them; he had about five of them there and got around twenty-five pounds – a fiver each is alright. He got nearly eight pounds each for the donkeys and he was happy as Larry. He said he was going to buy a box of a dozen young chickens. You had to have hens there: you couldn't live without them. They hatched quite a few themselves, but he would buy a fresh batch whenever he went to the big market. He was buying a bit of feed and looking around. I was looking at some of the rugs – if you had a truck out there, you'd be doing well: you could buy stuff and bring it home. There were some lovely Persian rugs – handmade ones too, not the machine-made ones they had in the big towns. The ones up there in the market would be made by the old people in the hills. They were selling for around ten pounds. If you were to buy one in the city it would've cost you twenty-five for a machine-made one.

It was a great day! Up the town, a man had a big open fire, and he had this charcoal mix, with racks at different levels. He had fantastic-looking kebabs, so I was definitely going to have a couple of those! The kebabs were made up of lumps of sweet corn, onion, pepper and camel beef on a big skewer. Oh, the flavour on them! The smell off them! They were well spiced meat and they'd wipe a little sauce up and down on them as they were being cooked evenly on a foot-long bar. They'd hang the cooked kebabs on a hook, then you'd get a small bowl and help yourself. There was a good bit of wine in the market, so I was sitting with a glass of wine with this kebab and small roast potatoes, done on a tray on the end of the fire. It was the nicest meal I'd had in a while. It was amazing to see the men out on a wooden veranda, just across the road from the market area, with their beards and turbans and hats and big long djellabas. I was beginning to look a bit like one of them at the time! My beard had grown quite long, and my hair. I had one of their jackets with the hood on it; they were quite good – you could nearly sleep in them. I was glad I wasn't wearing shoes! Nobody had shoes on. But we were sitting there, having the wine and talking; Al was telling me that that market actually went on once a month in that area, and it was one of the best markets around for selling and buying. He grew all his own corn and stuff too. They were quite lucky where he lived because there was a large well in the area and they all had pumps. It was very good land where they were as they were one of the few places that got water all the year long.

It was gas now going back, bringing the chickens back to the house. He was delighted with himself. He said that what he had made there would keep him going for three to four months. He'd bought a couple of big bags of different types of flour and different kinds of oils. He wouldn't have spent more than a fiver on all the stuff that he'd buy for the house for a month. They had their own meat, they had their own vegetables, they made their own bread – they'd just get the flour in and the oil – they'd have a chicken out of the yard now and again if they wanted one. They cooked chickens really nicely out there – like a tagine.

I had been with Al now for two and a half weeks and was getting lazy. It was a really lovely place. You could walk around all day, up round the donkey field. I was very glad I'd met him, as I'd have known nothing about the area – nothing about the people. He was teaching his own kids. His kids were about seven and nine; they had a few words of English. They had great fun watching me riding the donkey – or trying to! Quare funny! He said there was no panic on when I wanted to leave, but I figured I should be heading off in about a week. I was getting too fond of good food and nice people. I wanted to head on towards the border. It was still very early in the year, only the beginning of April then. I hadn't seen one drop of rain in the month since I left Turkey. It was getting hotter the further I got; it was twenty-seven or twenty-eight degrees around that time. I had a hat on all the time now.

I was eating too much of this sweet almondy cake bread that his wife made! They had a good life – they lived quite well, they'd no hassles with anything. They were ninety percent self-sufficient and they bought about ten percent in. He'd had the old truck for years. The brakes used to give trouble on it, but he would have a go at fixing it himself – there were plenty of spare parts in the yard out the back!

12

IT WAS TIME FOR ME TO TRAVEL ON. My plan was to head towards the town where I would get a bus to the border with Afghanistan. Saying goodbye to Al and his family we agreed that, if everything went according to plan, I would drop in on the way back, because I'd be welcome there any time. Ah, it had been good bringing in and out the goats, working with them. When I was a young fella back in Ireland, we used to have pigs, and a horse and a lot of hens. My mother used to talk about goats, but I don't remember having them. They're very good to milk, for a small animal. They milk camels too. Everyone thinks milk comes from cows and that's it, but goats are a very efficient animal.

From the town where the buses were, the border would be about a ten-hour drive. Al was telling me that the penalty for heavy drugs offences – no matter where you came from, what you were – was all the same: for opium and heroin, it was the death penalty. Not that I'd go near anything like that, I can tell you – I just smoked a couple of pipes of hash with him there in the three weeks I'd been there.

Al dropped me to the bus. It was a battered old Merc – some of the windows were missing too. I went to pay the driver in dollars. He was looking for five dollars and I said to Al, "Are you mad? I'm not getting on that for five dollars! I'll give him three at the very most!" It was half full and they were getting ready to leave. Al told me to just sit back and wait my turn, feel them out. He wasn't wrong either – the driver took three dollars off me and told me to get on. There would probably be a stopover on the way, or else he'd be driving halfway through the night. The buses always left a bit late. I didn't want to get into a border area at midnight, not there anyhow, because I'd heard there was a ten- or twenty-minute walk between the borders across no-man's land. You'd get off that bus, take your bag and you'd walk, and you'd meet a bus on the Afghan side. We were heading up into the hills again.

There was a young Swiss guy called Tom on the bus, heading for Kabul, and I told him that I was heading for the border. Early in the previous year I wouldn't have been allowed in, because Afghanistan was a kingdom and no Irish were allowed in, being so-called revolutionaries! I had been talking to a few people the year before that hadn't been allowed in. However, they had ousted the king in July of '73. There was a bloodless coup while he was in Italy and he stayed there, so in August the republic was declared, which was cool for me as this was now spring of '74. I was sitting with Tom, chatting away about different things, and he said he'd had a hell of a time in Turkey as he had been caught up in the same landslide as myself.

The bus stopped after a while for prayers. Everybody except me and Tom – including the driver – got out, rolled out their prayer rugs and they were all praying to Mecca. It was fine, not interfering with anybody, just stopping for a while with the engine turned off.

I'd got a nice block of cheese when I was leaving Al's house, six boiled eggs, one and a half loaves of bread and a big bottle of the red berry juice that they made. I must say I hadn't felt bad from any of the food anywhere. It was important to watch what you were eating – to be careful with salads and if the leaves were very wet, dry them off completely. I ate oranges and apples too. Dates were everywhere and I ate a few of them. I'd been caught out with figs before, so I wouldn't eat too many of them – I didn't realise what they could do to you!

We were coming up to the border area and there were only about four of us left on the bus. I got off with Tom. They told us to walk now, so we walked two hundred and fifty yards or so, then we got to the next bus, which was going to Herat in Afghanistan. When we got to the border it was about ten dollars for the visa, the passports were okay, so we filled in our details on a bit of paper and gave it to them, then got back on the bus.

From there we headed on to Herat. It was like being in a scene from the bible. We were on some winding roads and saw quite a few horsemen, and when we got down into the town, there were little shops on one side, two hotels on the far side, a truck and bus yard – all the towns seemed to have these truck and bus depots. We found a hotel with about ten rooms in it. You couldn't say it was a hundred years old, but it looked like something we might have had in Ireland two hundred years ago. There was a couple of wooden stools with sack bottoms in them on each side as you went in the doorway, a fella there with a djellaba down to the ground and the old Afghan hat. The two of us stayed in the one room – it was only a small little room; I think it was about twenty pence each. You could lock the door, but I wouldn't say it made any difference. There was a little tea room downstairs, that was all they had. We had a roll each – I still had about three boiled eggs of my own – and a cup of chai tea. We definitely wouldn't drink anything cold now, or anything watery. It was just as well we'd got vaccinations for smallpox, as it was the first thing you'd see – people with it. There were lots of cripples and beggars. It was in a poor state with open sewers. You'd be waiting for Genghis Khan to come down the road, it was so backward! I knew it would be something like that, but to see it in real life was still … unbelievable!

Most of the men on horseback were carrying rifles. The policemen had a grey uniform – it was like an old grey blanket from the fifties in Ireland that had been made into a jacket and trousers. It was a hard life for them. The police were quite nice, they just told us in no circumstances were we to take rides on the roofs of the trucks going up the North passage to Mazar-e Sharif, that they watched the trucks every day leaving, checking them. They warned us, "If you go up there, you'll never be seen again; we have no way of finding out who goes and what happens. Just don't go there. You're going to Kabul, you leave here for Kandahar and from Kandahar to Kabul. It's a hell of a long way but it's the only thing you can do."

I'd no intentions of moving on for a few days; there were loads

of little shops to explore. It was much the same food as in Iran –
probably mostly camel, but I'd say they didn't kill the cats there
just for the skins. Hanging outside the butchers' shops were camel
skins, goat skins and cat skins, so I reckoned if you got a nice small
stew it could be chicken or cat. Wouldn't matter anyhow, it's all
edible!

I'd been talking to one of the guys in the shop there – the prices
were amazing: you'd get enough food for the day for ten pence.
It'd be good quality too: a couple of boiled eggs, an onion, a full
circle of bread, two oranges and an apple. You weren't going to get
lumps of beef or anything like that, but you wouldn't need it. There
was more in the way of rice dishes there than I'd seen in Iran.
There was a little restaurant near the hotel, so myself and Tom
were going in there for dinner that evening. We had the best stew,
which came with a big bowl of rice, and a basket of bread. There
was an old radio playing in the background. At that time there was
no television. There was no television station in Afghanistan, there
was Afghan radio which was just about okay.

They had electricity – it was a big enough town – but there
wouldn't have been electricity in the smaller towns or villages,
or on the hillsides: out there you went to bed when it got dark.
There were no railways and one or two roads; ninety-five percent
of the transport was by horse or camel. The trucks dated back to
just after World War II, cars were jalopies, and on the buses you
had to watch your step inside – unbelievable stuff. There were no
glass windows in most of the buildings – the shops had shutters
and they would just pull it down when it was closed; there was no
window frame, no glass. There were all these shops – little places
with boards outside for counters, stacked with all these pies and
things you could buy: yoghurt pies and apple pies, whatever else
you wanted to buy.

I was chatting with one of the policemen again. "There's a
couple of us," he said, "keeping an eye on this truck yard area when
there's a few foreigners in town. There's a few other people around
from France and there's a few others around. We're just making
sure they're all getting on a bus, not on the roof of the trucks."
They were all heading off in the morning but not me; I wasn't in

that much of a rush. It was not a bad town and I wanted to have a good look around in it, even if it was the sort of place I'd probably just zoom through on the way back. There were a few small back streets. They said there was a school at the end of the town, but it was very hard to keep kids in the schools. You might have twenty kids one day and ten the next, they were telling me. They weren't really pushed about it. I suppose that's the way it was at that time. The horsemen were something else; you'd hear them half the night in the town, charging around, almost like the Wild West.

I went into a little antique shop – Jesus, there must have been fifty types of old rifles. They looked like they were hundreds of years old. I had a good look at some of them and I'd say half of them were made-up souvenir jobs – they didn't look real. You wouldn't want to say too much about it though! I picked up a little trinket one day, it was a brass piece with a stone, carved to look like a guy with a lasso on it. It only cost me a few cents. I got an old silver ten Afghani coin – paid a bit for that, but I wanted it. The fella who sold it was happy enough and I was happy enough. I'd say what I gave him was worth less than what he gave me. One thing I did want to make sure about there was to have dollars and pounds – they'd trade with any of them. There wasn't much problem with the currency, I believe they would even pay in little pieces of gold bars – tiny little squares. I did a fair bit of looking around the shop with the old rifles in it – there was a lot of stuff in it: leather bags and boxes of semi-precious stones. However, I had heard there was a much bigger selection of stuff in Pakistan, so I wouldn't bother buying anything. I wasn't intending to buy too much at that stage anyhow, because I'd be carrying it around for weeks. I had a leather band and there were two small holes in the Afghani coin, so I put that on to the band and wore it. The other little thing I stuck into the bottom of my bag, in a little box where I had bits and pieces, coins from different countries – you never knew when you'd need it. I had a heap of old guilders and Deutsche Marks.

There was a little bar up the road from where I was and, amazingly enough, I heard English music being played just as I was walking by. They had a few tourists going into it. In another month there'd be a lot more people around there. At that time I was nearly on my own in the town. A few Afghans spoke a fair bit of English, but up in the hills it mightn't be the same.

There had been a lot of fighting through the years in Afghanistan. I saw a young kid there sitting on the roadside with a gash in his leg, poking at it to make it worse, and with his hand out begging. I gave him an apple, and he was grateful to get anything.

I had decided that at the end of the week I was going to head to Kandahar. It would be a long bus drive as Afghanistan is very, very mountainous. The whole place is full of mountains, a bit of forest and not much else. The houses we passed were very small, square mud huts with windows and doors stuck on the front, with a sack over the window like a curtain. In the towns some of them had glass windows, but not many. There were a lot of women with the veils that fully covered their faces and just a slit like a little net curtain over their eyes. You'd hardly even see their hands, except now and again in a shop. Younger girls were dressed quite normally, it was just the adult women. You wouldn't see too many women around doing anything. You'd see some of the Afghan men with big old black bicycles carrying all sorts on the back of them. A lot of them come into town to get a bit of weekend stuff, I suppose. It was a real eye-opener coming into Afghanistan because I never realised it would be so far behind with water, sanitation, everything. It was unbelievable! Even counting the windows on the bus – I think there were about eight with glass left in them and about twelve with it missing. It was painted all colours and covered in beads on the windscreen. All of the buses were ancient!

13

ON THE MORNING I WAS READY TO leave, I headed up to the yard where the buses pulled out. There were about fourteen or fifteen people getting on, quite a few animals, boxes of chickens as usual and a few goats. I'd never been on a bus out there without squawking, bleating livestock! The road was okay, nothing fantastic – there was only one real road in Afghanistan anyhow. The one we were on went to Kandahar and then Kabul. It would be a long enough drive, probably with a stopover. There was nothing much around. The little houses were strange: everywhere you went there were sods of manure stuck to buildings, to be dried and used for fuel. It must have been quite tough, living there. I hadn't a clue what Kandahar would be like though. We stopped at one or two small villages along the way. We pulled into the first village after about four hours' driving. There was nothing much in it, just people selling stuff out of baskets and quite a lot of beggars. There was a tea shop, so I got a bit of their bread with a lump of goat's cheese on it – it would do for the morning. The bus stopped for an hour, so I just walked around. There didn't seem to be a school. It was strange to see loads of kids, with very little covering their bodies.

Back on the bus I reckoned there would be an overnight stop, given the speed he was driving. You would normally do the journey in about a day, but even if he kept going non-stop, we wouldn't be in till about two in the morning. The bus had a petrol engine and you wouldn't believe the size of it! We passed another village and a few horsemen and nothing much else. I ate the last bit of bread and realised I should have got a lump of yoghurt, but I'd have to do without it now. It's a wild country, just full of hills and mountains and a few trees. There was very little other transport to be seen along the way.

There wasn't a stop in the end and we pulled into Kandahar in the early hours. It was a big enough place: the centre was a half circle with walls and one or two old hotels in it. I couldn't see much so I was looking forward to the morning, but first of all I got into a hotel. They were all around the same price – very cheap, but you didn't get much: a wooden frame on the bed and a woven base of reeds like heavy straw on the bottom. You'd pop your sleeping bag onto that because there was nothing else in it. They had dry toilets in the back room, like a little cubicle with a hole in the floor and two places for your feet – pretty primitive.

In the morning I went downstairs and there was a fella at the reception area and his beard must have been about two foot long. I thought mine was a big beard! They all wore a djellaba nearly to the ground and sandals; some wore the Afghan hats, some wore more of a rolled-up turban that you could put across your face. It'd be for the sand and wind blowing across the deserts. You'd get sand in your eyes anyhow.

I asked the man in the hotel where was the best place to get something to eat. He said there were only two places there and they were both fairly similar, so I went down and had a couple of cups of mint tea in a little bakery. The bread wasn't bad – sort of in between white and grey, softer than the usual ones at the fires on the side of the road. I got a little bowl of oil, a lump of yoghurt, cheese and a boiled egg – the usual breakfast out there most of the time.

After breakfast I headed off for a bit of a walk down round the bottom of the town. There were the same kind of antique shops with the old guns and stones and statues. They had skins, Afghan clothes like the nomadic tribes – I think they're called Kuchi – wore and some of their traditional clothes. It was big money to buy some of the tribal stuff though – full of beads and metal things, decorated with hand embroidery stitched on with gold thread. I wouldn't be buying anything on the way out – coming back I might have a look around. There were some fairly old buildings there. A lot of them were built out of timber with straw and mud plaster. I stopped to watch some fellas doing a bit of building, to see how they were working on it. They were chopping up straw with a machete-type tool, throwing it into the mud base with water, swirling it around, and then they put it in by hand in between the timbers and rubbed it in. Same with the floors – when it dried up it would be like a rock. There was a big camel yard there as well: the noise of them! You'd see the occasional group coming in with them; they'd be collecting stores and different things and heading off.

I met an American guy there but he was going the other way. He had come down from Kabul: said it was wild up there! You'd meet the odd traveller going through. A few days later I was having a look around a crowded market square, where there were a lot of animals for sale. I was walking around trying to find out what villages were in the area and what the places were like, so I got talking to a local lad who spoke a fair bit of English. He said they used to have a market once every two or three weeks there where you could buy anything. They'd sell all sorts of things that were growing around the place, like different types of vegetables and beans, and anything from a hen to a camel. There were lots of donkeys and lots of good horses around that area. There were villages within three to five miles of there, so I thought I'd try and link up with one of the lads and head out to a village for a few days. After about a week in Kandahar you'd get tired of looking at it! I met this lad, Sohrab, who had a place in a village about six miles out of town. He said there was nothing much out there, just a few houses. There wasn't much money spent in those places, it was usually trading – a barter system. The Afghani is a strange currency anyhow, but anyone would take a dollar off you.

That evening, after Sohrab had sold some goats, we headed off in his dilapidated Fiat type car with a trailer on it. I could go back to his village, and I'd hang around there for a while. It would take nearly an hour to get there – they weren't real roads, just tracks. There was very little green – just a few trees – and the houses were all square, mud huts. They were very, very primitive areas. We got to the village and there were seven or eight houses and a couple of water pumps – there were no real water systems. There were some nice fields around – they were well taken care of. They'd be small holdings with about two acres of vegetables. They'd buy very little in the shops. They'd have their own meat from goats; sometimes they'd have lamb, or camel. I didn't see many cows. Most of the places you'd still see what looked like soda bread stuck to the walls: they all seemed to make their own manure briquettes. Sohrab's house had three rooms in it: the living room-kitchen-sitting room was all one room, and there were two little bedrooms. He'd no children: the only one living there with him was his mother. It just showed a different side of life, the whole thing – it was really fascinating. He was telling me it had only been nine months since they had a king in the country, but since it became a republic it had been a little bit easier for them. They were getting along a bit better anyhow – it was more opened up. He had about fifty goats and a couple of camels. He did alright really, selling some of the vegetables and some of the goats and trading with the camels.

There were a lot of big black bicycles in that town. The old Afghan bike was huge – a big high nelly type with big carriers. Nearly every town had a place that fixed them or sold them. A good friend of Sohrab's had the bike shop in that town. While I was staying with him, I gave him a hand clearing up the back area. Nearly everything was done by hand; gardening was very like it was in Ireland in the fifties – digging, turning everything by hand, hoes and rakes, forks and spades. There was no shortage of milk with all the goats, and he had very good coffee in his house. I was also drinking a lot of herbal teas, still laying off the water. A few of them were making wine there too – just the odd person. A lot of them didn't drink at all. Radios were worked by battery – batteries were bloody expensive though.

In the mornings we'd be out the back, working in the garden. Mainly what he'd get out of that would be some vegetables to keep, and some to sell on. He had about ten hens as well and chickens: he could wheel and deal with the eggs, swap them for flour and such. They grew lots of different types of beans there.

It was nice to sit down in the evenings there. They'd make these flour balls with spices – they're the equivalent of potatoes for us I suppose – something between a dumpling and a spice burger. They were very nice in a stew with a few beans in it and good enough flavour from the goat. It's quite a nice meat when it's done really well – not too hot, just fresh spices in it, served up with freshly baked bread, and a glass of wine. We'd have home-made wine and the little old radio playing a bit of their own kind of music. It was a bit like the Arabic music, singing about love and different stories going through them. He was telling me that to get to the nearest school was a four-mile walk – that's if it was even open. There were a lot of places out there where no one really went to school that much – there weren't that many schools.

We'd go down to where his friend was, in the bicycle shop. There would be a small bit of a session going on in there, some of the lads on their pipes. I think there was quite a lot of opium smoked. I was not bothered with it myself. I had the odd bit of grass – like the kif in Morocco. Quite a few of them were on the peppermint tobacco in the water pipes. They'd all sit around and talk, all wearing sandals, and what I learned was called *perahan tunban*, which is like a shalwar kameez – a long loose tunic and pants, and hats. Some of them wore the Afghan hats, some wore a turban-type wraparound. I'd been wearing one of them myself for a while; it covers your face when you're out walking. Some days the air was full of sand and dust.

They were nice people in this little village – very easy going. I found them quite a lot easier to get on with than the Turks, they were more friendly. They wouldn't have many from the West up in the small villages.

I borrowed one of the bicycles from Sohrab's friend for a day or two. I was telling him that I used to repair bicycles back in Ireland when I was only a young fella – the old bikes in the early sixties, with black twenty-six-inch frames. These were more like twenty-eight-inch with big wheels and massive carriers on them. Some of the stuff they put on the back of these bikes, you wouldn't put onto a horse and cart!

In the morning I got the bike and I headed up into the mountain area. I took a bag with some bread and cooked meat – a bit of lamb in a flask with a lid. Stew is okay if it's cold. I also had a bottle of mint tea. It was pretty barren up there, just the odd house here and there. It was very mountainous, with some nice valleys where they had pastures for the sheep. The only people I saw around there were some of the young lads – shepherds, looking after the sheep and goats, walking with them, making sure nothing bad was happening. They would bring them up to the higher ground for about six hours a day and then bring them back down to where they could see them. I believe there were a lot of wolves; I hadn't seen any but they were around. I saw the odd horseman. They had beautiful horses – very pretty looking, streamlined, jet black and dark brown – not too big, and well kept. The horses were probably the best kept of all the animals or vehicles! You'd get used to seeing the locals riding by, carrying a rifle on their back. It was getting quite warm there by then– I'd say about thirty-two degrees. You'd need your neck and ears covered, if you hadn't got your hair long enough. My face and hands had got used to getting the sun, but I'm very pale skinned so I had to wear some kind of covering most of the time I was out. I was wearing the old Afghan style clothing – a kaftan-type top with long sleeves, and wide loose-fitting trousers. It was nice on a bike, especially when you got an area you could free-wheel or pedal on. I spent a lot of time walking that day as well, and in the evening I headed back down to the little village. The children just looked at you and smiled – you'd get the odd wave. I probably looked strange to them, and they looked strange to me at times. I got back to the house around seven or eight o'clock that evening and I told him I would give him a hand next day outside in the garden.

Land was quite valuable, if you had any that would grow anything. He was putting down a white turnip seed, and some kind of butter bean or kidney bean and a few rows of leaf vegetables, like spinach. There were no packets of seeds, it was all little bags with names on them. He had about a half stone bag of little potatoes. He used all the manure from the goats and hens – most of the camel dung was made into briquettes for fuel. Hen and goat manure is good fertiliser – everything grew quite well from then till the end of September. We got a lot of work done in a couple of days. He had a harrow that he put behind a camel to break the ground up, but there was no furrow for making drills. He made beds, a bit like my father and mother used to make. They were lucky with where the water was: there were two pumps in that town, and they were very close to the houses. They were manual pumps, just like the big old pumps we used to have. In the fourth house down the town, they did most of the bread making – it was easier for them to make a lot of bread on one fire. They mainly made the big flat bread. In the house where Sohrab lived everything was done on an open fire with a frame over it. There was no oven in his house, no oven in quite a few of them. We were talking about the possibility of making them – metal boxes to one side of the fire with a heater system and a door, they probably would work okay.

He said he could see that I knew what I was doing with the planting. Well, it's the same depth for most seeds as we have – beans go down about forty millimetres, other seeds only go down about twelve to fifteen millimetres. He still used a lot of beans from the previous year; they could dry them, as it gets very hot, and then could store them easily. There were no freezers as there was no electricity in the village, but you wouldn't miss it after a few days. They cooked kebabs on the open fire; it was quite good – hot ash on the bars. That's the way they did the bread too. You'd eat when you wanted to, there was no worry about eating at any particular time – whenever you'd finished working out the back. Milking the goats was an absolute panic, I wasn't that good at them at all! I got used to it though, just learned how to be easy with them. I was surprised how much milk you'd get. They were a small breed of goat, but you'd get two or three pints a day per goat. They had a nice bit of ground out the back to graze on. There was no such thing as buying nuts for them or that – he said they'd get the waste leaves when there were a lot of vegetables being done, other than that you'd pick the greens for them and they'd get a bit of grass. Goat farming was big in most of those places. He said some people milk the camels as well, but he didn't milk his because he only had one or two of them. I suppose there's no difference: we use cows milk – some countries use horse milk, camels' milk, doesn't matter what it is. They eat them too; I'd seen them in Kandahar in the butcher's shops.

Travel with Moon

I was thinking that in about a week's time I'd head for Kabul. I had the bike for a few days so I would bring it back the morning I was leaving. There were very few people in the town at the time. You wouldn't see a car from one end of the week to the other there. You'd get the occasional small carts pulled in and out of the town by donkeys or ponies. Some of them had rubber wheels, some didn't. They sold a lot of goat skins in the markets – there would be all sorts of skins for sale. There was nothing much to work at out there, most people just worked for themselves. There would have been a certain amount of work in Kandahar itself, but not in the countryside.

I was amazed at the toilet systems, I hadn't seen flush toilets anywhere. It was usually a hole in the floor, and there would be a big eastern-type jug with water and a basin where you rinse your hands after the toilet and throw the water down the hole. I'd been washing my clothes by hand and hanging them out. It was always cold water but it didn't matter. In the same way, you'd wash yourself from head to toe, using one of those jugs – pour it over yourself. It's not like you'd walk into showers everywhere! It was a different lifestyle – they lived a very beautiful lifestyle, very relaxed.

One Friday I had arranged to get a lift down with Sohrab into Kandahar. I had only seen his mother and one other woman in the village. You didn't see a lot of women: they'd be fully veiled. They wore the burqa – a veil with a little window in the face, probably like looking through a heavy lace curtain – you'd see them walking around the town in them. His mother wasn't covered up, she just wore a black headscarf – a hijab.

On the Friday morning I left back the bicycle and thanked your man a thousand times – he wouldn't even take one Afghani off me. Back into the old Fiat 1500 for the drive down. We said our goodbyes and I went back to the same hotel in Kandahar, just to stay one or two nights in it.

I GOT THE BUS TICKET FOR KABUL and it would be a good few hours' drive. There was some bustle, I can tell you, unbelievable! They were sixteen- to twenty-seater buses, they weren't big and they had bags stacked on the roof. It was hard to tell whether it was an old Mercedes or what it was – it made plenty of noise anyhow. It was back to the boiled eggs and onions – the easiest thing to carry – and I guess you'd call it mint water rather than mint tea, because it was cold, but it tasted alright, having been boiled with mint in it. You could put a slice of lemon in it when boiling, if you wanted to. The sun was baking down and the bus was full of dust. I got talking with a German fella on the bus who said he was heading to India. He was going to Kabul for a few days, then heading up through the Khyber Pass into Pakistan, down to the Indian border. I was planning to stay in Kabul for a while.

We arrived into Kabul and, oh, it was wild! There were a lot of people there, a lot more people than anywhere else I'd been for a while. There was very little transport: the odd small bus, a few cars, one or two vans. There were plenty of people walking, plenty of bicycles, and there seemed to be a good bit of life around. Look down any side street, though, and they were not very clean – no hygiene whatsoever. I got off the bus and walked down to the corner of Chicken Street, which was just off the main street. I think it used to be a huge market area for hens, that's why it was called Chicken Street. It would have been a bit like the cattle market in Dublin, around Smithfield – cattle and horse markets.

I picked a hotel a fella said would be a good one, the Steakhouse Hotel. It had a side garden to it, which was nice enough. In general, you'd get a room – just a bed – stick your bag in the room, and anything very valuable you'd keep on your body. It was essential to keep all your paperwork in a bag round your neck with your money; any bit of money for daily spending you'd keep separate.

They were nice lads in the hotel, Mohamed and Al; they spoke pretty good English too. Kabul was wild looking alright! There were quite a few nice little places in it, a lot of knick-knack shops. I spotted a butcher's and at the back they had four or five different pens: goats in one pen, hens in another; it was a pretty big place. There was an open front on the shop, with meat just hanging on hooks and lying on boards – lots of flies around the place, but when it's cooked it's cooked – it'd definitely be fresh anyhow! The most amazing thing there was the shops where they had everything hanging outside. I'd never seen as many cat skins – and they definitely didn't throw away the cat! It was quite a different city, a lot of horsemen, and evening time was like a parade. Just sitting in the hotel room looking out the window, they were amazing looking. I noticed that the buses were segregated – women and children on one side and men on the other – and I had seen another bus earlier, it stopped where a lot of school children got off, and they were wearing uniforms, which I couldn't believe, dark red blazers – so they must have had proper schools in Kabul.

Myself and the German guy I'd met on the bus went to the little restaurant just off the corner of Chicken Street that evening. It was his first time over there as well. He was from Bavaria, had been in the army for the past year, and had wanted to get away for a while. There was the strangest sign of all on the door going into this restaurant, "shoes off", and it had a drawing of a leg wearing a boot, with a broken ankle, meaning, definitely leave your shoes at the door! They had low tables with little stools. The smell coming from the kitchen was great, and you could buy a beer there as well. I hadn't had a beer for about two months. So they had a big stew on anyhow and they had potatoes with it. Bread, potatoes, stew and a beer – I reckoned that'd be alright! The people in the restaurant were quite nice, good portions of food and if you wanted more, you just had to ask. The beer wasn't bad either. They'd a nice rice pudding with cream in it. We each had a big bowl of that as well. They had a few western tapes playing in the restaurant.

Someone said there was a club on the main street, run by two Austrian guys, which sounded quite strange, but we'd have to go and have a look. It was supposed to be like a good late sixties, early seventies music bar. We got in anyhow and, yeah, there were a couple of very tall Austrian guys, with black suits and black hats on them – a bit mental! They were quite spaced-out guys, they'd been there a couple of years with the place, but they only ran it from season to season. It would be an interesting thing to have I suppose, where you don't have anything else from the West. They even had those weird ultraviolet lights and they were playing Led Zeppelin music, all that kind of stuff. There were only five or six customers in the place and they were all foreigners! There were one or two Afghani fellas behind the bar, making teas and there were pipes being handed around as well. Afghanistan, of course, was famous for the black Afghan hash, and the poppy plantations. We smoked the pipe a bit, and the beers were around ten cents a bottle, so you could afford a couple of bottles. It didn't taste great but it was alright; they were only small bottles – about 250 millilitres. It was nice though sitting around listening to a bit of music, and we hadn't that far to walk back to the hotel. I decided I'd hang around there for a few weeks. I'd get to know the scene a bit more and explore the streets and huge market areas.

I liked the markets: from live animals to clothes to soap bars to powders to snake medicine – you could get anything you wanted! It was a bit like the old American West ... the head of the snake does this, the middle part is good for your back, drink the juice for this part and that part ... incredible! There were quite a lot of nice stones and beads. And huge pipes: glass water pipes with big bowls, then you had the clay water pipes – earthenware with a bamboo smoking end and three different size bowls on them. The markets were full of everything. You could buy pistols, swords, knives, rifles, rabbits, hens, ducks – and goats of course! The only thing you didn't see was a pig. There were a couple of cattle there as well. That market was on every week and they came to Kabul from all over for it. There were two or three big cycle shops in Kabul, with all the black bicycles. They had a few mopeds too: old pedal type 50cc things, Gorellis and Bianchis – they had a different sound – and old three-wheel Lambrettas or Vespas with the one wheel in the front, two in the back. It's an interesting city.

I slept after that night out in the club, and I didn't wake up till around eleven o'clock the next day. I hadn't been sleeping late, but you could lie on for a few hours in Kabul. In the mornings you'd be woken early with the prayer calls, but you could turn over and go back to sleep. There was a good shower in the hotel, so it was the first time in three weeks or more that I'd got a half decent warm shower. The weather was pleasant – fantastically bright skies, so blue it was unbelievable. There was a lot of dust and quite a smell around the city itself and a lot of people around – it was a busy spot. I took a walk down to some of the clothes shops. I wanted a top and another pair of light trousers. I got a pale green top and trousers: very light material but hard wearing. It only cost about fifty cents for the lot.

I was talking to the German guy that morning. He was heading on out to Pakistan the following day. I was planning to head up into Mazar-e Sharif and out into Balkh, up at the Russian border, in a week or so. You could see the mountains from all over the place there. We were not that far from the Khyber Pass and only a couple of hours from the Pakistani border. It's a fantastic looking place, with all the mountains and valleys!

There were quite a few other tourists around Kabul then: you'd see a lot of western people there. The airport was fairly busy but I hadn't even thought of getting on a plane. I wouldn't bother – you'd miss too much, you'd land in a city and see the people and walk around and leave, and that'd be it. I wanted to get to know more of the people and the cities. I wanted to get to know more people outside the cities, if I could. There was a big horse fair there, as well. I wanted to be there for the major market day – I heard that it was unbelievable what came into town! Kandahar was like a mini market compared to this place.

It was a good little hotel. The garden at the side was a decent size, with orange and lemon trees in it. You could sit out there, and they did good food on an open-air chargrill. I was going to eat there that evening. A few of the other people I'd been talking to had said they'd be there that evening too. There were a few Canadians around – you could spot them a mile away as they always had a huge maple leaf on their bag or their jacket!

I was talking to a policeman there who told me they could do military service in the army when they were called up, or they could do the police service. According to him, you were given a book to read up on the rules and regulations. The uniform wasn't up to much, I can tell you! They got a hairy pair of trousers and a jacket, old boots and an old rifle to walk around the streets. There weren't that many of them around either.

As I wandered around the many small back streets, I wished to Jesus there were more toilets around the place; everywhere you went there were people just dropping their trousers and squatting. There were no TV stations, no railways; there was just one road in and out and a few old buses. There wasn't much of a local bus service; you walked around and that was it. A bus would bring you from one town to the next now and again but transport was very scarce. There was a radio station, I don't know whether it was Radio Afghanistan or Radio Kabul, but you could hear it in the shops, and you'd hear the prayer call in the mornings, afternoon time and evenings – it was very loud alright! There were plenty of shops selling rugs and textiles. The nomadic Kuchis would bring goods in to trade. I bought a traditional hand-embroidered Kuchi robe.

I was going to rest up there for the next couple of weeks, after all the running around for the previous three weeks from one town to the next. I still had a good few bob as I'd spent very little in the previous few weeks, mostly on bus fares and visas. I'd have to watch the Afghan visa though, as it was only valid for one month and they didn't like you going over the time. They also wanted to know where you were staying. They'd rather have you registered in a hotel so they would know where people were. Now and again, while I was there, I stayed outside the city – I couldn't get over looking at the mountain ranges and the skyline.

Back in the hotel that evening, I met the Canadian guys, Jack and Paul; they were staying there too. There would be a bit of a session that night. I had told the German guy I'd meet him later on, so I tried to get the Canadian guys to come out as well. We all had a meal at the hotel that evening, sitting around there in the garden. As we were living on Chicken Street, we thought we might as well have chicken for dinner! There were nice rice dishes there too. You could order what you liked, although there weren't too many choices. We had rice with the chicken dish that night, and some locally-made wine. There wasn't much alcohol around there anyhow – just in a few of the hotels.

The Canadians had flown in, and they were going to be hanging around for a few weeks. One of them worked in the timber industry in Canada.

We headed out at nine or ten o'clock. There were a good few horsemen around, and camels with their drivers. We'd have to be careful not to walk out in front of those camels and watch where we were walking – especially down those side streets – taking care not to step in anything. So much shit around, it didn't bear thinking about … and the lads laughing! The four of us headed out to the club that evening. There was a little doorway into it, then a little corridor, then into a room. The music was playing away, weird lights, smell of incense, smell of black hash and a good few people there. We got a couple of beers and you could order one or two pipes and a bit of smoke if you wanted it. The Canadian guys were well into it, and the German guy – I'd have a bit myself too. They were playing the Rolling Stones there, and they were going to play Zeppelin. It was such a weird club to have in the place – but they were doing no harm! There was no food at all, just a few crisps in a bowl when you bought the beers. The pipes were fairly strong: the German guy was used to it, but the Canadians – they really enjoyed it! The beer tasted like a cross between Harp and Heineken, a strange sort of lager. I told the lads I was heading up into the hills the next day, on a bike. I was going to pick up a bicycle in the morning.

Coming up to midnight, the music was still going full belt. We left though as we didn't want to get too stoned! Jesus, I could hardly walk after this stuff, and we'd had a good few beers as well. We staggered back to the hotel and sat in the lobby for a while chatting. You could get a round of flat bread with a bit of cheese if you wanted it, even that late. We were laughing about the state of the cars and trucks we'd seen – you wouldn't believe it; they might as well be held together with string! The Canadians reckoned there wouldn't be any of that transport allowed out on the roads where they were from, but – Jaysus – some of the stuff we had back in Ireland in the sixties wouldn't be too far behind them. I had been looking at a family on a moped earlier – I think there were three or four on it – all you could see were bodies and hear a bit of engine noise.

I'd have to pay for the bike hire in the morning, but it would only be something like ten or twenty cents a day. They didn't mind renting them to you, if you were in a hotel and you put the bike in the hotel grounds. I got the bike for one American dollar and the guy said that I'd get nearly half of it back if I only had it for a couple of days. I packed up some bread and a stew in a flask, a bottle of mint tea and lemon, tied everything on the carrier and I headed out of town. There was a small roadway where you could go two or three miles up into the hill area. I kept looking at the great long mountain range. I heard that near the Chinese border is where Genghis Khan came through and killed everything. Now I don't know – could be true – they said there wasn't even a rat left alive.

I met a policeman up there one day and got talking to him. He said you wouldn't know what the mountains were until you got near Mazar-e Sharif, and all around the Hindu Kush. He was really friendly and invited me to stay at his place for a day or two. I knew that you were only supposed to stay in a hotel, but I reckoned as he was a policeman it would be okay. The strange thing was I never saw any women while I was there; you'd hear them laughing and talking in the other room but they seemed to have a completely separate existence.

It was getting warm in the mornings now – you wouldn't want to be powering along on a bicycle. It was only a single speed thing. I was out on open land now and there were plenty of space around and a good few trees – more than I thought there would be. I came upon a little village where there was a load of barrels outside and some planking and bundles of straw that they were chopping up with a big machete. They were bringing out wheelbarrows and sacks full of earth from the inside of the building and throwing it into a mixing area, then they were breaking up any of the hard lumps and mixing it up with water and straw. I went over and I

Policeman between Mazar-e Sharif and Kabul.

started talking to them. They didn't speak much English, but I understood that they were building, and what they were doing was putting an extension onto a house – re-doing the floor and then adding extra walls with a timber frame. They didn't throw anything away – that was re-mixed straw and mud for the floor area between the boards and the sides of the building; it kept out the heat and the cold. The buildings were like square blocks. There was power in Kabul, but once you got outside the city there was no power or telephone lines or anything like that. I was amazed at the materials they used – they packed it all in with little timber blocks into the crevices and smoothed it all off. The houses were just like a small cowshed – they weren't much different from where they kept goats. All they had in the houses were doors – most of them didn't have windows as such, just squares with a little wooden hatch that could be closed over. There were one or two little shops in this village. There was one – a pudding shop – and I went over to it thinking they had blackberry pies, until they chased the flies off! There was a good lot of smallpox though. There was nothing much for most people. A lot of people were working out in the fields and everything was done by hand – just a hoe and a rake and a shovel or a spade. They mostly grew their own food, like the beans I'd seen growing in Kandahar. They tasted alright. They were yellow in the middle and didn't really have a hard skin like the red kidney beans and they had a nicer shape and taste. The lads said they grew a lot of stuff like that there. There were a good few rows of potatoes too, four or five inches high. I was surprised they used that many. It was like the fifties in Ireland, when everyone had their own vegetable gardens and hens everywhere.

On my way back to Kabul I noticed a moped shop on the outskirts, so I decided to stop and have a look around. The state of some of the motorbikes or moped yokes! I hadn't seen any filling stations, so I didn't know where they got the fuel for them! It must have been supplied by the bike crowd or a pump at the side of the shop or something. I'd say they were all hand pumps anyhow. Even on the old trucks and buses we were on, they never pulled in for fuel anywhere; the yard must be where they filled up. Walking around the old bike shop, I saw a couple of really old Honda 50s with push rod engines, a couple of old double seater 2-stroke mopeds and a few of those three-wheel Vespas. There was an old garage down the road, round the corner from the shop. I don't think they threw anything away there – everything was used ten times over. Even the tyres were used to the very last.

I went back to the hotel to lie down for an hour or two, having baked in the sun all day. I'd meet the Canadians later on. I put the bike in a little lean-to at the side of the hotel. I'd been given a lock for it.

I was planning to look into how much it cost to get to Mazar-e Sharif towards the end of the week. I wasn't going before Saturday anyway, because the big market would be on then. I had asked the hotel guy and he said that would be the big one, that there were two or three medium-sized market days in the month but that Saturday would be the full market. You could buy anything, he said, anything! There should be some amount of horses at the market and there'd probably be hundreds of people at it.

There were twenty-nine rooms in the hotel. He said half the year there'd be nobody in it, that it wouldn't really be open. It was even worse, he told me, before they became a republic. There wasn't half the tension anymore. Word had it, the old king had a big boat in Kabul, but you might as well be a million miles from the sea! There was a big old military barracks down the road too. The army didn't have anything – even the police only had a couple of cars.

I told Jack and Paul that we'd be going to the restaurant in the town – the one with the "no shoes" sign at the door – to get a big curry. They were leaving the following morning, flying into India. You wouldn't know what you'd be doing flying like that – completely out of one culture into another mad culture. This place was hard enough on me head! One place you'd go to, they'd kids with no clothes on their back, next part you'd go to they'd have a few. There were a lot of half-mad people as well; you'd hear them roaring at night-time.

Some of the beards were amazing! There were men sitting in doorways with worry beads and big old pipes outside the tea shops. It was great sitting outside the tea shops, drinking chai and listening to stories of the wolves in the mountains and hills. They were saying the greatest horsemen in the world, and the greatest horses, came from Afghanistan. Some of them would be fairly getting on – the younger fellas would be telling you that some of the men you'd be sitting beside were nearly eighty years of age – and they had had their troubles in the past thirty or forty years.

They said it would be ten to twelve hours on the buses to Mazar-e

Sharif. The buses wouldn't be going any more than twenty-five or thirty miles an hour and it looked like a long distance on a map. The older guys were saying that the market on Saturday covered about nine hundred metres by six hundred metres. It was a big area. There would be some trucks parked there and lots of pens for the livestock, which would be left up all the time. They didn't let anyone drive in around it – trucks were parked on the edge at one end. You could pull a trailer in and leave it there but you had to take the cars out. They said that from Friday afternoon the area would be filling up.

By Friday morning most of the guys I'd been talking to had left. Some had flown out, some had gone by bus, so I was just hanging around with a few of the guys that worked in the hotel. I took a walk around the town. There were a lot of people about and the sun was getting well up. There was a lot of hustle and bustle in the town that day. I'd say a lot of people were staying overnight and going to the market in the morning.

A lot of old trucks arrived in the afternoon. I suspected there'd be a big racket in the town that night with a couple of thousand extra arriving in and hanging around. I took the bike down the road for a spin before I left it back. There was nothing in most of the side streets, just houses. I was talking to the man where I got the bike and he said, "When you come back down from Mazar-e Sharif, you can use the bike for another four or five days. You've only spent about fifty cents out of the dollar." They didn't normally rent bikes but the guy in the hotel knew him, so they'd let me have it. They wouldn't charge much anyhow. I was going to have a few shish kebabs that evening with a bowl of that good rice and spend an hour or two in the mad club run by the Austrian guys.

I met an English fella and girl that were just staying for the one night. They were going on into Pakistan and down to India. A lot of people headed for India.

I had a beer or two in the club and went to bed early. I wanted to get up early for the market. It'd be interesting. One of the old guys outside the hotel said it'd be jammed. I didn't mind; I'd have a look around at everything and see what was going on. I found out an old trick with the beds: you put the sheet down and lie on it, then you pull the sheet back really quickly and swipe it with a bar of soap. It takes a lot of the bed bugs out – you'd be eaten alive there at times! But once you put the soap down you get a good few on it and if you left a bit of soap, it kept them down a bit. The rooms were very bare, with just a bed and a chair in the corner to throw your stuff onto. There were no fancy lockers in these little hotels – I don't even think the bigger ones had them. It was just the bare bed, but you couldn't complain about the prices. Nice people as well.

In the morning I'd get a couple of fried eggs and bread. The coffee was gritty, but you'd get used to it too. It was like the grains were still in it, unfiltered. It tasted good though. I headed down to the market early. There was a stream of traffic going in to it – from a quarter of a mile away from it you could barely walk with the crowd! Everything on four legs and two legs was for sale. There were lots of bags of grain, all sorts of stuff, from leathers to clothes to rugs, knives, guns, camels, horses, donkeys, sheep, goats … everything! The pens were up, trucks with the sides down on them, old trailers for sale, car trailers, horse-drawn carts – anything you wanted was for sale. I went over to one of the gun stalls. Some of the rifles were something else! They had lots of old stuff: some small pistols and every shape knife you can think of. I couldn't buy anything but most of them could buy what they wanted there – guns and ammunition. It was all tribal there and the same down in Kandahar – different tribes around Kabul. It's a bit like Ireland hundreds of years ago. It was the same with Mazar-e Sharif, I was told; that was going to open my eyes when I got there.

You should have seen the amount of haggling going on there in the market, swapping and buying and money changing hands, shouting! I didn't understand a word of it. I was with one or two of the lads from the small villages outside that I knew. They were in there buying and selling. A mother and kid goat were fetching around seven or eight dollars, which sounded like a lot of money. Anyhow, I met up with Sohrab who I had been with out on the little farm for a few days. He said it was the biggest market of the year at that time, people buying in supplies for the year and changing their animals. There were a lot of good horses there that day. He said there'd be very high prices paid. The Afghan horse is amazing. You would see the tribal guys on the darkest brown and the blackest horses you would ever see – beautiful looking! The weren't monstrously big, but a fine animal. I wouldn't have a clue what they were worth but there was a lot of trading.

There were boxes of every type of hen you could think of and they were all going cheap. There were traders with bread stalls, eggs for sale, and there were butcher's stalls set up. Everything was in the open air – just buy what you want and take it with you. Some of the rugs were fantastic, but I wasn't going to be able to take anything like that. They were selling some old textiles and robes as well. There were quite a few kids around too but there was only the occasional woman, and they were nearly all fully covered. There was a big session in the corner with the fellas yapping and smoking pipes. It was only half eleven now and, beJesus, the place was booming. You'd wonder how they'd get out of there by the evening time. I'd say it'd be late enough when they'd be leaving. Some of the trucks and cars were from the late fifties, some from the early fifties – definitely nothing newer than 1965 or 1966.

A fella pulled up with a trailer and he must have had twenty sheep and lambs in the back – a strange enough looking breed, like a mixture between a Scotch Horny sheep and a Jacob sheep. They had long legs and I was fairly sure they'd be bought. There were all sorts of seeds for sale: all kinds of beans and peas and all kinds of little plants. They grow a plant that's like a beetroot or white turnip and they're fairly tasty when they're boiled. There were plants for sale in pots and trays, bundles of cabbage plants, all sorts! There were two mad stalls full of sandals. There were loads of old bicycles and mopeds, as well as parts for sale – all sorts of bits and pieces.

I sat to have a cup of chai and a chat with some of the lads I knew. They said some people had come thirty or forty miles to this market. On horseback it wouldn't take them that long, or driving old scooters or mopeds, or on camels. You should have heard the roars of them! There's two breeds of camel, a dromedary with one hump and the Bactrian with two humps. The lads ride in on them and then stop, the camels fold up their legs and get right down and they just walk off the top. It's the same getting up – not like climbing up onto a horse – the camel gets right down, you climb on and move off. They ride around cross-legged on these things. They can go all day on them.

I was amazed at the amount of stalls in the place. They were saying some of the best handmade rugs in the country were there. They were selling for fifteen or twenty dollars, but I had no way of getting them home. You go halfway round the world to get stuff and then you can't bring it back with you! Every size water pipe was for sale, and sebsi pipes, a whole stall full of pipes and pen knives all in the one place. I was glad I went to the market because I wouldn't have had a clue about the place otherwise. You couldn't sit quiet – everyone was running around the place. A guy pulled up on a motorbike and he must've had about twenty chickens in boxes on the back and hanging over the front of it! They came from everywhere, it was wild!

The market had my head flying around! The best of food was being cooked on big grills – basically timber and a bit of charcoal. It's the best way of cooking! You could get a big lump of chicken in a flat bread with a little bit of saucy juice in it and sit back there with a big glass of cold mint tea. I was still watching the water. I'd had a few frights already – once or twice up in the middle of the night. It was just a small dose of the runs, but I thought I was getting something bad. I also stayed off the very spicy food – just a little bit of chilli well cooked. Chicken's alright once it's done right. I ate a bit of lamb, beef, camel, all in kebabs and stews. There were quite a few from the Kandahar area there at the market. It was a long drive for them, but there were a few trucks. I think they did all the market areas, travelling from one place to the other, in big old weird canvas-backed trucks, painted up and with ribbons and colours and medals hanging out of them and huge petrol engines. There was nothing cheap about car parts or bits of trucks or anything like that. I never saw anything like a real garage there either – it would just be an open yard with a lean-to, a box of spanners and a sledgehammer.

Around five o'clock in the evening some of them had started

packing up in the market. There must have been three or four thousand people who went through there. There had been noise all day and you couldn't hear anything but horses, camels, bikes, cars, trucks and trailers going in and out. You'd think there was nothing sold the way it was done with the barter system there. I'll give you this for that, give you that for the other: goats for bags of food and meal, and large bags of rice. A lot of food was changing hands like that. The old hotel guys had been down there early. I was heading back to the hotel in a little while to get the meal with the lads there that evening. They made a lovely camel stew – it had to be camel, didn't taste like beef, could have been horse I suppose – I don't know! It was cooked in a lovely sauce and they did a few of those browned-up fried potatoes with a bowl of salad and a few tomatoes. I nearly went to dry the salads and stuff off, but I reckoned it should be okay. The hotel bread was nice.

I was just having a bit of craic with the lads in the hotel. I told them I'd see them in a week or two and I'd be back down that way because I wanted to spend a bit of time up in Mazar-e Sharif. I put my stuff together in the bag, I checked my passport – had to keep an eye on the visa, still a few weeks left on it – and I still had quite a few dollars and quite a few English pounds, a pocket full of change out of Afghanis and some Afghan paper notes. I'd started using the local money a little bit, but not that much.

In the morning the lads were joking with me about the breakfast, but they said they'd pack me up some nice breads with chicken and meat on them. You'd hardly push a dollar at them: they wouldn't take it off you. I gave them a few bob for the hotel room, paid for the meals each evening and paid for the breakfast, but they gave me a bag of food and two bottles of mint tea with lemon. That would keep me going until I got to Mazar-e Sharif.

Oh, Jesus, the bus was unbelievable! Lumps out of seats and sides missing off them and some parts of the floor missing! The bus was three-quarters full of people. I sat in the middle, two rows in front of the back axle, at least three rows down from the front. It was a weird thing I had about those yokes – I was afraid of a bang from behind or in front, so I sat in the middle, although I hadn't seen many accidents out there. They didn't go quickly enough!

We took off up into the hills. The road seemed reasonable. It was nicknamed 'the Russian road'. I had heard stories of one road that was built from Mazar-e Sharif to Kabul, by the Russians. The women on the bus were all covered up, wearing the burqa. It reminded me of Ireland in the fifties and sixties, and the women going to mass with a pair of gloves, headscarf, properly covered up, long coats. The children were on the left-hand side with the mother, men and older boys were on the right-hand side of the church. Getting into a bus here, sometimes it was men on one side, women on the other. It was always men first in the chapel in Ireland too.

We had to stop along the way, only an hour out of Kabul. There were two policemen with a guy handcuffed and legs shackled as well. I was wondering why there was no one sitting in the two front seats. They got in and they put him sitting in one of the seats and they opened one of the handcuffs and put it round the seat rail, and as they were sitting there one of them was carrying a gun and the other one was laughing about it. I wasn't taking too much notice. There were a few chickens squawking in boxes – not too many animals on this bus, just a few boxes of chickens. It was getting more mountainy as we headed on up. They said there was a village about an hour and a half away, where they were going to pull in. It was more like a crossroads with six or seven houses at it. If you wanted the toilet, you could just run behind a building. The driver got out and he was talking to a man at the roadside. It wasn't really a restaurant or a tea house or a shop, he was just selling bits of bread with boiled eggs, onions, that sort of thing. I had plenty of food, a nice bit of chicken meat on the sandwiches that were like a naan bread or flat bread. Your man was still handcuffed to the seat and the police were standing at the door of the bus, making signs about him getting hanged. Strange! They said he'd be hanged in Mazar-e Sharif. "Tomorrow, tomorrow," they kept shouting. Fuckin' weird!

The bus took off again, going incredibly slowly. After about an hour the bus slowed right down. The brakes weren't veroy strong. A poor old guy walked across with two donkeys and the policemen jumped out, gave him a kick in the arse and kicked the two donkeys. They gave out shit to him and banged the donkeys with the stick. They were yelling at him to get off the road because he'd nearly caused an accident. They got back on clapping and cheering and laughing. It was unbelievable – the man was miles away and we wouldn't have hit him.

We headed on again, getting really up into the hills now. We had another three or four hours to go – it was only about three in the afternoon and wouldn't get dark till nine o'clock or half nine. The sun was beaming down all day and it was hot and dusty. There was a lot of activity across the hillsides. People were out working in the fields: goatherds and shepherds. They always seemed to be with the animals. They didn't have big fenced-in fields and I think they watched the animals the whole time. They were young kids really – twelve or fourteen – and sometimes ther was an older guy with them, sitting on a rock looking at them. There was very little farm machinery; it all seemed to be done by hand. They used camels for ploughing. The ploughs looked like something from biblical times – a wooden peg in the ground. It was no bother to a camel or an ox to pull a plough – you wouldn't see many horses used. There was a lot of maize grown and poppy fields too, all over the place. It was a big enough country for drugs – I don't think there was much other income in the place.

The fella that was sitting across from me on the bus said we'd be in Mazar-e Sharif in less than an hour. It wasn't as big as Kabul, but it was well known. It's very tribal country so you had to watch what goes on there, keep an eye on things, don't go off the beaten track, and never take out a wallet of money – always have change in your pocket. The backpack I had was quite small. I still had a Bowie knife that I used for cutting things but didn't carry around much. A Swiss army knife was the only thing I used day and night – best yoke I ever bought! I must have had it about six years by then. There's nothing much you can't do once you have one.

At first sight of Mazar-e Sharif, it was hard to believe the state of the place! It was like it was half built and then abandoned. It was just incredible looking. There were hills all around. Balkh was just up the road – well, not too far away. There were a lot of horsemen there and I saw about eight camels walking one behind the other for the first time. There were quite a few horses tied up outside and mad looking men with them!

We all got off the bus and they kicked the shite out of the fella they were going to hang the next day as they were taking him off. I wouldn't be looking out for that anyhow. The police uniforms were unbelievable – big hairy blankets, old boots and hats. You'd see a lot of Afghan hats – they looked like a loaf of bread or a weird chef's hat. Children with bare feet were everywhere. The hotel looked like a three-storey shed. As a precaution, I took anything that I didn't want stolen out of the bag – not that they were going to take anything, but I didn't want to leave any temptation lying around. The guy at reception said not to leave the bag in the room, but to leave it in a little locker in the lobby where he was. There was nobody else staying in the hotel. There were a few people around the town – the occasional trader. There was a rich smell of food cooking on fires outside. I still didn't know how they got fuel for the vehicles. They did carry a lot of cans on them. I think the bus driver had got some in the village that we'd pulled into about four hours back, pumped in from one tank to another.

At the hotel, I walked down something like a mud corridor into a little room at the front: the window must have been about three foot by two foot. There was no glass, it was just a hole in the wall, with a curtain you could pull over. You'd hear everything from the street. I walked down another corridor to where there were supposed to be the toilets, and you're not going to believe what it was like! There was a round hole in the floor, about ten inches in diameter, and there were two square platforms for your feet. I was on the second floor at least and I looked down into the hole. There was a pile of shite – it looked like a pyramid – in the yard underneath! I'd say they must have cleared it once a year maybe! It was the same all over; there was no sewerage system anywhere. There were open sewers outside, so you really needed to watch your step! The whole place was mental – I was boggle-eyed looking at what was going on. Kids were running around playing and I didn't know what they were playing but it looked like they'd nothing to play with. There was the occasional woman running through the street dressed in black down to the ground, and men sitting around smoking joints. The smell of hash was unbelievable around the tea shop – there'd be a cop sitting there with them and everyone just sitting around smoking.

I stayed around the hotel that night. When you walked out the door, all the options were the same anyhow. There was a restaurant right beside the hotel and your man told me everyone ate there. It wasn't like a hotel, it was more like a place full of bedrooms with nothing much else in it. There were pumps on the street for water – a suction pump with a big handle on it, like the fifties in Kilmacanogue! There was hardly a car around.

I was sitting outside the restaurant and they were still talking about the great man Genghis Khan. It reminded me of a lot of parts of Iran, where they talked about the holy men as if they were superheroes. At the same time you could feel the tension that came from it being a tribal area. It was like, for instance, the O'Byrne and O'Toole clans in Ireland back in the Middle Ages: it's all tribal law out there in the mountains. You're not going to tell a man from the mountains of Mazar-e Sharif what to do!

The food was alright in that restaurant. I was sitting on a tiny stool at a low table. There was a fork and knife, but a lot of the food is eaten by hand. People were looking at me because I'm left-handed and I eat with my left hand. They've an old saying that the left hand is for wiping your backside. If you shake hands, you should always give out the right hand. The people were quite friendly, though, and I was surprised that a good few of them spoke English. A lot of guns were being carried. I suppose there were wolves and different things going on in the hills. I didn't know much about the tensions between the tribes – it seemed to be just that they had their own law and their own way of going on.

There was no beer to be had up there. I was sitting there in the restaurant and one of the men asked me if I wanted a smoke. There's a saying, when in Rome, do as the Romans do. Well, they were all smoking there, so I wasn't going to offend them by saying no! There was a little pipe passed around the table, and it was really enjoyable, even if it was like being hit by a small train, or a half ton of bricks! We were having the craic anyhow. They had lovely little desserts there too – they're famous for sweet stuff like that. It was full of fruit and rice. Then they'd bring you a cup of chai. I got fond of that.

By half ten there were just a few lights on. I don't know where the power was coming from; it didn't look like they had mainline power. There was no radio or television up there. I'd have one or two more pipes then off to bed. I'd sleep well that night – I was well stoned by the time I got to bed, I'll tell you. I had a pain in my back from the journey. It had been like being up the hills on an old school bus – noise and smell and dust. I brought my bag up to the room as I had paper I wanted to write some things down on. There was a nice man, Abdul, on the reception and your man in the restaurant was cool too. They were first cousins – I think that's the way it was there, probably another relation owned the butcher's. They were saying there was a bakery down the road too. I'd see what kind of sweet bread they did in the morning. The prayer call was taken very seriously. You didn't have to kneel down or bow, but if you just stopped and stood quietly it honoured the way they pray, like the Angelus in Ireland.

Breakfast in Mazar-e Sharif.

My first morning in Mazar-e Sharif, I was up about nine in the morning; the sun was well up and a lot of people were around. I washed my face and got down onto the street. The little café next door was like a one-room shack, with a little fire for cooking on. I ordered a cross between an omelette and scrambled egg. I could have it with or without spice. I said, "without spice" and they threw in a bit of onion and two eggs, whipped it up, cooked it and served it in a bit of bread. I had a cup of nice chai with it. There didn't seem to be any other foreigners in the area at all. It was very quiet: just a little bit of music, more likely a tape machine than a radio. I did hear a bit of a racket in the middle of the night – a lot of movement of men on horseback.

There were quite a lot of old people around. I reckoned I'd hang around for a few days. I had enjoyed the smoke with the lads the night before. After breakfast I took a walk around town. It was cool. I was getting used to it being so unbelievably different. There was just an odd old car here and there and the odd small camel herd passing through. The guy at the reception was part owner of the hotel. People had a fair bit of English, but you could walk up to someone and you'd think they were going to speak English but they wouldn't have a word.

I'd learned how to dress for the weather now: very light clothes, a good pair of sandals, and a little hat that was a bit like a turban. The hat was the best thing of all – it kept my neck from getting burned when I wrapped it around. I noticed a few small buses: they looked like really old Mercedes vans. I'd find out if any of them were going towards Balkh. Just down at the end of the town I was looking in a few shop windows – well, open holes really. Shop fronts were not the same as our shop fronts. One of the shops down there was doing some bread and sweet bread balls. The stuff they had was very sweet, almost like balls of sugar. There was even less money used around there – less need of money when you got to higher ground. You could trade anything if you had it, silver or gold, bits and pieces. I saw one transaction in a shop, trading with tiny gold bars – no actual cash. They had amazing saddles, quite different from ours but incredibly well made. The bridle gear and the saddles – anything they had on the horses – was all top class. Everything was kept clean and polished. I suppose it was their main means of transport, so they took care of it and they took pride in it. A lot of the roads were just tracks. There'd be a lot fewer roads from there out – none really. It wasn't that far from the Russian border there, nor even that far from the Chinese border.

There were a lot of fertile fields around too. They grew a lot of poppies in that area and there were small hash farms; I don't think there were many other ways of making money. They kept sheep and goats, and nearly everybody grew everything themselves. There were some very old carts around as well, pulled by ponies or donkeys. No one was in a hurry there. I hardly knew what day it was anymore; time didn't matter. Get up when you wake up; go to bed when you're tired; follow the seasons rather than days of the week.

You would get a bit intimidated at times when you'd see a lot of the men around, in the tea shops or sitting around with the pipes, but they were all quite friendly. Weapons were carried openly; even the police carried old rifles there, but they were quite friendly as well. It was like being in another world – not just another country. Everyone seemed to know everyone else. In that way it was similar to the small towns in Ireland, but everything was more primitive there. The only thing they listened to there was the prayer calls. The way of life was whatever you could make out of the ground and whatever you had was what you had. You wouldn't want to be depending on banking; the only currency exchange I ever found was in the markets where anyone would change money for you. You'd often get asked if you had any dollars or any English pounds. I changed a few but I wouldn't change that many. The rate of exchange on a pound varied widely. The difference would be enough for three or four extra nights in a hotel – mind you, that's at a few cents a night! There was never anything much, just a bed and cold showers. If you wanted to have a bath you had to pay for the sticks for the fire to heat the water.

A lot of the guys I was chatting with were interested in where I came from, but a lot of them didn't have much of an idea of the difference between England and Ireland. I tried explaining that we used to be ruled by England but that now the biggest part of the island was a Republic and that a small piece at the top was still ruled by England. Some of them understood that.

There was a good smell coming out of the little restaurant in the evening: they were baking nice fresh breads with local corn in them. They had a nice bit of fresh lamb there as well, that they were putting in kebabs with peppers and onions, cooked over the coals in the fire. The guy in the hotel said there was a bus going up to Balkh a couple of times a week. A relation of his wife lived up there, if I had any bother. They were all saying I should go by horseback, but I couldn't ride a horse! I wouldn't have a clue. I had sat on a donkey a few times and that was it!

The music got a bit louder that evening. I was sitting around in an open air place with seats and tables and there was a bit of craic going on. It'd be another good session that night. All the lads were on their old sweet tobacco pipes. I used to think there'd always be something else in them, but no. They'd usually go on to the hash or grass late in the evening. I'd smoke a bit with them, it was very strong up there though! It was okay if you took it easy. There was no alcohol around. Someone said you'd get the odd bottle of wine made locally, but they weren't pushed on alcohol. Some were strict because of the religion thing, but others not so much. There seemed to be only about two policemen around. They didn't do anything – just walked around, sat down and drank tea!

They were serving a meal for the whole table – big plates of kebabs, huge bowls of rice, plenty of bread, big bowls of salad and a lot of jugs with cold mint tea. The lamb was very tender. A fella arrived who had a huge dog with him – he had the dog tied up beside one of the horses. He was sitting at the other table. He was from the mountains alright – wild out! They were all carrying big guns, looked like old 303 rifles. When most of the food was eaten, they brought out the puddings – wouldn't finish up without one – a nice big rice pudding made on goat's milk with a lovely flavour. Big pots of chai were put out on the table then. They told me that at that time of the month a few locals came down there and a session would go on. A couple of them played a bit of music and you wouldn't know what the hell they were playing – one-string or two-string instruments. It sounded pretty good and there was the odd roar of a camel in the background. A camel will stand there all day once you give it a bit of something to eat –big cactus leaves and stuff like that. They'd sit there and chew all day. They never really get that uneasy – a horse gets unsettled a lot quicker.

Pipes were on the table and bags of grass were on the table. We were in for another night of indulging! Some of the older men just sat there swinging out of their beards, talking and fiddling with their beads. It was going to be some night! I got a blast out of the first pipe that went around and a cup of chai. They were getting into the swing of the music with three or four guys playing now. It looked like one was playing something between a fiddle and a lute, and another a cross between a clarinet and a whistle – nice sound anyway. There must have been about twenty lads sitting around now. When it got dark a few big oil lamps were lit and set on each end of the table. You'd miss a beer at this time, but sure, I had to get used to it. They might have some wine in the hotel at the weekend. The pipes were flying around. I was a bit more wrecked than the night before, but I wasn't going anywhere the next day. They put down some of that sweet bread, it was quite good – chewy, something of the texture of almond fingers. The party broke up eventually, the lads climbing on to their horses and heading off; I guess the horses knew where they were going!

View from the hotel roof, Mazar-e Sharif.

I took a walk down the town before breakfast next morning, to the mosque. A fella was telling me stories about the tribes around there and this mad game they played with the carcass of a goat, called buzkashi. It sounded like a mad sort of polo, with the players on horseback trying to score a goal with the carcass. It was a tough game, apparently played quite a lot up there with some of the best horsemen. I was still amazed at the shine off the horses there – I'd never seen a black horse as black, or brown as brown … glowing!

After breakfast I was talking to the man with the little bus; he said he'd be leaving at half nine or ten in the morning for Balkh.

It's a short distance so could be a day trip, but I wanted to go beyond to the Hindu Kush as well. They were saying that would be by camel train or horses, so I wasn't sure whether I'd be into that.

The following morning was very bright with blue skies; I hadn't seen rain for months now. I felt a bit of loneliness coming on: I hadn't been in touch with anyone in Ireland for a long time. It was strange – I was feeling a bit down after feeling great for a long time. I was just thinking of my parents and brothers and sisters. I'd get over it – it wasn't like I wanted to give up, just one of those days I was going to be a bit stuck in my head: "what am I doin' and why am I doin' it?"

I got the breakfast and got on the bus. I took a packed lunch off your man as well, and a couple of bottles of mint tea. From what I had heard about Balkh, it was a strange place. I just wanted to go there. It's very close to the Russian border. You could see a difference in the people in Mazar-e Sharif: they had a slightly different complexion than around Kabul.

The bus was a clapped-out heap, but it was going – just about! There were a few windows missing, as usual. There were two fellas there with a box of chickens and a few other things; they were probably heading back to Balkh. The bus stopped now and again to let people on or off. It was very dusty up there, just mountains all around. The Hindu Kush was not far from there but I still didn't know what I was going to do about that, whether I'd go there or look at it from a distance. It was a wild place.

Coming in to Balkh, wow! There was nothing really: a few droves of camels, horsemen, people walking around; a few small, low buildings like a row of garages with no front door on them. They were built mainly of clay and straw with a bit of timber. There were a few knick-knack shops, a little tea shop and the usual places selling bread and the like. I had heard that there was an English fella living around there for a while. Maybe he was gone. I wouldn't want to spend more than a day round there, anyhow. Being very close to Russia, someone said there was a road that went up to a huge tunnel there, but it was probably just a rumour. The country up there was genuinely one hundred percent tribal.

Balkh.

I picked up a nice belt there – it's probably one of the best belts I ever bought. I think it was about five shillings in old money. The buckle was moulded brass, probably worth five or ten dollars. It was definitely cow leather – you'd know by the strength of it. There were no other tourists around; they would just come in and leave. The bus driver was at the tea shop and probably wouldn't leave till around four or five o'clock. The bus went up and back a couple of times a week. I could see a few fields around with different things growing in them. There were the usual goats and a lot of sheep as well. The old wagons reminded me of the fifties at home, where they would have had milk churns on the back, pulled by a pony or a donkey. I would have loved to speak the language properly, but three or four words was all I had. I'd sit there and listen and the expressions and the laugh would pretty much tell you what was going on. You could pick out what was good and bad from that. I had a few words with the bus driver. He knew a little bit of English and could translate some of the stuff for me, if I really wanted to know what they were taking about. It was all about horses and what they were doing and what was going on, and that it hadn't rained for so long. It was dry alright – dust in your ears and your hair, and the beard was full of dust.

A couple of nice camels pulled up. The fella with them had four or five in a row, tied together with a bit of rope. I wouldn't have known what to do with them. I was amazed how many people did ride them around. The horses reminded me of the old cowboy movies – the Wild West: guns, horses and the men on them. The old movie *Lawrence of Arabia* would give you some idea.

Balkh was just one small street, and one small side street, then you were into no-man's land again.

I had two cups of chai with the lads there and I took a walk off down the side street. There was nothing much – I thought there'd be more there because I'd heard stories about it. I knew it was a large hash-growing area. There was a lot of opium around Mazar-e Sharif and Balkh too. I wouldn't get mixed up in too much stuff like that. You're on your own out there, y'know? The only one that can watch you is yourself. I was talking to another guy with the driver. He'd spent a lot of time in England. Now and again you'd meet people who had lived in Europe. Some of them didn't want to stay in Afghanistan, but for more of them, their land and their country was their own. They were very dignified about it. Like in Ireland – the land is your birthright, it is where you should live. Travel is travel, but home is home. That day I felt a little bit homesick. It was hard when you'd start thinking too much of the same thing; you'd have to try and clear it up. It's worse when you're sitting on a bus – what do you think about? What do you look at?

Another bus had pulled up. I'd seen about four cars in the whole day. The newest vehicle around those parts was nearly twenty years old, some of them more like forty. The buses were big, bull-nosed petrol-engine things.

There wasn't anything to stay around for, so I got back on the bus that evening. It was another rough, dusty trip back down. I wouldn't say it was a waste of a day – it had been an experience to see it. You couldn't say it was underdeveloped – there was nothing much to develop around it! There were more settlements outside of the town – farms in the countryside. The nomadic tribes moved from one green area to a warmer area, pulling their tents behind their camels, or strapped to the sides. It was amazing when they'd put them up. It was a bit like a circus – full of animals, mainly goats, sheep, horses and a few camels carrying stuff. They'd put up one big tent and some smaller ones,

Camel caravan in Balkh.

making a big circle. They would always have people minding the animals – they had to. It was some way of life! They're beautiful looking people – the children were always smiling. They used the land and lived from the land. They only took what they needed and

Horseman in Balkh.

a little bit of a profit at times. There was no greed with those people.

I arrived back at the hotel. It had been a strange sort of a day. I suppose every day can't be enjoyable all the time –you have ups and downs, but I wasn't sorry that day was just about over. It had been my most pissed-off day in the last five months, I reckoned. I resolved to find a bit of a party and some wine that evening – Abdul in the hotel would pull a bottle out of somewhere. He said he'd have it for the weekend anyhow. I was going to have a good wash to get the dust off myself and wash a few bits of clothes and hang them on the balcony.

Street scene in Balkh.

The music was good that evening and stopped me wondering too much. There were a good few around as well … Abdul and his cousins were there, so there was a good few to sit around and have a bit of a chat; they were speaking Afghan on one side of the table and English on the other. I told Abdul I was heading back to

Kabul at the weekend. It was one interesting area alright, Mazar-e Sharif – a wild beautiful place. There were no more than five or six hundred people living around the place and they'd come in and out quite a lot from the outlying areas. It still amazed me that there was so little machinery – although it wouldn't be much use having a tractor up there and no fuel to put into it! Everything was done by hand. Ploughing with a camel and an old wooden plough – just barely pierce the ground and throw the grain in. You'd see a half-acre plot squared off – they'd be well irrigated and watered and good food grown in them. Otherwise nothing would grow there.

The food was all laid out on the table and we ate for an hour or two, chatting away. There was a bottle of home-made wine on the table. There were only one or two who drank it – Abdul would have a glass of wine but very few of the others. The baked potatoes weren't bad – just salt them a bit and eat them with the kebabs. There was no Kerrygold there, but I was well used to that! I wouldn't have minded a lump of butter sometimes but that was a long way away. It would be a night on the pipe there. They were always sucking on their tobacco pipes; they'd be calling for water pipes all evening. When it got to eight or nine o'clock, the music was still playing and it was still daylight, getting a bit dusky. There was light from the cooking area – a few lamps – but very little electricity at all there. I was amazed at what there was. I didn't see wires around much, but there must have been some way of generating it. There were no town councils there or anything like that.

You'd very seldom see the police – I think they only walked around occasionally. There was very little trouble there anyhow. They'd take your hand off for thievery, so I suppose you wouldn't find much shoplifting – or adultery: you'd get stoned to death. They were tough laws, for a hard country. But then again, most of the countries there – Iran and Iraq and all – they all had the same laws: capital punishment, beheading, hanging. It was just a matter of keeping yourself straight – if you can't pay for it then leave it behind you. I wanted to keep a fair amount of my English pounds for buying in Pakistan. I wanted to go to the big market in Peshawar.

Travel with Moon

When I told Abdul I would be heading back down on Saturday, he said he was delighted that I had been there for a while. He hadn't been speaking English much. I had been just over a week there and it would be ten days by the time I left, down another rocky, bumpy, dusty road! I had drunk a good bit of the wine and the food was great – the pipes were too fuckin' good! At least I'd sleep like a log – I'd done nothing but walking all day. They were playing a weird game with what looked like a couple of dice. You'd see the old guys banging away on the tables and other fellas sitting there playing with their beards all day, or the worry beads.

In the morning I decided I'd walk the back streets right down to the end of the town. I'd heard there were a few areas of cultivated land and I was mainly wondering where they kept the stock that they used in the town. There was no such thing as a meat van coming in – nearly everything was killed in the area and it came in, onto the table. One thing I noticed everywhere was eggs – everyone eats an egg and everybody had hens. They used camels' milk, and it could have been in some of the dishes I'd eaten, but I didn't know.

By Friday morning I didn't feel as bad. I'd had a good sleep. I tried some of their coffee for a change instead of tea – it was very bitter but something different. I was looking forward to Saturday morning. I felt like I had to move on. I had two coffees, a nice bit of their bread and an egg, and a bit of yoghurt – that was all I wanted for breakfast. The yoghurt keeps the system good. You cut it up with a spoon into big lumps and it's nice with a little bit of sugar cane juice on it.

Down at the very end of the town I found an old place making jackets and another place fixing leathers and making stuff up. They used very few tools there but they could make anything. It was unbelievable looking at your man making what looked like horse bridles – he'd no big sewing machine there. I hadn't thought about it, but they had to get stuff made somewhere! Your man was making the jackets and cutting up shirts and sewing away – everything done by hand. I had bought a new top and trousers a while back, so I had two or three sets of light clothes by now. It was enough. You could buy a ton of stuff there if you had a way of bringing it back, but I wanted to keep any space I had in the bag for stuff that I could buy to sell – rings and semi-precious stones: cat's eyes, agates. Pakistan would be a great place for them.

The bus was leaving around nine. If I remembered right, it had been uphill nearly all the way there so it should be downhill going back, with a few flat sections. Back at the hotel, in one way I was sorry to be leaving in the morning. I had gotten really friendly with a lot of them – even the ones who didn't speak English: they'd still clap you on the back and give you a good handshake. A lot of the older people were amazing, if you could only get the stories from them.

I'd only seen the Hindu Kush from a distance and I wouldn't be going any nearer to it. Right behind that was the Chinese border.

I'd take it easy that evening – sit around, get a bit of food, drink a few teas, one or two glasses of wine; I'd have that and a small pipe and that'd be it. I was looking forward to getting back to Kabul. It'd be a trip down and a stop overnight and then a bus to Peshawar. I got my passport checked out and got everything ready. I checked my visa and vaccination papers. I got a new strap for the wallet that I kept all that stuff in. I would get freaked out at the thought of what would happen if I lost those papers! I said goodnight to Abdul and the lads and went to bed a bit early.

There was a good old handshake and a hug each in the morning. I was sad enough leaving them – it's amazing how attached you get when you hang around a place for a while. There was no rip-off there anyhow. When I got to the bus stop, there was a fair bit of stuff going on the roof. It was about a twenty-one-seater bus and was fairly full. Two women sat up the front at one side. I thought the men were meant to be with them, but they didn't say a word. They were wearing the burqa, so you couldn't see anything of them.

As we were heading down the mountain, I was reminded that it's a huge country – the range of the mountains is something else! We passed fields of poppy plantations, going down the hills. You needed the few stops on the way; after an hour on that bus you'd want to straighten up and dust yourself down a bit. The dust would poison you! I was glad I had a couple of scarves to tie around my head and over my mouth, across my face and tucked up in the side under my ear. My beard was very long now.

When the bus pulled up in Kabul I was half deaf with the noise of it. I had to shake myself for half an hour after I got off to get rid of the dust! We were only a block down from the Steakhouse hotel. I didn't have to collect a bag off the roof – I never let it out of my sight and it wasn't that big – about fourteen inches square and two foot high with a roll on top. I had a small shoulder bag too with my daily bits in it – food and a light jacket. Back at the hotel I got the same room – it was like I hadn't been away at all. I said I'd go for a wash before having something to eat.

The bus I had come in on was the same one going on the run to Peshawar. That would be a couple of hours, I reckoned. I had always dreamt about the Khyber Pass – it's a beautiful name for a place, quite a heavy border too.

There were a few people around. They said there'd been a few foreigners staying at the hotel over the last few days. I decided I would eat at the hotel that evening. I'd have a bit of a chat and I wouldn't bother going down the town. I had to get an exit visa in the morning, and an entry visa to Pakistan. The exit visa was about two dollars – that was to get out of Afghanistan. I checked all my papers again, especially the vaccinations. Smallpox was on my mind – I got frightened when I saw so many people with the scars. The amount of people begging was shocking too. It'd be the same the next evening when I got into Pakistan.

I SAID GOODBYE TO THE LADS IN the hotel and they just said, "Mind yourself in the mountains – be careful!" You can only be as careful as you possibly can. The bus was packed to the gills, no empty seats, baggage on the roof. It was no distance to the border where I got out and handed over the passport. The guard wrote a few lines in it and put a stamp on it, I paid him the two dollars and got the passport back. Easy enough, then another one – into Pakistan. I don't think I paid anything that time. They talked about Irish, English, Commonwealth … I didn't know what they were going on about, but I didn't object.

We got through the border at the Khyber Pass. Peshawar was just over the border. Wow! Fuckin' mad there, mad! They had double decker buses, like the old English London bus, but with no paint on them – just silver. There were hundreds of little two-stroke machines with three or four seats on the back flying around. Lots of dust. Crowds of people, lots of children as well – it was hard enough to take in this one. There were railways as well, and it was really, really noisy! You'd know there was a lot of English influence in the country. There wasn't much wealth though. People and kids were nearly in their bare skin, except for a little T-shirt, or jacket on them – no shoes, nothing! Anyway, I was in Peshawar! It was strange – the amount of people and the hustle and bustle was overwhelming: mud roads, lots of beggars and cripples, little shanty town shops full of plastic shoes. There was a guy making footwear out of old car tyres – unbelievable! You could smell the

tea shops there, chai tea, full of cinnamon – beautiful smell. They
had a little counter with boilers making tea; they boil up milk and
tea and spices, and pour it into little teapots. The teapots were
ancient –lots of them had been broken lots of times. They were
delft, put together with little pins and nothing wasted or thrown
out. I took a seat on a little bench with straw – it was practically
on the floor – and ordered some tea. The whole area seemed to be
smoking tobacco and whatever else. It was lovely tea – had a much
better flavour than the Afghan tea; you could taste the English
influence.

There were rolling hills and mountains everywhere. I went to
look for a hotel room and there were plenty of little cheap places.
Nearly everywhere was painted white, so you'd want to know where
you were going and coming back to, not to get lost! There was a lot
more noise than in Afghanistan. There were big markets all over
the place. I got talking to a policeman in the tea shop, and he told
me there was a hotel on the corner of the street we were in and
that the rooms there were probably the cheapest. You wouldn't pay
much more than a pound a week. It was a small little cubby hole
of a room with just a bed. They weren't really hotels, more like a
downgraded youth hostel. Like before, I left the bag down in the
reception area and kept my passport and money on me.

You'd hear lots of old motorbikes and old scooter-type three-
wheel vans, that would carry three or four people in them. The
trucks and buses were amazing: coloured and painted to the last,
with ribbons and decorations all over them. I figured I'd hang
around there for a few days then go up into the mountain areas of
Jalalabad. I thought I might make it into Rawalpindi. The trains
went straight through the middle of nowhere: you'd just see a
steam train appearing out of the sunrise or sunset. There were
no level crossings, or anything like that. They must have been put
in by the English years ago, mainly for carrying cargo around. I
was told that in Jalalabad the railways were brutal – mountains,
bridges, tunnels, single track. It hadn't been raining there in a long
time either, just dust.

I'd have a good look in the market, at the perfumes and semi-
precious stones and beads. Lots of people in Pakistan speak

English. You'd meet loads of people that had been in England, or their brother or sister or cousin lived there. I saw an unfortunate guy with no legs. He had a little wooden trolley with four ball-bearing wheels on it, two blocks of timber, and he was just scooting around the town. I don't think they had mental institutions either: there seemed to be lots of wild guys hanging around the streets. There weren't as many horses or camels down there. I could smell a lot of curry there and spice dishes.

In the hotel they asked for my passport, but I said, "No, just take the details. I'm not letting it out of me hand. I'll pay you in advance for the room." Everywhere you'd go they were trying to take money. Exchange rates varied from street to street – people trying to get your dollar and get your pound. Around the market there were lots of dealers in the currencies. I had my eye on large bottles of musk oil and patchouli and jasmine; if I got the right price on them, I'd get one of each. I'd get a cloth and put timber packing between them. I wouldn't get them till I was leaving anyhow.

There were a few other Europeans around the town. I'd seen the English fella and girl that I'd seen in Kabul in the market earlier.

They would sell anything on the streets. I saw one guy there who had bottles of liquid for stomachache, headache, backache, pains – cures for all those things. They were selling snake heads and tails. There was another guy selling what must have been toothpaste or something to clean your teeth – it looked like Omo or Daz in a big unmarked box. He had a few brown horse teeth – he put water on the brush and dipped the brush into the powder and cleaned the teeth. Lord Jaysus! Rough! There were people buying the snake juice or whatever it was, Jaysus I wouldn't go near it! They did sell though. Then there was another fella haggling about land he was selling. There were a lot of good vegetables for sale too. There was another place in the market with birds in cages – they looked like small eagles or birds of prey.

I'd been looking at boxes of semi-precious stones, cat's eyes for rings, and old cheap silver rings with good stones in them. I wasn't asking any prices – there was no one around to ask! I decided to book a ticket for the middle of the week to go up into the hills and spend a day or two trekking round up there. There were a lot of military around too. They could hop on and off the buses, checking things. Any time a bus got near a bridge, there was always a checkpoint. I was talking to a few of the people there and they said that if you were riding a bus up into the hills you should get onto the ladder on the back and go up on to the roof with your bag. There were rails there and, if there was a crash, you'd probably be safer than sitting inside.

There were old donkeys carrying bits of timber around – most places still used fire for cooking. I don't think I had seen anything new out there – they'd fix anything. There were lads working on the old cars, trucks, motorbikes, everything … nothing was wasted. There was a man cutting shoes out of car tyres, adding a leather sole inside and a few straps to make sandals. They were better than bare feet, anyhow. The heat was unbelievable – must have been about thirty-eight degrees. The cripples were everywhere with bent legs and arms, begging. The nearly naked children looked happy, running around. Very busy. I met the English fella: he was called Peter and he said he didn't know what to think of the place. He and his girlfriend were heading on to India. I said I wasn't going near it – not this trip anyhow. I had enough on my plate as it was. In four or five weeks, I wanted to be back in Istanbul or Ankara. They had come overland as well and I think they were heading for Delhi. He was from the Manchester area and his girlfriend was from near Sheffield. They had saved up money for this trip for a long time. I told them I was heading up into the mountains. He was saying there was an American guy in the hotel where they were. There were no other foreigners in the one I was in, the staff were nice people though.

I'd have boiled eggs in the morning with the yoghurt, which seemed to be very plentiful. The area would be in trouble without hens and the goats for fresh milk and yoghurt. The bread was quite nice, although you'd miss butter. I was eating tomatoes quite a bit as well, when they were clean and rubbed. I saw they had Pepsi or Coca Cola there too and lots of machines selling sugar cane juice. I think the machine they had to roll it was originally built by the Romans. They still worked very well though, even if they were mental looking things! They had a radio station as well. I hadn't seen a television – I hadn't heard any news from home.

A couple of days later I was heading for the mountains, for Jalalabad. The bus must have been from around 1956 or even earlier … ancient! It sounded perfectly alright though – the usual big petrol engine and brightly painted, with ribbons and beads hanging out of everywhere. I think they must have been privately owned – they're very individual buses. The trucks were the same. There were lots of people walking on the roadsides and working in the small fields. I heard something about salt mines in some places but there was no other industry that I could see there. There was a huge population in Pakistan too; I had never realised that it was such a big country. We weren't going any more than twenty-five miles an hour. There had been a checkpoint on one of the bridges we crossed. Soldiers got on to the bus and walked along inside. I was on the roof, they didn't say much to me or to the few old Pakistani guys lying up there on the top. Always keep your head down!

We came onto a part of the road then where the bus slowed right down and I saw this guy sitting on a rock with a rifle, and around the next corner was a chain gang. They must have been prisoners. They were wearing stripey suits and were chained together, breaking stones for the road with sledgehammers. It was hard to believe but it was there in front of me. They'd probably get put on a truck in the evening and brought back to the prison. I'd only seen it in the movies!

There was very little timber there – just a few stands growing in the parched ground. There were a few old cars in Jalalabad, and motorbikes with three or four on each bike. Like in Afghanistan, I was often amazed that you'd never see a filling station or anywhere to get fuel. There were a few horses and camels up there, and the donkeys were used there just like they used to be in the west of Ireland – everything was carried on them. At least there was electricity there, whether it was mains or not I didn't know. Didn't think so. I got off the bus and sat down for an hour or two, had a pot of chai and some sweet bread with an almond taste. There was only the one small hotel, like a bed and breakfast. Not many people stayed up there. I had noticed, driving along, marijuana plants were growing all along the edge of the roads and the hillsides were covered in them – it was like the nettles we have all over Ireland! There was a huge market there for that. All the lads were sitting down with their pipes there too – you'd see them all rolling up smoke and you could smell it. They'd be very offended if you didn't take a pipe off them, so now and again I did. It was quite strong. There was a bit of music goin' down, again there was practically no alcohol … just chai tea, which was alright too. I got talking to one of the lads living locally. He made a living out of sheep and goats, selling the milk, the kids, the lambs and the wool; he didn't need that much to get by. Back in the evening the same fellas were hanging around the place. I just paid for two nights there.

I was knackered anyhow, I wanted to get a good night's sleep. I checked the room out and was just lying in the bed thinking, having visions of lovely pints of lager – one thing I did miss! I crashed out then and I'd get up in the morning when I felt like it.

There was a fella called the Monkey Man, who seemed to be the organised dealer of the town. Anything you wanted to buy, he'd bring you to the people. It was just a service that he provided I suppose! I bought four pounds' weight of top-quality black hash from him, for four pounds sterling.

The man I was talking to, with the goats and sheep, had a fairly well put-together little place. He had his father and a sister living with him. You'd see the women walking around there a bit more; they were actually allowed to talk to you there. He was milking thirty goats, all by hand, and making yoghurt. Water was scarce too. They all kept around a dozen hens. He was telling me there were eagles there –you'd see them flying around – and vultures as well. I don't know what kind they were but they looked weird – baldy necks with ugly heads! I don't know how they could stick the heat and the dust. There was a small school in this town, with only a handful of pupils in it. Their education was a little bit better than in Afghanistan.

I was heading back down to Peshawar the next day and I wanted to find out how far it was to Rawalpindi and decide whether I'd go there or not. I had only planned a week or two in Pakistan, mainly

to go to the markets. You could be offered anything in the hills –
weapons, or kilos of this, that and the other. I knew I'd be better
off doing the markets, like I had planned to do. Even in the shops
back in Amsterdam, the price of the perfume was mental. I'd get
my own large bottles and fill them. I'd get some beads and stones,
and the rings. I had come up to have a look around and that's what
I did. It was just unbelievable the way they lived. I'm not saying
they had an easy life, but it was peaceful, hassle free. Peshawar was
quite big in comparison. There were a lot more people and shops
and hostels. There were people selling anything you wanted and
beggars looking for everything. What bit of traffic there was didn't
slow down much either.

On the way down from the hills there were at least three
checkpoints, looking for terrorists blowing up bridges, or whatever
– I didn't know. There were only a handful of people on the bus
going back down – but it was full of chickens! Back at the bus
station in Peshawar, I was worn out with the heat. I was thinking
about the ad back home in Ireland, with Sally O'Brien and the pint
of Harp. I wouldn't have minded a pint of Harp now! I got back to
the hotel and booked in for another couple of days.

Waking up in the hotel room in Peshawar next morning, I
determined I was going to get organised and buy the stuff I wanted
to bring back with me. I took two English fivers from my wallet,
where I had it around my neck with the passport. I reckoned I
could buy quite a bit of stuff with that. It was a very hot, clammy,
still day. There was noise on the streets, a lot of people around and
dust everywhere.

I left my bag down in the lobby and headed off after breakfast
with just a small bag. I headed down to the market, passing old
bicycle shops, little moped shops, all sorts of stuff. The butcher
shops were mad, with goats and lambs hanging around and pieces
of every kind of meat, and chickens. There were flies everywhere
and a good few donkeys around.

The market was just rows of stalls, like a market anywhere, but
it didn't move. They would just fold everything up. There was a bit
of a roofed area in the middle. I had my eye on large pint-bottles
of good perfumes, if I could get the right price on them. I wanted

to get musk, patchouli and jasmine. I wouldn't even dream of going near the boxes of rings with individual prices. I'd buy maybe fifty or a hundred; same with the semi-precious stones. They were beautiful looking, and any decent sort of jeweller would set them in rings or pendants for you. I was at a stall negotiating on three bottles of perfume and one small box of rings and was going to try and get a hundred semi-precious stones and thirty cat's eyes. The cat's eyes would be a little bit dearer than the other ones. I might only be able to sell fifty or sixty of the stones and the rest mightn't be any good, but the chances were I'd be able to make some money on them.

We were haggling away over the perfumes. They'd wrap them in a cloth, but I told him what I wanted was wood – like an orange crate – and wood around each bottle, so they wouldn't knock together. They had proper lids on them. I had looked carefully at them and they were genuine oils – I didn't want any diluted stuff. I was on the verge of buying three bottles, a hundred stones and a box of forty or fifty rings. He was looking for fifteen pounds. I said he was fuckin' mad. We were dealing in sterling. Standing back, I said I'd been on the road for months now and I'd been wheeling and dealing and haggling. I remembered the trips to Morocco a couple of years before – you'd learn about haggling there alright. We were at twelve pounds and I wasn't budging.

I took out the two fivers and I said, "There's your pretty English queen fivers – you can have the two of them!" That went on and on for ages … we were going to have to have a cup of tea now and a bit more of a chat. "I've a long journey back, even as far as Switzerland – it's a long way back yet. I need money to get back with. I have to eat for the next couple of weeks, pay a new entrance visa into Afghanistan – it's not easy."

He had very good English, this fella – relations living in London I suppose. We were sealing the deal at ten pounds. "No, you're not getting eleven – I'm not breaking another fiver. No, no rupees either man, just ten pounds even. You won't sell that much in the next two weeks here. How many times do people come in to buy that much off you?"

"Go on then, take it."

Deal made! Good for him but very good for me. I had it sorted for the way back. I wasn't planning on buying anything in Afghanistan or Iran. I'd probably get some of the Turkish rings, but I wouldn't buy them in Istanbul.

I was happy out now that I'd got that deal. I got my knife and cut up the box and got a cloth on the bottles, like two pairs of socks on each bottle. I wanted wood on them though. Your man didn't mind me doing anything in the hotel room – it was only a concrete floor with a bed. I spotted a stall selling Coca Cola there and I got myself a bottle. It was warmish, a bit flat – horrible in a way. The only thing you could say about it was, it was wet! It was like treacle. I think I did the wrong thing buying that – it was bottled there. Half an hour passed and I was in bits! I puked the whole thing back up and nearly shit on myself! I felt like crap. I waddled back to the hotel, felt like I was dyin' now … I'd had it. I was warned about them but I wouldn't listen – I said I'd try one. I went back to the hotel, but Jaysus I was dyin! Out to the jacks again, sick again – I had picked up dysentery off the Coke. I lay in the hotel room for a while, luckily the jacks was in the same hallway. I'd got the best deal, and then got that bottle of shit! God! My stomach was doing ninety, galloping out to the jacks every half hour, back in, lie down! I was supposed to be leaving in two days to get to the Afghan border. I put one box together for posting back to Ireland. I put in some of the rings and some of the stones and some of the odds and ends that I had bought, including two little rugs. I put one pound of the dope in there as well. I sold the rest to some Americans.

The post offices seemed to be quite strange places. It was expensive to post anything. It was nearly dearer to post it than to buy the stuff to go into it. I decided to send one box and carry everything else with me.

Oh my stomach! I'd just have to get on with it, stop when I had to and start when I could. I tried a small meal in the evening, mainly yoghurt, a few potatoes and a bit of chicken. I was hoping for the best. There was very little you could take for it – it would run its course, I was told. It would probably be a week. I wasn't looking forward to getting on a bus for hours either. I sat around in the hotel in the evening, didn't feel like walking around that much.

I took apart the other wooden box that I had and, with the good old Bowie knife, got the laths made into about two-inch sections and taped about eight around each bottle. I left them sticking up a bit at the top, then stacked more papers or cloth down into the top of the bottle area. I could put the three in a row in one part of my bag, once they were packed right. I got a little pair of pliers off your man in the hotel, so I could tie the wire in around the bottom, the middle and near the top. It was fine, soft wire I had picked up. It was boiling hot in the room. The bag was now about five kilos heavier, maybe six when I put the stones and rings in. I was very happy with the stuff I got: some lovely coloured stones, like a half circle, flat on the bottom. I'd make money on them.

I got my bottle filled with mint and lemon tea, let it go cold and sipped it when I needed it. I wasn't going near any doctors – I'd let it take its own course. I had met a fella one day in Afghanistan, he'd got it too and said it was a bastard of a thing. It was bound to happen at some time or another. I hadn't been sick once. It was pure stupidity – I should've known. The top was nearly loose on the bottle. I felt alright lying down for a while and I reckoned if I got a good sleep, I might be okay. I'd have to stay off any spicy food for a while.

I slept alright that night – only had to get up once. I was a bit weak. I had a cup of chai and some bread and yoghurt in the morning, for breakfast. Your man told me not to eat any hot foods at all, like cooked kebabs or chicken, for a while. I'd only upset myself worse. Stick to boiled eggs, yoghurt and bread.

I staggered up to the main post office later in the morning with the box in my arms to get the stupid thing weighed. The guy weighed it and said, "Three dollars fifty." He said they'd sew it up in a cloth – a big printed thing with the name and address in Ireland on it. I could probably get in touch with them in Ireland when I got to Denmark in a couple of months and see if it had got there.

I felt a rumbling in my stomach. I thought food poisoning was bad but that goes away. This thing kept coming and going. I'd have to make a run for a bush somewhere, or a laneway. I couldn't hold anything in.

Travel with Moon

I booked a ticket on one of the very colourful buses for some time the following day. I didn't know what time I'd be going at though, as there were a few running that day. A German couple, from Hanover, had moved into the hotel too. They could speak a bit of English. They'd only just arrived. I warned them not to drink any of the Coca Cola there. Water even shot back up when I drank it – well, tea, not water, I wouldn't touch the water. I sat around with the Germans that evening for a bit of a chat. They said it was shit weather back over there. I hadn't seen rain now for three or four months. I didn't really miss it, but I missed it getting a bit cooler and I missed the green. It's a strange place. The young German fella still couldn't get over the amount of beggars and cripples either. They'd only just arrived but they weren't hanging around; they were going on to Karachi. I told them I would be heading out in the morning, about eleven o'clock. Sometime in the afternoon I'd be back in Kabul. I wasn't looking forward to the bus. There they were having a nice kebab meal and I was on yoghurt and boiled potato and egg. Ah well, I only had one more night in that place. The German guy offered me a joint but I didn't bother with it. I wasn't trying to say I didn't smoke, I told him I enjoyed a smoke, but not at the moment, with the stomach I had. My head wasn't in great order either.

I said my goodnights and headed up to bed. I checked everything in the bag and made sure it was all sitting well on my back. It might not sound like much, but five or six kilos is a fair bit of extra weight in a bag, especially when you're walking around with it, lifting it on and off buses and in and out of old vans. My stomach was slowing down a bit but I was still staying off the food, just trying to eat something that would soak things up. Yoghurt lines your stomach, bread does a bit of soaking, and the chai, the tea with the cinnamon, is nice. I didn't drink too much but it was refreshing. But I never wanted to see another bottle of Coke – unless I saw them bottling it in America or somewhere! I had a mild headache with it too.

In the morning I got ready to go. You wouldn't want to be moaning about your back in the beds. I was thinking that we should get the van back on the road – it was like a palace compared to these rooms. I missed the van and Clob, but sure you can't live together forever. I'd meet him again when I got back to Denmark. When you spend too long together you need a bit of time off. We never had rows, we just decided we wanted to go different ways. Sometimes I'd think of him a bit and the craic we had in that van.

Anyhow, I got a bit of breakfast, had a chat with the hotel owner before I left and gave the Germans a wave. I checked my papers and it was all still okay for a few months. I got some money out for the hotel – it was only a couple of rupees for the two or three days I'd been there. I hoisted the bag on my back and I could feel the extra weight, especially as I was still a bit weak. I felt like I'd lost a couple of stone in the past few days.

There were a few Europeans on the bus when I got on. After an hour, everyone got off at the border. If I could hold on for the next hour without running into the jacks that would be great. I'd already ruined one pair of trousers yesterday and had to wash them. All went well at the Pakistan side, then back on the bus and out again at the Afghan end to get the entrance visa. I paid roughly two American dollars – it was crazy! I had never realised it would cost so much in visas going out there and back. I didn't have to pay in Pakistan but I had to pay for entry and exit visas in Afghanistan. Iran was an expensive visa too, as were Yugoslavia and Bulgaria later on. I made sure I used the jacks at that border check area. It was just a hole in the road with a hut on it, but it did the job.

At last we got into Kabul. The bag was weighing heavy now. I went back to the steakhouse hotel. Your man remembered my name. They all called me Moon – I never told anyone my other name. We were always just Moon and Clob.

So, back in the hotel: "Hey Moon, how are you?"

"Not bad. Here for a few nights," I said. "I got fuckin' dysentery off a bottle of Coke!"

"Ah," he nodded sympathetically. "You'll have that for a while now, I can tell you. You can have the same room."

"I'm going to beg you for sticks to boil water," I said. "I need a good wash in that little bath thing upstairs – my hair and beard's manky!"

I got hot water and washed the clothes too. I could hang them on the window ledge and they'd dry okay. I told him to be very careful with the bag. I took all the clothes out of it and left the big bag down there – I didn't want to leave that in the room. Even while I was having a good wash, I kept the pouch I had with my passport in it beside me. I took it off for the length of time it took to wash and dry, and then put it back on. I could have done with a few new pairs of underpants, but what I had would have to do until I got back. I hadn't worn socks for four months.

I felt a good bit better after a good wash and with clean clothes on. I went down to the lobby to sit down and have a chat with Al and Mohamed. They said there had been a good few people around the last couple of weeks. They asked if I got what I wanted to get and I said I did. They said, "You get the best prices there. In Karachi you'd pay twice as much for the stuff you bought. They don't haggle as much." The sun was beating down on the walls outside. It was bright as hell there. I still couldn't believe that sky – you couldn't get that colour blue anywhere else. I could smell the food cooking, but I wouldn't be able to have much of it. I wasn't too bad – it had been about four hours since I had been to the toilet. I was watching everything, though. The stomach was still rumbling. I met a Chinese guy in the hotel and he said to ask the kitchen if they had any semi-cooked rice. He said that would bring my stomach back in good order and stop it heaving all the time: semi-cooked rice and yoghurt a couple of times a day. I was going to hang around till I was a bit better anyhow. The last few hours on the bus had been rough enough.

I saw the two Austrian fellas that had the club. They looked amazing – big tall hats and long coats on them! I went into the little restaurant I used to go to, just to have tea and a slice of bread. I had nothing on it, just a lump of bread to chew up with the tea, mint and lemon. I must say the chai in Pakistan had been amazing. A strange thing I noticed, there was quite a lot of them drinking tea off the saucers. I remember when I was a little kid, about eight or nine, my grandfather used to drink his tea off the saucer. He'd make an awful slobbery sound, slurping it. But he spent a lot of time in India and probably got it from there. I drank coffee that way – sipped it, but the coffee was full of grains; you had to filter it through your teeth. I said I'd come back in the evening and get a little bit to eat there. I felt refreshed after a good wash, clean clothes and when my beard wasn't stuck together; it was quite long and so was my hair. I still wore a little hat. I suppose you could say I'd quite a high forehead – I was a bit bald at the front, but I always wore a hat anyhow.

I was talking to Mohamed about where I was heading to from there. He was saying he might get to Europe sometime, you'd never know. It was so different to be back in Afghanistan – it was a lot slower going, with different rules and regulations. Even between Mazar-e Sharif and Kabul, there was a big difference. The laws were slightly different too.

I headed out for a walk around the town for a while. You'd never get fed up looking in the shop windows and the shop doorways, at what was hanging up and what was for sale. I wanted to get a Kuchi robe. There was a beautiful one there: it was jet black with gold edges and very, very colourful embroidery. It was a really old one, well used. It cost a couple of Afghanis. I didn't mind paying that – I had intended to buy one of those. I'd only really got three things from Afghanistan, the old silver coin, the little Afghan with a lasso in a brass setting and the robe. I was talking to the man in the bicycle shop and I said I might and I might not hire the bike again. I said that I wasn't in great form for riding a bike. I had intended to use it again and had left the money with him, but there was

Steakhouse Hotel Kabul; Al, Mohamed and Moon.

only a few cents in the difference, so I told him he could keep the few bob.

There was a lovely bit of ground around that little hotel. You could sit outside there all day. It was just amazing to hear the horses and a few cars going by, guys in carts with donkeys, the occasional old bus, old noisy trucks now and again. I was taking a bit of a rest. The old belt had gotten a bit loose. I had the dose about five days now, so if I hung around there for another four or five days, I should be okay. I didn't mind. I liked that hotel anyway. I'd been in it three times now. I was on top of the world with all the things I had bought and couldn't wait to get back and set up my stall. I love selling things – haggling. That little Kuchi robe would be grand for setting up my little table. I had a little eighteen-inch square rug, like a little Persian rug that I used for sitting on most of the time.

There was a young Swiss guy called Jan at the hotel and I wanted to talk to him later on. Someone had said he was heading back home and it would be nice to travel back with him. The big Canadian guy, Jack, was still in the hotel. I was heading up to my room when I saw them in the bar. I wouldn't have a beer yet – I'd leave me stomach alone for a while. I was half afraid to drink anything. I'd go over to the club with them alright.

Jack was a big hairy mountain man. He was a lumberjack in Canada, a very sound man. When I told him where I was from, he said he was going to Ireland in four or five weeks. I suggested we all meet for dinner later on.

"Ah, we'll go to the club because that little restaurant stays open pretty late. Then, if you don't want to go to the restaurant, there's probably a bit of food in the club. They have beers, good pipes, usually a bit of sweet cake. It's a nice place – usually a bit of Black Sabbath music playing, and the Austrian guys look like them anyhow! Right, I'll see yous all in about an hour."

After lying down for a while, I didn't feel too bad, so I wandered out to meet Jack and Jan and head over to the little Austrian club house, have a few beers, smoke and tea and whatever. Jan was from just outside Zurich in Switzerland. He was heading back in a few days, so I said I'd see what happened and I might head on with him. Sitting around in the club, I was just having mint tea, not going on the beer yet, but the lads were having a beer. There were pipes going around, but I wasn't even going to bother with that. I didn't feel half as bad and I wasn't getting sick anymore.

There were a few people in but not that many around. There never were that many in that place. It was mainly westerners who came in. Johan was one of the owners of the club, a big tall fella. They were nice guys.

Jack was well amazed at the place – he said he hadn't thought there'd be anything like that out there. He was heading back fairly soon too. He was going to Istanbul and then he was flying from Istanbul to London. He said he was going to Ireland, so I gave him my parents' address and a note to give them. If he made it there, he could hang around for a few days. He had given me twenty dollars, because I was a bit low on cash, so I said, "If you go to my mother's, you can stay there for a few days." I'd have to watch the money from now on, until I got back to Switzerland. I'd make money there selling a bit of jewellery and perfume.

A couple of hours later we were heading back up the street, looking in a few windows. I wasn't up to hanging round too late – you're not into much when you're not feeling great. The lads were heading on up the town, so I said I'd see them in the morning about ten. I was planning to leave in three or four days. I'd head down to Kandahar and back into Iran. I wanted to be fairly fresh sitting on the buses for that length – there wouldn't be too many stops. I wanted to have a chat with Jan in the morning, see what he was up to. He was a nice fella and I was hoping I could head back with him for a few days anyhow. It would be good to travel with someone else for company. He had pretty good English. His parents had a cabin up in the Alps and they didn't live too far from Zurich either.

The mornings seemed to come around very quickly there, so by nine o'clock I was up, enjoying bright sunshine and a beautiful sky. I decided to get a decent bit of a breakfast this morning – a couple of eggs whipped up and a sort of soft roll. I'd have their coffee – it wasn't too bad – and a bit of yoghurt as well. It smelled good and tasted good; I hadn't had a decent breakfast for weeks.

"Good morning Jack, how's things? You all right after last night?"

"Ehh, not too bad."

"I was going to say to you, Jan, when you're leaving on Wednesday or Thursday, I might head along with you."

He said it was a good idea anyhow, so we were half planning to leave on Thursday. I told him we'd want to stop in Tehran for a day or two and have a look around the market areas. I had very little money to buy anything, but I had kept a few bob as I definitely wanted to buy some puzzle rings in Turkey. I'd probably get them in Ankara.

I got down to the little market and took a walk around there with the lads. Jack said he was looking for a few small things to buy, like a little bit of clothing or a small rug or something, and the market was the best place to buy them.

"Don't bother with the antique guy," I said. "You only get fuckin' hassle. They're not very much of an antique either. Yeah, they've big water pipes there alright. Depends how much weight you want to carry on your back. The small rugs are nice: three foot long and about eighteen inches wide. Quite a nice little thing, but they are handmade – you can notice the ones on the other stall there, they're not done the same at all. Three or four dollars is nothing for them; you'll even get two for six dollars. Just tell him you have Canadian dollars and that's it, whatever he gives you. They'll take them once the queen's head is on the dollar. That's a good deal!"

We went down to the little restaurant place, as it was getting near lunchtime. I hadn't had a decent bit of meat for days! I got a shish kebab, a small roll and minty lemon tea. I tried a goat kebab – they were lovely. "Go on, Jack, for fuck's sake – it won't kill ya! You eat hens and you eat cows and you eat sheep, it tastes no different. Ask Jan, he's eating it, not a bother on him. When you're hungry you'd eat anything. I must've eaten about a hundred eggs in the last two months, more, a hundred and fifty. When you're getting on a bus you just bring three or four boiled eggs, onion, a knife, big flat bread, and away you go. If you can get a tomato, you get one – not always easy. Best thing I ever had was that container I keep the food in – keeps it hot or cold. I often put stew in it. It's brilliant if you're in a place overnight with nowhere to eat."

"Mmmm," he mumbled round a mouthful, "that kebab is good!"

"Haha, told you," I laughed. "Are you flying or are you going overland?"

"I'm flying from Tehran to London."

"Well, call into that woman there in Avondale Park, Bray, Co. Wicklow. It's only half an hour from Dublin city. You'll be very welcome and I'll give you this note to give her. Let her know I'm getting on alright, might be home by the end of the year. I'll get in touch with her when I get back to Denmark. You won't be the first one sitting on the wall outside the mother's – I often send people there."

"Cool, thanks, man! I will."

"No bother, thanks for the twenty dollars. I have your address, I'll send it on to you, or else see what happens at the mother's when you get there. Fair exchange, okay. You get a couple of days there we'll call it quits. She'll feed you and there's always a spare bed in that house."

I went back to the hotel to stretch out for an hour or two; it had been really hot all day.

It was a strange place. In the hotel room there was a window, not much of a window but you could look out through it. There was a cloth pulled down over it and no glass in it. When you'd been there for a while, you'd get used to seeing people in the streets with smallpox, and beggars and cripples. Life must be hard for them. There were a lot of differences between the people in the cities and the ones up in the farming areas. There was always someone looking for something in the city – probably the same in every city. They seemed to be getting it a little bit together – compared to what it had been like when the king was there about a year before. The only place I'd seen school uniforms was in Kabul. I couldn't tell if they were secondary school or primary, I wouldn't know the difference. They looked very young.

Later that evening the three of us met for dinner. I was going to have half a roast chicken, done on the grill outside, fired up with timbers, cooked the way you wanted. "You going for the same, Jack? Ah you're going for the big lamb rack, fair play to you."

They said they'd do anything we wanted. Well, I wanted an onion as well, cut in halves, a couple of those long mild chillis and a couple of the big potatoes. We got a bottle of home-made wine to go with it. The whole meal, between the three of us, cost about a pound. Two or three courses each and the wine. We gave a two Afghani tip as well. They were really nice people. Never once did they try to overcharge us. We'd haggle on the price before we started, and they'd leave it at that.

It was Wednesday, and we were leaving the next day. "You're going in the morning, Jack?" I asked. "I'll have a pipe with you this evening then. Al, can I borrow your pipe?"

"Yeah, no bother. I'll join you later."

I'd a couple of glasses of wine and a lovely meal. I was feeling good again. Just as well there was elastic in the trousers that I was wearing, they would have fallen off me I'd lost so much weight.

"Ah, you light it, come on, Jan, light that up!"

"Yeah, that's … you wouldn't find better. What do you think, Jack?"

"Never had anything like it until I got to Afghanistan."

"I had something close to it a couple of years ago in Morocco. Nice country too, quite wild but not as wild as here."

"Ah, if we get fairly fucked we'll go for a walk, sure."

We picked up the wine and we headed down the town. There were still a lot of people around.

"Alright, Jack, you're heading off to bed? Ah, we'll see you in the morning. You're not leaving till ten anyhow and we'll be up at nine. You'll be sitting in Piccadilly when we're only arriving in Tehran. See you in the morning."

Jan and I headed on. "Okay, we'll go into the lad's club for an hour, get a beer. One beer and one more pipe and then we'll go back."

There weren't many there in the club, so after a beer and a pipe we headed back to the hotel. I did the usual checks, passport, the money, the lot, made sure everything was ready. I took the haversack up to the room to check everything was tightly packed. I didn't want to break any of the perfume, and I had a little bag of bottles he had given me. There must have been a hundred or two hundred miniature bottles with corks in them. He didn't even charge for them. I put a kind of tape on each side of them, I put them together like a row of bullets – they'd be broken in bits otherwise.

In the morning I went up the town to have a wander around, talk to your man at the bicycle shop and the moped place, since I'd told him I'd see him before I left.

"There's been no one around, no? Just the few repairs you're getting. We're leaving today. Thanks for everything. I'll see you again sometime, maybe. If I'm ever back, I'll call in to you."

Then back to the hotel, to Al and the boys, bit of hugging and goodbye. I'd been in that hotel a good few times. If I ever came back I would definitely go back there. I got a photograph of Al and the lads outside the hotel and put the name and address in my little book. They had mine but I doubted I'd ever see them again.

On the bus down to Kandahar, it was the usual hot, dry, dusty journey with one or two stops on the way. There was the usual couple of boxes of chickens, a few goats and a fella with a box of pups. We stayed overnight in Kandahar, then got onto the bus for Herat the following day.

In Herat, we noticed two young German fellas and I wondered what they were up to. They'd be on the bus to the border in the morning too.

"If he picks the radio up anymore and puts it back down, I'll ask him what the fuck are they at. Can they turn it on? If not, we should tell them to leave it where it is, not to take it with them."

They'd be picked up immediately if the border guards went near the radio. First thing they'd do is open the battery section to check if they were smuggling drugs.

"Jan, you speak to them. I don't know if they understand much English. Tell them what they're doing with the radio is crazy – to fuckin' leave it there."

I was crashing out anyhow, going back to the room. I was still a little bit weak – not too bad though.

It was my last day in Afghanistan – I was looking at the last of the trucks there, camels and still quite a few horsemen around. I had a good breakfast – and my bottle of mint tea with lemon. That'd do me. Jan was looking forward to being home as well. It was a couple of hours to the border check and then that was us out of Afghanistan. We spotted the German lads but there was no sign of the radio. I'd never carry anything through a border other than perfumes, jewellery, rings, stuff like that. No hash or any other drugs – it's not worth the hassle. They lock you up and throw away the key out there. But there's always someone doing it. You watch the guys when they get near the borders, they'd be having kittens if they've anything on them. It was the last chance to chuck out anything you didn't want. There would be nothing in my bag except the few clothes, the food bag and the perfumes and jewellery that I was bringing back to sell.

AT THE IRANIAN BORDER, THERE WAS A higher charge for the
visa. "I just need a couple of days," I complained. "I'm only passing
through." But no excuses, paid, stamped, back on the bus. There'd
be a few stops on the way. We were crossing the desert now for a
while, then another overnight stop in a small town. They didn't
really have hotels, it was more like a shed with beds in it, four beds
to a room. The two young Germans and ourselves stayed in the
same room. It cost practically nothing. At least we got a bit of a
sleep. It was quite hot on the bus and the only air conditioning was
when there was a broken window. They didn't drive all night, they
always stopped. We'd get a train in Tehran, for a change. There
wasn't much difference in prices, or the speed of them.

When we had been on the bus for about six hours, I thought
the main stop would be Mashhad, further into the mountains. We
hoped to get into Tehran in another day or so and we'd probably
spend a few days there. Jan wasn't bothered about what time we
got into Istanbul, he wasn't in too much of a hurry and still had a
few things to do on the way.

It was quite an interesting town we were coming to, near the
border area with Russia. You'd see the influence between the two
countries when you got close to the border. It was a big enough
town – very dusty. We could see there was a train that ran into
Tehran. There wasn't too much livestock on this bus. We stopped
here and there – always stopped for prayer call. After another three
hours travelling, we stopped for about an hour, to get out for a walk

around. It was just a crossroads. We could have got some food if we wanted it, but I still had a small amount left. We passed some nomadic tribes there and herds of goats, some camels. I could just watch the animals all day and all night. When you're in a country, you don't realise how big it is until you have to go right through it. Iran was as big as Pakistan and Afghanistan put together, maybe even more. There was a good bit of money in Tehran but not so much when you got outside the bigger towns – nothing in most of the villages. You wouldn't have a hope of getting a beer there, I can tell you that much. Jan hadn't been in the smaller villages that much and I said we'd try and hit a few on the way back.

When you got into Mashhad, you could hang around for a day if you wanted, because the ticket covered you – you could get off that bus and on to another one. They came past there once a day. It's a big town, I'd say there were a couple of hundred thousand people in it anyhow, and it looked lively. It had big marketplaces as well. We decided to hang around there. You'd get a bed for fifteen or twenty pence. A dollar a day was my budget for getting back. I wouldn't have any money to spend in Tehran, but it didn't matter; I wasn't that interested. I had been thinking about getting some agate but I wasn't well up on it so I wouldn't know what was good or bad. Some would tell you it's worth a lot, some would tell you it's worth very little, so I decided to leave it.

We found a decent enough place to stay and paid for the one night, with the option for another.

We took a walk around the centre. It was mad lookin' there too! I hadn't realised it was so big. Jan said he had come out through Kerman: "it was said to be a roundabout way to get to Herat but this is quite different."

There were a lot of shops but we decided to find a place to sit down and have some tea and some sort of a sweet bread. They all love their sweet stuff. You get Danish marzipan and it's very heavy, but the stuff you get out there was double the strength of that. We got a coconut one each, and they were quite nice.

"Wait till we get to your place," I said, "we'll have some of that Swiss chocolate, that'll be something else! First pub I get to there I'm going to stay in it for a day or two."

"Ah, we can have a decent session on the beer in Turkey – cheap as well."

There were some nice clothes in the shops there, and rugs – if you had the money and a way of carrying them. You'd get a handmade one, almost two metres by a metre wide, for ten pounds sterling. They looked great and you'd pay a fortune for them back home. I thought I might come back this way sometime in another year or two.

We could smell the food out of one place that had two fires going. They had shish kebab in a bread roll, with a bit of beef for a change. We might go there later on. It wasn't as dear as Tehran. Tehran would be ten or twenty percent more expensive for food. We were looking at the old guys, hanging around, playing with their beards, the worry beads, sucking on the pipes. They'd play with the beads, pet the beards for hours, looking across, talking to one another, sucking on the pipes and drinking mint tea. You'd get used to seeing them. You could hire a pipe there if you wanted to, but I wondered how hygienic they were.

There were quite a few old motorbikes, a few carts and a lot of shops. You could smell the spice shops – they were deadly! The world stops when you're in these places. It could start off again in a day or two, when we got into Tehran. Tehran was a bit Americanised at the time – because of the Shah.

When we'd been walking for an hour, we decided to go back up and copy the older guys, sit down, sipping on tea or something. I had never tried those big water pipes, with the sweet flavoured tobacco. They could be on that from early morning till night. I suppose it was no different from the guys in Ireland, some of them went into the pub around twelve in the day and stayed there till about six or eight o'clock in the evening, drinking pints and looking at the television. I always said there were more things to do.

We were sitting chatting about our future plans. Jan reckoned he'd be heading off again soon after he got home, whereas I wasn't even heading back to Ireland and had taken Copenhagen as my base for a while. We talked about maybe going on to Tehran the following day. I was telling him about the hotel where I'd stayed the last time and about staying with Al on his farm on the way out. We'd come back a different way, so I wouldn't be calling this time. We chatted a bit about our families: he was one of four kids and I was one of seven. I explained that my father worked in CIE; his worked in the postal service. His mother was a nurse and we talked about how, at the time, it was more common for women to work on the Continent than it was in Ireland or the UK. We talked about our countries and how Ireland had joined the EEC, while Switzerland stayed out of most things – except banking.

We reckoned we'd be at Jan's house in a couple of weeks. He assured me his parents wouldn't mind me coming to stay and I said he'd be similarly welcome in my house. I explained that I had done an apprenticeship and gone to Bolton Street technical college for drawing and had qualified a couple of years before. He had another year and a half to go at university, studying engineering.

We were up by half seven for the bus to Tehran at half eight. I'd a feeling this bus would only stop about once on the way and it would be packed, once you're going from one big town to the next. We got the bags and got tea and a roll next door. We packed something for the journey as well: the big flat breads, two eggs, and onion as well and got the bottle filled with mint tea and a dash of lemon in it. I had salt and pepper – I always carried them. I got pepper in my eye sometimes from my hands in my pocket!

The bus pulled up and we saw straight away that the rack was full outside, so we fought our way into two seats in the middle, one on each side. I didn't want to put my bag up in the rack, I'd fit it under my legs. If the bottles got broken now, I'd freak out! The bus filled up quickly, the door was closed and off we went. I hadn't been on one as full as this for a long time. The road wasn't bad, better than the last one. It was the most sheep and goats I'd seen along the road – there must have been a thousand of them. Men on horseback were herding them along and the children were all running behind, clapping their hands and chasing them. I suppose they must have been to feed Tehran. In a couple of hours they'd be in the markets. We passed two lorry loads of hens; they'd be going there too. I hadn't a clue what the population was, a million or more? Two million? It was huge. You wouldn't leave your bag or anything down. There was always someone trying to sell you something or ask for something; you just had to keep walking straight when you got there – don't slow down when someone tries to say something, speed up. There was plenty of hustling going on. Coming into Tehran, we drove past a cinema. I hadn't been at one for six months or a year. The last movie I had seen had been subtitled in Arabic and the dialogue was Russian! The last big movie I'd seen was *Custer's Last Stand* in Bremen in Germany, and it wasn't subtitled – it was in German! I broke me heart laughing at Geronimo and the Indians, and General Custer speaking German.

Back to the bright lights of downtown Tehran. If you closed your eyes and opened them quickly, you'd think you were in the States with their big American cars and flags – plenty of Cadillacs. It was a far cry from Afghanistan. The bus depot was just around the corner from where the hotels were. I found the same hotel and two nights, in the same room, cost a dollar. They didn't do food, but there was a bath and a shower. We brought the bags up to the room there. It was fairly safe, with a decent lock on the door. I had no soap left but there was a smelly weird soap there which would do. I threw the clothes into the shower and stood on them. They were light green turning blackish grey. I washed out an incredible amount of sandy dust and hung them on the windowsill. They'd be dry by the evening. It was baking hot there too. I lay on the bed for a while in me underpants, sweating. There'd be western music and a few beers – later on. I wasn't moving for a couple of hours. I had a sore foot and my back was broken from that bus ride! I was definitely going to try a train in a couple of days. I'd had one ride in a train there. I took one out the last time. They had a good sound, and the smell of burning coal.

We went out to find a western cafe, as I'd a craving for chips! I put on my sandals and trousers and a top and we took the little bag. I took the key of the room with me. There was a fair bit of hustle and bustle outside. Down the road I could definitely see an American style cafe – it was the only one around with the Coca Cola and 7up signs hanging out of it. They had chips and burgers and hot dogs, the whole lot. It was dearer than normal, but we couldn't complain really – burger, chips and a bottle of Coke for forty-five cents. We could see that it was a large portion of chips and a big burger as well, so we decided we'd both have the same. They were playing the Rolling Stones.

But what a disappointment: the chips weren't great and the burgers were okay, but had nothing on them by way of a dressing. We'd go back to the kebabs, the shish kebabs were about the best of them.

"Jan, I think we'll hit the sack a bit early tonight and in the morning we'll go down to the bazaar area and look at stuff that I can't afford to buy – rugs and turquoise. Don't know much about it but I want to go down and have a good look around, spend one more day. We'll just tell the hotel we're staying tomorrow night."

Jan had about thirty dollars and I had about twenty-two, and we would need that I can tell you. Rooms were cheap here, but Istanbul would be different, you'd never know what you were going to be charged. We'd have to stay in north Turkey as well for a night. We had a couple of days left that we had to feed ourselves and it would be a long enough trip. That bag of mine was getting heavier every day. I just wanted to make sure it would still be intact when I got to Switzerland. Jan was looking forward to getting home as well, probably to steep in a bath for a month! We'd do a lot of walking the next day but I didn't mind that. The bags were very safe in that hotel; it was a good cheap hotel but it was nice. It was a long way from there to Istanbul though – about two and a half thousand kilometres. Yeah, I suppose we should've gone up around the Caspian Sea but you can't go everywhere.

It was very different from Kabul there in Tehran, they used a lot of neon fluorescent tubes in the evening time, a lot of colour around. You wouldn't get much of it outside of the city though.

We got a coffee in the lobby and sat down for a while. The coffee was alright.

"We'll start at the top end of the market tomorrow, we can work our way down through all the stalls. There's old antique stuff, there's everything new, there's Persian rugs, from a foot square to twenty foot square. There's quite a few dealers coming down from Europe buying here now, and with the Shah in power there is huge American influence everywhere."

Talking about getting back into Europe, Jan had a plan. "I reckon, when we're in Istanbul we can go down to the truck park, look for a Swiss truck and get a ride the whole way. That would be cool."

"Yeah, I don't mind hitching in Bulgaria, but I don't like hitching in Yugoslavia."

"There's a good few companies dealing there from Switzerland, so we've a good chance really. We can check for a day or two before we do anything."

With that, we agreed to meet for coffee around ten in the morning and headed off to bed.

There was a bit of traffic noise coming through the windows from outside. It had been hot all day, the temperature was in the mid thirties. My feet were like rocks, probably from the sandals, my hair was long and knotty, and my beard had grown to about eight inches. I hardly ever shaved – I'd never really got into it. I hadn't been clean shaven for six years, had always had a beard of some shape. I never liked razors.

At nine twenty I got up and had a quick wash. When I came back that evening I'd make sure any of the clothes I had to wash were washed. It would be the last chance until we got to Istanbul. I wasn't intending to spend any money there because I didn't have it. I was very interested in looking at the turquoise. There's a beautiful green one they all talked about and you could get a good blue with no marks on it. You could get a lovely piece for a dollar. The one with the white lines – forget about it – it was rubbish. Jan spotted a nice triangular piece that would make a nice pendant. The guy was looking for two dollars, but with a little bit of haggling he got it for a dollar. The rugs were beautiful, but that would be for another time, if we were ever back that way. I thought I might come back that way sometime. I'd like to have gone back across the east.

There was a live market around the corner, with every kind of chicken, goat, sheep, camel, anything you wanted.

I was looking forward to the next part of the trip. "You think I look rough? I think you look not much better yourself. Gone weird! The clothes we'll sort out this evening. I've no heavy clothes at all now so it wouldn't want to be too cold when we get back. I have sandals and an old jacket. No heavy trousers, two pairs of socks, two pairs of underpants, light trousers – about three pairs. Maybe

177

the next wash I do will be in your mother's washing machine!"

In the morning we got on the bus after a bit of breakfast. We took a small bit of lunch from the hotel, to keep us going. I had checked all the bags again before I went to bed: everything was perfectly okay. I was still a bit nervous with my bags of bottles. It would be a good long trip to the border of Turkey – probably take a day and a half. We'd probably stop at one or two places on the way. The bus was fairly full. It was another scorching day – hadn't seen rain at all. Tabriz was a stop on the way but that was over six hundred kilometres away, so it'd be a good while before we got there. Time passed slowly – the buses were quite slow, lots of nomadic tribes outside. We'd get off for a day or two on the way – you couldn't do it without stopping. We were passing within fifty miles of the Caspian Sea. There would be small unmarked towns we'd pull into on the way – it depended on the bus driver of course. This bus was quite an old bus but it wasn't as bad as the usual ones. We'd probably change buses along the way anyhow.

Over halfway between Tehran and the Turkish border we pulled in for a couple of hours, a chance to have something to eat. We'd been chewing on the bits and pieces I'd brought in the bag all day, so we hadn't much left. I couldn't see us making the border by midnight – or anywhere near it. We were all sitting round having something to eat, some of the passengers moving seats, other people trying to get on. There was never much to do when they stopped like that, nothing to look for or to look at either. We got back on the bus, ready to go again, and it would be another three or four hours before we stopped again. I didn't like this part, looking out the windows was all you could do, or try and sleep for a while. At least the driver was going flat out to the border now: he was making good time.

Everyone got off the bus, which was now pulled over to one side, for the usual border checks. There was only one American on it; we were getting no hassle. They were asking what was in the bags: perfume, jewellery, clothes – that was it. We got our passports stamped and a short-time visa: we'd only be a couple of days. So we were heading on again now, over to a bus depot. Your man wasn't driving any further and it was after midnight. There

was a motel bunkhouse thing: you'd get a room for nothing there
– a little wooden bed with a light mattress. I had one or two cups
of Turkish coffee. I was surprised that the little shop was open – I
suppose because of the buses … One night there wouldn't kill us
anyhow. We'd get a few beers the next night. We'd get as far as
Erzurum, a big enough town. It had been hard going the last four
weeks. The dysentery had fucked me up for two weeks – I'd got a
bit of strength back but wasn't a hundred percent yet.

It was a weird place to wake up in the morning. It was only
seven o'clock but looking around, there were a few people standing
around the bus. The sun was coming up too. There were a couple
of old scrap cars around the side of the building. Wild enough! It
looked like there were a few farms dotted around the hillsides. I
was happy enough to be back in Turkey. The bus would be leaving
at half eight or nine, so I went off to give the face and hands a
bit of a wash and get a bit of breakfast. It was all fresh bread
made there, goats' cheese and the coffee was good, if gritty and
unfiltered. I got a couple of boiled eggs to take with me; it would
be maybe another six hours to Erzurum. We should get to Ankara
by Thursday or Friday and it shouldn't be too bad from there on:
Istanbul, Bulgaria, Yugoslavia.

When we got into Erzurum, I didn't feel like staying around any
more than one night. There was a restaurant beside the small hotel
where I'd stayed on the way out and the food was good in it. They
did lovely Turkish stews, and I recognised the waiters and the fella
behind the counter. As far as I knew there was a Tuborg brewery
in Ankara and they had the sign in the restaurant in Erzurum. We
got a half litre anyhow, and it tasted good. We'd be paying more
next week – Swiss prices – but we wouldn't worry about that yet.
Two pints was enough and we got to bed a bit early as the next
day would be flat out. As far as I knew, the bus would go through
Ankara and then up into Istanbul. There was one little market
there that I had to go to. I wanted to get a small box of three- and
four-piece Turkish puzzle wedding rings.

It was hard to believe we'd be in Istanbul the next night. The
last couple of days on the way back were always half boring. It'd
be grand when we got into Ankara and Istanbul. We'd only be

stopping in Ankara for a few minutes, I hoped. If the marketplace was open I wouldn't stay overnight, but I wasn't sure. If it was still bright enough in the evening, the little shopping mall area could be open.

Just after six in the morning, the sun was well up for another scorching hot day. It was some difference from the rain on the journey out! The bus had pulled in at the vegetable market and there was a lot of fresh stuff there. We went to get a bit of breakfast on the corner. I wouldn't mind spending a night and a day in Istanbul anyhow – leaving on Saturday morning would be grand. When we were on the bus we could see the buzzards flying around, sheep all over there too, and goats – everywhere you looked someone had them. There was a fair crowd on this bus. It was one of the better ones. At least the seats were fairly comfortable and I had my bag safely tucked under mine.

We were making two stops before Istanbul, for toilets and food, and maybe a prayer call too. We pulled into Ankara around the market. The shops were all still open anyhow. Five dollars' worth of rings would leave me with about three dollars. That should be okay. If I got broke, I'd get money from somewhere. We would only be stopping for an hour, so I ran into the shop. I got a bag full of rings –small and medium; I didn't really want the large ones. I haggled for four dollars. That was it, I left the rest, and ran back to get back on the bus. I had saved a dollar and I would need it.

Getting close to Istanbul, the first thing we could see was the war college on the Bosphorus, as we were coming over the big bridge. It was still daylight and people were running around everywhere. There were fifty- or sixty-year-old taxis – mad looking. People were selling everything and anything. We got off the bus on the western side. The truck stop was down around the corner and we were right beside the marketplace. The hotel I had stayed in on the way out was just down the road, so we headed straight there. There were a couple of good restaurants right beside it. We would get one or two nights depending on when the truck was going out, once we made sure we could get a truck. We paid for the room and made sure the bags were safe. We just paid

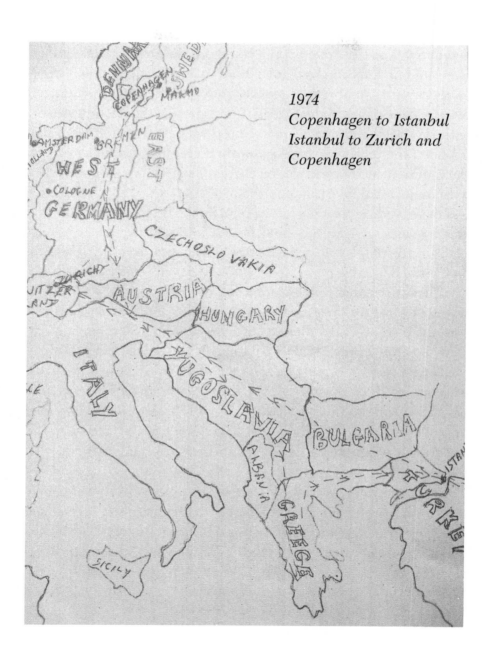

1974
Copenhagen to Istanbul
Istanbul to Zurich and
Copenhagen

for the one night; we'd know by the morning if we could get a lift. Then we went for a pint and to get something to eat.

First we had a look around the area and spotted a couple of Swiss trucks; they'd probably be leaving in a day or so. Jan went down to talk to the drivers. If he could organise a lift, it'd be great. He would probably be back in an hour so. In the meantime, I went to get a pint. Istanbul was usually packed with people – a lot of people there, and ancient taxis. I recognised the Dolmus ones, with the black and white squares on the sides, from the last time I'd been there. There were obviously no regulations on the tyres there or how much wear was on them – I saw things going by with what looked like four tubes on them!

Jan arrived back saying, we were in luck. The following morning at six o'clock, the truck would be leaving, so that was only one night in the hotel. "He said he lives sixty miles from my house in Switzerland."

"That's cool, that's fuckin' amazing. I wasn't looking forward to trying to get across Yugoslavia again. Brilliant!" With our transport sorted we went to get dinner, into the Pudding Shop for a lamb stew, red sauce, nice boiled potatoes in the sauce and a pint of Carlsberg. It was always a busy enough little spot there and meals were cheap. They'd want to be when you'd no money! We should be in Switzerland in about two days, with a bit of luck. A couple of pints then off to bed and up at five. We'd take the bags now on the way in and pay for the room, so there'd be no hassle in the morning.

In the morning we walked down to the truck yard. It was a nice truck; the driver said he wouldn't normally take people, but Jan was from near the same town as himself. We got underway quickly and it was an hour or two to the border with Bulgaria. They were chatting away in Swiss Deutch. I didn't understand much of what they were talking about.

Beer delivery, Greencamp, 1973.

Tent 7, Greencamp, 1973.

Greencamp wagons.

Border Town, Northern Turkey, 1974.

No-man's land, Turkey-Iran border, 1974.

Colourful trucks in Herat, 1974.

Herat, 1974.

Moon ready for work, 1975.

18

At the border our passports were checked and all was in order. We got back in the truck but, just as we left the border area, there were huge checkpoints, police all over the roads checking everything that moved. They pulled our truck in and they said he had to get something done with the turbo, so we drove to the next town, about thirty kilometres from the border. The driver had to phone the company he worked for and sort out a part. It would take one or two days. We had to make up our minds whether we'd stay or try our luck on the road. I thought we'd lose too much time if we got out of there now and tried to get all the way to Switzerland. It was a long distance and the driver was going almost to Zurich. There was accommodation in the truck for the driver, but we'd have to stay in a guest house. He said he'd give Jan a few bob if he was stuck anyhow; he could pay it back to him in Switzerland. Five English pounds each would cover us for a day or two and I could give it back to Jan when we got to Zurich.

So we were there for a few days, in a small town in Bulgaria. We walked around town for hours and we found a bar and a restaurant where the people were very friendly. They were playing very loud dance music, so we had a few bottles of Bulgarian beer, and got a meal. They had two rooms that they let out there, so we took one room for the two nights. We put the bags in the room and got a key. At last we had a room we could lock up, decent beds, shower and toilet. I hoped to God that we could leave on the third morning. Of all the things to happen! They were very fussy about noisy trucks and noisy vehicles in general. The driver of the truck was a really nice fella, probably about thirty-five or forty, and he had a small bit of English. He said he did a lot of running up and down to Turkey, Italy and Greece. He was telling Jan that he had thought the truck was a bit noisy on this trip, but never looked into it. The Bulgarians didn't want you breaking down there or causing hassle. The weather was still quite warm, so a day or two wouldn't harm us. He said he should have the part the next morning; there was a big truck garage in the town and it'd be delivered and fitted there.

The part arrived on time and he was hoping to get on the road, if he got the truck back by lunchtime … but it didn't happen, so we had another night there.

The people in the bar where we were staying got into a session. BeJaysus, they sang and danced half the night! They were very happy people. I had a better time there than afterwards in Yugoslavia. Once we left there we wouldn't be stopping, going through Sofia, but straight into Yugoslavia. We were fed up waiting around – we should've been in Zurich by now or in Switzerland anyhow. But it was fine, because we had two nights of mad craic with the people in that restaurant. They drank a lot there too!

We paid the guesthouse and had a good breakfast before we left. We were going to drive and drive and drive, not going to stop much. Yugoslavia was quite big and the people weren't as friendly, but they had decent roads. We cut across near Venice on our way to the Italian border. We didn't expect any hassle there, and didn't get any. It was getting cooler the further north we went, but we still hadn't seen any rain. Finally, we got into Switzerland and it was only a three-hour trip from that border. We couldn't thank that truck driver enough when he dropped us off in Basel. Jan had his name and address so we could send the money on to him.

It was strange being back in Europe; it would take a while to get used to it. We got a taxi the three miles to Jan's house. His brother made tea and coffee for us and Jan lent me a pair of jeans. I washed the hair and beard. We had nice coffee, fresh bread and Swiss cheese. His mother arrived and introductions were made, and we talked about the trip and where we had met. I told her I hadn't been home to Ireland and that I was staying in Denmark.

She said I was welcome to stay for a few days. It was the first time I'd had shoes and socks on for a long time. Jan's brother Peter's shoes were the same size as mine. I had a pair of shoes, jeans and my own jacket. It was a good bit cooler there and you needed a jacket and jeans. I had two or three different types of hat. The three of us would go out that evening. His father wouldn't be home till late and they might join us in the pub which was just around the corner. There were real seats in the bar and I got a half litre of Swiss lager.

"Cheers, Peter, and cheers, Jan! Good trip. Yeah, we'll lie on in the morning alright … three beers is enough."

We headed back to the house and his father was at home, so more introductions.

"You're welcome in this house."

I decided I would head into Zurich at the weekend – another two days there would be nice.

It was so nice having a good bed to sleep in and I was enjoying myself there, but I'd a good bit to go before I got to Denmark. I wanted to set up the stall in Zurich and sell a few perfumes. We'd go out that night and have a few beers in Basel. It's a nice little town. I had to get used to wearing shoes and socks again too! It wasn't that cold there either, once you had the right clothes on.

I said goodbye to Jan and his family. I would catch up with Jan in Zurich as I'd probably spend four or five days there, selling. I'd get a few bob then; I hated having no money at all. Only for Jan and his parents, I wouldn't have had anything to go to Zurich with, but I'd pay him back when he got there. I got on the train on Saturday morning. Time didn't seem to matter anymore – hours and minutes. I hadn't really thought about it until now. I was looking forward to Zurich.

I got into Zurich around midday. It was a huge busy place – people, trams, buses, trains – a fine looking city. I had been in it a year or two ago but hadn't really spent much time in it – had just been passing through. I booked into a hostel the first night and, if it was any good, I'd stay on in it. It was only a pound a night anyway. You'd get a small breakfast with that – cheese and bread. It was just a bed in a room, with anyone else. You locked your bag up when you were leaving, like any hostel. There were a lot of cheap restaurants, if you knew where to go – just follow the students.

I crossed over the bridge and the area I was looking at was ideal. There were people there already with small stalls. They sprang up across the bridge and down the side ways. You'd want to get into the section where all the schools were for selling what I had. I'd set up in the evening for an hour or two and see what happened.

I got the smallest funnel I could find for filling the little bottles. I'd bring the little rug that I had for sitting on and put them up on a little table. I put the bag in the hostel, got a key to the locker and was told to get back before twelve. I had a look around at the other stalls and checked out the prices. I was sure there'd be another stall selling something similar, but maybe not the original good strong perfumes. A lot of the patchouli and musk were watered down.

When I did set up there were a lot of people around watching what I was doing, putting the little coloured cloth on the table, putting the little bag there, taking out the bottles and putting them in rows. I had the initials on the bottles, so I knew what they were. I started my sales patter anyway. Around ninety pence a bottle seemed to be a reasonable price.

"They're all pure oils – there's one open bottle there you can smell it. Try it, if you want to. It's very, very strong – one little drop is all you need. What's in the bottle there would be pure, usually they are diluted with different oil to make it stretch. There's nothing extra in those. I brought them back myself in large bottles. These are the same size and price as the Indian shops around – but these are top class. The rings and stones? They vary in price: five francs for the good one, other rings four francs. That ring and a bottle of musk? Eight francs."

First sale and I'd only been there about ten minutes! "You'll tell your friends? Be back later? I'll be here for a couple of hours anyhow. I'm only back from Pakistan and Afghanistan. I brought it back with me. I bought the perfumes in Peshawar, most of the rings, the stones, in the large market out there. The Turkish rings I bought in Ankara. All the rings are around four or five francs, the stones are the same. Perfumes are four. Yeah, if you buy a ring, a stone and some perfume, I'll knock something off for you. Twelve for the three. Yeah, I'll take eleven. You'll get a good deal!"

They were starting to sell now. There were two policemen looking over, but they didn't say anything. There were other stalls and I wasn't blocking anywhere and I had my passport. I'd be selling for four or five days before I left. Every time I went to fold up someone else came up to buy. I took in 125 Swiss francs, and I was delighted. I'd sold about half of what I took out of the bag that day and I'd only taken a little bit out. The perfumes were starting to fly. I folded up anyway. It had been a big hit – the perfumes and rings and stones. I had noticed it the year before, coming through London. Amsterdam was the same; I could sell a good bit to the stallholders at the flea market and still make a load of money, but I'd rather do my own stall. I wasn't going to sell any of this in bulk. The smell of the perfume was amazing; it was all over the bag that I was carrying the stuff in.

There was a triangle near the hostel, with a restaurant with seating outside that looked alright. That evening I got a salad, fries, a large spicy sausage and a half litre of lager. There was a decent bit of music on the radio and a couple of nice waitresses working there. Gillian was the girl who served me. She was a student and worked in the cafe on the weekends. I was eating there for less than the price of a bottle of perfume. The lager was good. It was alright being back on my own; you always meet someone. Gillian said she was working the next day and I told her I'd call in for a meal and show her the rings and the perfume. It was still only eight o'clock, so I took a walk up around the main drag to see what was happening. There was a lot of traffic around. A lot of bars with music in them too. Of course it was Saturday night, it would be packed around. I picked a bar to go into and got one or two beers. There were a lot of young people there, and they all seemed to have good English. The music was loud but it was alright.

Sunday morning started a bit cloudy, but I didn't think it was going to rain. I had coffee, a small yoghurt, a roll and a bit of cheese for breakfast. Good coffee too. At least you could drink the Coca Cola there. I would have to get used to not being afraid of the water.

I headed up to have a look around and see how many were at the station area. It wasn't looking like a bad day after all, a lot of movement. I was thinking I might stay another night in the hostel. It was about ten or fifteen francs for a single room with a bed in it, but you'd get nothing extra, just a key to your room, a sink in it and a toilet. I'd have a think about it. It would mean I wouldn't be walking round all day. I could go back and lie down for a while. It was almost three o'clock, so I got set up in the same place as yesterday. It wasn't long till there was a crowd coming over. By five o'clock, I'd sold nearly as much as the previous day, so I decided to go and get something to eat as I was starving. It was about a ten-minute walk to the restaurant. I was happy enough; everything was selling very well.

Three guys from a band called The Minstrels were sitting there. Gillian introduced me as a guy from Ireland.

"Ah, we've played in Ireland; we know the Dubliners. We're the Minstrels, a Swiss folk band."

"Far out! Yeah, I'll be here for a few days. I'll have my dinner and listen to you playing. Brilliant, we'll have a session going in a minute." I called across to Gillian. "You're finishing at ten, aren't you? D'you wanna have a beer before you go home?"

"I don't mind, yeah, okay, Moon."

There was a bit of a session going on, the doors were open and the restaurant was fairly full. Good music, good wine, good food and good people.

I was chatting to Gillian at the bar. "You'll be getting off university in a week or two?"

"Yeah. I'll get a full-time job here for the summer, if I want it. It's handy because the university is close by, the job is here and I share a two-room apartment nearby with two other girls. It's handy."

"You'll have a lager? You order then, I'll have a half litre. What are you studying?" I asked.

"Actually, I'm hoping to be a medic, if I can stick it – nursing. I'm only in second year."

"I didn't go to university," I told her. "I ended up being an apprentice. I'm from Wicklow, probably about twenty-five kilometres from Dublin. I haven't been home for a while." Another beer: she pays for this one. "The hostel locks up at twelve, so I can't stay out till all hours. Yeah, I wouldn't mind seeing you again."

"I'm off on Monday. I only work the weekends."

"Well, I'll be selling on the bridge from two o'clock till about five."

"I'll be finished college about half three, so yeah, I'll meet you there about five."

"Yeah, I'd like to stay out a bit later, but …. Goodnight. See you tomorrow …"

I had a couple of things to do on the Monday morning anyhow. I wanted to look around the city for a while. I hoped to get out of the hostel that day. It was bloody annoying going back so early in the evening times. I'd rather have a room or something. I was getting used to setting up and selling on the street. I'd be starting at about two o'clock that day and do three or four hours there. I had nearly enough bottles filled, I just needed to top up a few more small ones. I'd a hell of a lot of stuff left, but I didn't mind that. I was getting pretty good money for it.

Zurich is quite an interesting city – fairly big, with a big enough population. It's a clean city. Switzerland is a pretty wealthy country. Things were a bit expensive in the shops there. I wanted to give Jan a call at home. He was supposed to be coming in to Zurich the next day and I wanted to meet him to give him that few bob I owed him. If I got enough money, I'd take a train to Munich and then to Copenhagen. It had been a good while since I was on the trains in Europe.

The little table I had was like a chessboard. It was easy to move – it wasn't heavy and not that big either. I laid out the perfumes again in rows, a few rings, stones and the Turkish rings. I bought a Coke. It got warm there in the daytime. There weren't that many around this time, but when I'd been there a couple of hours, I'd sold a good bit. Gillian would be there in a few minutes, so I'd pack it in at five.

"Hi, Gillian. Yeah, I'm bored sitting here. I'll pack up and we'll go for a beer."

"I was talking to the girls in the flat. They said you can stay for a few days."

"That's cool. We'll have another beer on that, and I'll cook you an Italian dinner tonight."

"There's only a small kitchen in the flat."

"It's okay, it'll be big enough for that. You're on the second floor? That's okay, the bag's not too big – just heavy. We'll leave it in your place and go do a little bit of shopping. You know where the good places are."

It was a nice flat – double bedroom and a single bedroom, which was Gillian's. The kitchen wasn't bad either. It was nice up there on the second floor, looking out the windows.

There was quite a big shop nearby selling all sorts of vegetables, and cheese and meats as well. I got a couple of coloured peppers, half a kilo of plum tomatoes, minced beef and garlic and got the bread in the little bakery.

We headed back down to the flat and Gillian introduced Pauline and Francesca, the two girls she shared the flat with. We went into the kitchen to start the food. First we got boiling water to peel the tomatoes, then chopped the garlic and put it into some olive oil and sizzled it up for a while. I threw in the mince, chopped the tomatoes and peppers, and added them with some black pepper and a little salt. I made a small bowl of salad and sliced the bread. The red wine I bought was quite a good one – a Swiss wine.

"I like you, Moon," she whispered later on, after dinner.

"Yeah, I am quite fond of you too. I haven't been with a girl for six months or more. Yeah, I'm delighted with you. Don't mind me if I'm a bit nervous. You enjoyed your dinner?"

"Yeah. You were right, you do make a lovely Bolognese sauce."

"I learned it in Italy a few years ago," I told her. "I was there for four or five months. A good friend of mine had a bad accident and was in hospital in Pisa. I was lucky enough to stay with a really good family while he was recovering."

"Wow, unlucky and lucky! Why don't we head down town, go to a bar? I've no class in the morning, only two more days to the holidays."

"Cool! Can you try that phone number for me again? I was

190

trying to ring Jan, that fella I was with."

I got through at last.

"Hi Jan. I'll meet you tomorrow at that coffee shop on the corner there. I'll be there for my lunch anytime between one and two. Cheers!"

I was happy that was set up anyhow. We headed down the town, into a bar that played a bit of music; it was a nice place. I was looking forward to this evening. Two half litres. "To friendship! Cheers!"

I was so glad I wouldn't have to go back to the hostel again. I'd be on my way to Denmark by the weekend. There was quite a crowd in the bar – it was the local bar for the young people around there. We had another one or two beers and stopped for a hot dog on the way home. I liked the Swiss sausages – nice flavour to them. Every country I was in had different food: it was either hot, medium, spicy; some good flavour, some not. Ireland – back then – was a land of bacon, cabbage and potatoes.

It was quite late when we got back. Everyone else seemed to be in bed in the flat.

"I haven't made love for six months ... just want to hold you for a while. That was brilliant, thank you so much! Goodnight. See you in the morning."

At breakfast time in the morning: "I'll make a coffee for you. No sugar, no milk, just black? Yeah, it was a lovely night. I'm going down to the cafe around half twelve, and I'll probably do the stall for three or four hours. I should be back around half five or six. See you later."

Jan was already there when I arrived. "Hey, Moon!"

"Hiya, Jan. How's it going? You're lookin' well. You getting used to being home?"

"Yeah, I've got a job for the summer."

"That's good. I'm just doing the markets for the moment, so by the weekend I should be heading for Denmark. I met a girl here called Gillian. She works in the cafe here. I'm staying with her for a few days. Ah, we just like one another, you know. She shares a flat with a couple of other girls, there's two bedrooms in it. It's only ten minutes from here, so it's handy enough."

"Ah, I wondered where you would stay."

"Well, I was in the hostel for three days but I didn't like it that much, so when she offered, I didn't say no."

"Cool, so how did you get on with the perfume and stuff?"

"Very well, actually. I sold a lot of it, and the jewellery. Sometimes 130, 140 francs in an afternoon. Another three days and I'll have plenty of money to head on with."

"Wow! That's good going. Well done!"

"Come on and I'll show you where I've set up. There's a few stalls along here: couple of those freaky guys with the horseshoe nails and the wire ones for making little earrings. The perfume's a big hit, and I've only got a handful of puzzle rings left. I sold about half the stones and half the cat's eyes."

We chatted for a while longer while I was getting set up, then he had to go catch his train. "Sure, Jan, we will meet again. Lovely travelling with you and thanks for the loan. If you're ever in Ireland you'll be welcome at my house, even if I'm not there. You have the address. Say hello to your parents and your brothers. Cheers!"

I was still selling a bit that day but decided to jack it in around five o'clock as it was looking like it might rain in the evening – overcast, not quite as warm as usual. There were lots of people around still. It seemed to keep going round the clock there. My average day's take was 130–145 francs. It was enough. I reckoned I should have 140–150 pounds by Friday. I might even get close to 200, if things got better. I wasn't worried about Denmark; I knew where I was going there, and I had accommodation anyhow.

I headed back to the flat. Gillian was there with the radio on. "Hi, Gillian. Yeah, I'd a good day. How about you?"

"All is cool. I've got one more class, and I've got my full-time job for the summer."

"We'll hang around for a while and then go out. Don't mind, we can eat out eitherways."

"Okay, I'll close the door then. Yeah, I missed you during the day as well. Probably was because of the Minstrels. You told me who they were and that started us."

"You're away from home and I'm away from home: two hours away for me, probably about two days for you."

We had a coffee and then went out for something to eat. Pizza and a glass of wine, perfect! Maybe we'd just go to the bar for an hour or two, better to go for a walk after a meal anyhow.

"Yeah, I'm happy too," she said. "It's good to share a few days with somebody. Nice walking down the streets here holding hands, lots of traffic and lights. It's quite a bright city at night-time."

"Well," I said, "I'm going to be leaving on Friday or Saturday morning, more likely Saturday, so that's two days, so we'll make the best of it. I want to check the station for trains to Munich. Might get a ticket to Copenhagen. I'm enjoying Switzerland: the market, selling, people I meet – including you. Nice to have a bit of money again."

"For sure. My summer job is pretty good and I have the weekends as well, otherwise I wouldn't be in college – my parents don't have that much money."

"Neither do mine. No, my mother never worked. Most married women in the fifties and sixties never worked outside of the house. It might change eventually, but not at the moment. Ireland has problems all the time now, low wages and not many jobs. One of the main reasons I left was because I was living in a small house full of grown-up brothers. I decided to pull out. Best thing I ever did. I learned so much in the last few years: different cultures, the ranges of food, the amazing people. When you get your qualification, you can travel with it. I still have my papers. I'd never be stuck for work – not in Europe anyhow."

After a couple of drinks in the bar we headed back to the flat and shared a bag of chips. In Ireland we had a lot of Italian chippers, doing fish and chips – fresh chips. They didn't have them there, so it wasn't the same.

Gillian was finished college now and she had started the full-time job in the restaurant. In the morning I went down a bit earlier, and set up the stall around eleven, so I could have one or two long days at it before I got out of there. I also wanted to organise my ticket to Copenhagen via Munich. I was having a good time there. People were very easy going, though they wouldn't be quite as easy going as Irish people. In the cities, of course, people moved around a lot quicker. It was a bit overcrowded. Myself and

Gillian were having a good time, anyway. It was nice to stay in the apartment as well; I didn't like those hostel places at all, with their rules and regulations. I hadn't had that for a long time. When I was travelling, I liked having the freedom to move or stay. It was just a different way of life.

I told Gillian I'd meet her in the restaurant later. She would be working there in the evening. By half two I'd had a good enough morning, so I folded up for half an hour and took a break to go and have a bit of lunch. I'd a coffee, a large sausage and a roll. I was trying to work out how much money I had – about 150 quid anyhow. I reckoned it'd be 200 by Friday. There were quite a few people on the bridge, and I was selling a lot.

It was a bit overcast when I got back to it, not too cold though. I had a good few sales in the afternoon too – I had sold close to half of what I'd brought back. I'd have to get more bottles somewhere. I'd try and get them in Denmark.

At the restaurant that evening, I met Gillian and had something to eat and a glass of wine. She'd be getting off about ten so we'd go out for a while. "No, we won't stay out late. I'm a bit tired myself, did the stall nearly all day. I left the bag back in the apartment so …"

"Yeah, we'll get a couple beers and head home."

The girls were away. They wouldn't be back till Monday.

"I wouldn't mind if I was staying longer, but I have to move on. Let's make the most of it. Get a coffee and go to bed early." Nice to have a comfortable room, good views too.

On Thursday I set up the stall for a couple of hours. Gillian was working from four till ten, so I'd call in when I was finished. Maybe she could change her hours to six on Friday and we'd do something. That was it now – finished, wrapped up. I was delighted – I'd say I made about twenty-five percent more than I thought I would.

Over Friday morning breakfast, we decided we'd have a bit of craic that day – take the tram to the big park. We didn't have trams then in Ireland, I'd only seen photographs. We stopped by the restaurant and got a picnic put together, with some rolls and cake and a couple of beers. It was a nice day out there. Later on, when Gillian went to work, I had to go back to the apartment and sort out my bag, then I went to the restaurant around eight. It was

one of those departures when you really don't want to go or stay –
you're not in love and you are in love, hard to say goodbye.

I had dinner in the restaurant, and we drank to our friendship.
We both knew it was only for a while; it was sad. We'd go out and
get a few beers. It would be our last night together. I didn't mean
to get so involved, but what can you do? Always think of the good
times: if we hadn't met, sure we wouldn't have the memories! I
suppose that's what life is – every day has a story, and life goes on.
We'd walk back to her apartment, we'd hug, kiss, make love, and
in the morning, we'd say goodbye.

In the morning I was up at six, I made coffee and picked up my
bag. "No, you don't have to get up. No, don't say anything. I had a
wonderful time here, keep the memories."

I had settled on getting an open ticket; it was better because
you could take two or three days then. Going to Munich would
make it a bit longer, but I didn't mind. I could've gone straight
up to Frankfurt, but I wasn't in a rush. I wouldn't have taken the
train, only that I had the money and I was fed up with buses. It
was a good train ride, with a bar and buffet with good food, and
I could stay a day in Munich, and then go on to Frankfurt and
Copenhagen. It cost about thirty pounds. I wondered if I'd paid
too much, but I didn't think so as I reckoned the ferry to Denmark
was included. We would be in Munich by lunchtime. It was a fast
train, and clean – I hadn't been on a train as clean as this for six
months. I was looking forward to Denmark. I'd be in Copenhagen
for the summer, I guessed. When I got there, I'd go and see Claus
from Greencamp, who was running Huset at this stage, and set up
something for the rest of the summer.

I was going spend a day in Munich, but I changed my mind and
decided to just hang around for a few hours and get the evening
train. I had been there a year and a half ago anyhow. I had to
change money again. I walked around, got a hot dog from the
stand at the station and a German beer. I was back in the station
around seven, and the train was leaving around eight. Sometime
on Sunday, I'd be in Copenhagen – change in Frankfurt and then
straight on. I woke up just as it was coming into daylight. I'd fallen

asleep looking out the window. We were just about to load onto the boat. I couldn't believe it – I'd be in Copenhagen in a couple of hours.

So, I was back in Copenhagen at last. I had an early-morning cup
of coffee in the station. It was just a couple of minutes' walk to the
centre. I could relax at last – go and visit a few of the lads, and
try and get in touch with Claus. I headed down to the pedestrian
street, past Tivoli, just past the square. As usual, there were quite
a few people in Copenhagen at that time of year. The population
almost doubled in the summer. I was thinking I might drop in to
Huset for a bit of lunch when I spotted Big Erik coming down the
street.

"Ah, Erik, how's it going? Hiya, man, how are you?"

"Great, Moon. I'm working at the moment, with the city council
here. When did you get back?"

"Ah," I said, "I just got back this morning, I had a cool time.
I'm going down to Huset for lunch. Wanna come down? And how's
everybody else in Copenhagen?"

"Ah, they're all fine. Claus is still running Huset and there's new
sleep-ins opening."

"Cool! I'll get in contact with him about that. He told me he'd
have a job for me this year, if I was around, maybe some kind of a
venture we could get going. Are you still living on the outskirts in
that nice little wooden house?"

"Yeah, everything's fine out there. I've been talking to Sven and
loads of others. I meet them quite regularly."

"Ole still got the old Nimbus motorbike?"

"Yeah, I don't think he's going to get rid of that!"

"I ran out of money on the way back. I've been selling perfume and jewellery. Yeah, I'll give you a bottle. I'll drop over some day to you. It was quiet in the winter, was it? I'd a mad time myself, travelling. I think it was February when I left here. It's unbelievable out there in Afghanistan and Pakistan. Time warp. Lovely people." I figured I'd walk down to the USIT information office, get the addresses of the new sleep-ins and head over there that evening. "See you later, Erik. Take care, man. Yeah, I'll see you soon. I'll be here for the rest of the year."

There were always loads of people sitting around USIT, looking for lifts and information about flights and trains. You could get all the information you needed there. I heard City Camp was open, but I didn't really want to go there. Greencamp was no more. The address of the new sleep-in was in a building called Valhalla. I knew where it was – I'd find it easily. It was about four stops on the number eighteen bus. As usual, I stuck the ticket into the timetable board getting off – there was about three-quarters of an hour left on it. I walked into the sleep-in.

"Ah Jack, how's it going?"

"Hiya, Moon, okay?"

"Is Claus around?"

"Yeah, he's up in the office. Want a coffee?"

"Yeah, cheers. This used to be a big nursing home? Nice lawn area, nice buildings."

"There's a big kitchen in this place."

"Hmmm? I'll talk to Claus about that."

"He said you'd probably be here this year."

"Hiya, Claus."

"Hiya, Moon, how's it goin'?"

"Okay, just came back from Afghanistan."

"Oh, fuck! Cool! Yeah, we were actually wondering if you'd be interested in opening the restaurant section – the big kitchen – and do the evening meals. Have a look around, anyhow."

Looking at the boilers, man – the size of them! Jaysus, it was some kitchen! You could boil 150kg of potatoes in one go, ten large heads of cabbage – anything you wanted could go into those boilers!

"Oh, I'm going to give it a lash alright," I said.

He said he still had the Volkswagen van there, so I reckoned I'd find our one – the Transit – and we could use that as well. It would have been lying up for a while, but I'd get it going alright. I'd have to arrange to go to the green market – the *grøn torv* as they call it – to check the prices of everything. I'd give it a lash alright.

"On the second floor, at the end of the landing area, there's a large room to the left, with two windows. You can take that room as your own accommodation."

"Cheers, that's great! I need a bit of space now, a place to put the bags and have a key to the door. Great to be here anyhow – I'm lookin' forward to this one. Cheers, Claus! I'll call back in to you later. I'll see you later, Jack."

Wow, that was like a dream, almost – back onto the cooking scene. I'd probably go for a mainly vegetarian menu. The sleep-in would hold about seventy-five to a hundred people. Then, thinking about City Camp, they'd probably take a hundred meals from the restaurant in the evening times. We could open four o'clock to about eight. We were going to do a meal for possibly ten kroner – that was equivalent to about sixty-five pence for a dinner. Most of the city restaurants charged the equivalent of about three pounds for a bit of lunch or an evening meal. I'd do big vegetable stews and I'd bring an old Irish meal into it, fried cabbage and potatoes – bubble and squeak – with a fried egg on top. I could do salads. Claus said I could use the van in the morning to go over to the green market and have a look around. Jack would come with me.

The room was fantastic – a large bed, nice locker and a table, a place to store a few things, and – best of all – my own key to lock up. I was thinking I could also probably sell a lot of perfume. There was a bar area in this place – not a full bar, but it sold beer. I heard Clob was in town as well. I'd surely bump into him in the next day or two. Someone said he was going to Morocco. A few of the Green Family from Greencamp were still hanging around. Sabine and Päivi were still living around, still arguing with the city council about proper accommodation. They had a child each now.

We went up to the market and had a good look around, checked the prices and checked everything out. We could get fifty percent off bent and broken carrots and cucumbers, there were deals on mixed peppers of all sizes. They'd be okay – they were going to be cut up anyhow. Tomatoes close to the use-by date were also fifty percent off. We got a box of each and I'd make dinner for the staff in the kitchen that evening, to see what it was like. I could take on one or two of the people that were staying there – if they worked in the kitchen they'd get a free night or two. I'm not a vegetarian but we'd do the meals that way. If you wanted steak, you could bring them up and I'd cook them.

I'd have to go and get the Transit out of storage and see what it was like. The battery would be dead, unless Clob had been running it. I was going down to see him later on – he was living in Brumleby with Mike. I'd pick an old bike up as well, just to get around on.

"Hiya, Mike. Hiya, Clob boy! How's it goin'?"

"Fuckin' far out, Moon! How are you?"

"I'm alright – had a great time. I only came back a couple of days ago. Someone said you were staying down with Mike. You're heading on, I believe?"

"Yeah, I'm heading down to Morocco – back to the mountains for a while."

"Is the van running?"

"Should be, I've been driving it for the last week! Yeah, it's still in the same place – it's free to store it there."

"Ah, the key, thanks. I'm thinking of opening a restaurant – well, not thinking of, I am going to – over in the sleep-in."

"That's a good idea."

"Ah, you would've loved Afghanistan, Clob. The last time we went out we couldn't get in there, but it's a republic now, so no problem! Yeah, you would've enjoyed it – like another world."

"What've you been up to, Mike?"

"The usual: doin' a bit of haulage, transporting stuff around. I still have the big van. I run a small removal service, get a bit of work."

"How's Butch?"

"Yeah, in great order."

"Yeah, I'll have a beer thanks, nothing like a good cold Carlsberg."

"Ah, we still all have the crates in the fridge – bottom of the fridge is just beer, the usual!"

"I want to get a fridge for my room, a small one. What d'you say, Mike?"

"I'll pick one of them up for you."

"Far out! Mainly for keeping beer and cheese and stuff in me own room. Fuck a television – I don't want that! Radio and a tape cassette thing'll do me grand. Lot of sales on anyhow. A fridge would be cool though – I'll take you up on that, Mike. You know where I am down at the new sleep-in. I'll be doing two or three runs a week now to the green market. All the boilers are working, all the cookers are working, potato peeler's working … everything. I checked all the prices out with Jack there the other day. We can easily sell the food at ten kroner. I have the notices up, 'All dinners are ten kroner – and you must have ten kroner. There'll be no change!' It'll be a rush to get everyone served. We can do small pieces in the evening in the bar area. There won't be dinners served there in the evening time, that'll be just salad dishes and sandwiches – stuff like that. Coffees and beers. Yeah, I'm looking forward to it. Should be good craic!"

I got into the Transit and started it up. It was driving okay. I checked the tyre pressures. It could have done with being cleaned, inside and outside. I got in early to the market on the Wednesday. I figured we'd do the bubble and squeak, so I only needed three items for that – two or three boxes of cabbage, 200 kilos of potatoes and two hundred eggs. I also got a box each of lettuce, tomatoes and peppers and a sack of onions. There was no need to take the beds out of the van – everything we got fitted in one side. We put the boxes of eggs and tomatoes on the low bed. The other stuff could go down the far side.

I had two helpers lined up for the kitchen, an English girl called Jane, and a young Dutch guy, so …

"No, you don't put fuckin' onions in a potato peeler, you peel them by hand! We're not using that many of them. Take all the outer leaves off the cabbage, check them, wash the rest and chop them up. Use the big sink with the rinser on it. You need a gallon or two of water in the bottom of the boilers – need more for the potatoes. They're electric boilers, close the lids tightly. We have large drains, we can drain all the water off. Take half the potatoes and half the cabbage out and put them into the bigger pot. We'll mix them with a tub of butter and salt. Then the mix gets fried in one of those big frying pans and the eggs get fried in the other. Bubble and squeak served with an egg on top. We're serving in about an hour. It'll be grand!"

There were some people outside already. We put a table across the back door and served from there.

"All knives and forks and plates should be put back on the table at one end when you're finished; please don't leave them out on the other tables. No, we're not selling cans of anything, just meals. The kiosk is on the side there in the entrance hall. There's an outside tap and disposable cups on the table, just please don't leave the cups lying around."

It wasn't bad. We'd fed seventy of them by quarter to six, and we'd started at half three. We'd get another twenty or thirty out of what was left – there was still plenty.

I agreed to pay twenty kroner for gas and electricity. That wouldn't be a problem if we could do a hundred or two hundred dinners. All the dishes, knives and forks had to be washed and put away before the kitchen was locked up. The floors had to be washed and the boilers cleaned out.

"Well, Claus, that went smoothly: everyone was delighted."

"Good one! Relax with a few beers now."

"Yeah, we'll have the vegetable stew on Friday. When we get it more together we can do bubble and squeak and a stew – and we can do fluffy rice and vegetables. We can make spicy vegetables, not too hot!"

Well, I was tired after that. In the morning I was going to fill the van with the vegetables for the rest of the week. The cold store worked pretty well – the building must have been hundreds of years old and there were big marble counters in the back room. Jack said he was going to have a few beers, so I sat around there with him and had a few beers and made a pipe. I said we'd do a few steaks there some evening, check out that supermarket and see what special offers they had. Mike said he'd have the fridge for me the next day. I'd get some of the dark bread and a few prawns ... liver pate, cheese, a few beers in the fridge. Perfect!

I was planning to go over to City Camp and have a look around, and find out what they wanted me to make for them. They'd have to have their own large pots: they could bring them over and we'd fill them. I'd get out of the kitchen the following evening at about half eight, as I was going down to meet a few people in Huset. Big Erik and a few lads would be down there. I reckoned the restaurant would be in full swing by the weekend. I was surprised that there were quite a few young Danish people having meals. I suppose in most restaurants it was twenty or twenty-five kroner, so we were giving good value. I reckoned the vegetarian meals would take off.

On day two we served over a hundred, so it was working alright. After it was all cleaned up, I borrowed a bike and cycled down to Huset.

"How are you, Erik?"

"Not bad, Moon."

"Yeah. I got that restaurant running. It's going fairly well. No, I haven't even taken the perfume out of the bags, nor anything else. Yeah, I might put up a sign in the sleep-in in a corner of the bar, sell them from there rather than down in one of the squares."

"There's plenty of tourists around anyway, all nationalities. You can hardly move in the pedestrian street with them, so the sleep-ins will be kept busy."

"Yeah, it's good cos we're flat out, but I get plenty of help in the kitchen."

One of the new helpers was a Canadian who'd arrived recently, Laurie Bacon. She said she'd work in the kitchen a couple of days a week, so she'd get free accommodation. Claus and Jack were saying the Hare Krishna group in Copenhagen might want to rent our kitchens for maybe two or three mornings a week, so we'd have to have a meeting about that. It'd be no problem if they paid for half the electricity and gas. It would be interesting – our restaurant was vegetarian, but the staff ate meat and eggs. They would be much more strict. We'd see how the meeting went anyhow.

Clob was heading off to Morocco on Saturday. Most of the rest of the lads would be around. I took the Mondays off – there was no point in trying to work seven days in a kitchen. I had good part-time staff coming in, which gave me a few breaks as well. We decided to leave the kitchen closed on a Monday, mainly for proper cleaning. The place had to be scrubbed out at least once a week.

I'd have the van for the summer with Clob away, so I headed off to the market again. Weird-shaped peppers were no problem – I got a box of each: red, green and yellow. I got a sack of medium onions and large onions, and then we had eight bags of potatoes. I got tomatoes – very ripe ones would be okay – lettuce, cucumbers – bent ones would be fine – and some celery. We were going to make the big vegetable stew that day. That veg would do for the weekend. We were having a special session in the gardens on Sunday. Claus had given me the whole run of the kitchen and we were expecting a lot of people over that weekend. One of the small bakeries near us would do a deal on boxes of bread. We'd need at least three hundred eggs too. One day we were going to do a salad with a boiled egg, baked potato and a small roll – that'd be a good meal too, all for ten kroner.

Down in the kitchen, we had to get to work. I started it off with ten kilos of chopped onions, two full heads of garlic and a pint of olive oil into the big boiler. I let it get red hot, added half a packet of paprika, a quarter pack of black pepper, three large spoons of salt and stirred it well. After ten or fifteen minutes we put in the carrots. Four celery heads would be enough – you didn't want too much of the celery, just a little flavour. Next in went most of a box of peppers, chopped in big chunks. I took the pot of boiling water off the gas and poured it in slowly. You'd see a shine of red and there'd be a lovely smell coming out of it. Any of the very large potatoes were cut in half. The courgettes went in last. Laurie was making up the menus – one to go on the main door coming in, one outside on the notice board and one in the garden: "Lightly spiced vegetable stew with boiled potatoes and half a brown roll – ten kroner". It did taste good, not overseasoned with salt and pepper.

All the peelings and all waste went into the bin. They had to be taken away every morning. You could get the health inspectors around at any time and you'd be in shit street if everything wasn't done right. We were serving from four o'clock till eight o'clock in the evenings – Friday, Saturday and Sunday.

There was a queue already now, and it was a lot of the same

faces on the second day, along with a few of their friends. City Camp hadn't said how many dinners they wanted. We could only give them the vegetable stews and the bubble and squeak – they weren't going to get egg and salad delivered over there.

Soon enough, we were down to the last ten portions – that was eighty or ninety served, and it was just a quarter past seven. Anyone who wanted a quick meal at that point would just get a salad, boiled egg, brown roll and potato. I hadn't expected that many people! Claus was happy anyhow, said it was a great idea, making use of the kitchens. I was looking forward to locking it up. There were two lads in now to clean down the floors and wash out the boilers. We used all paper plates, some regular knives and forks were used, the rest were disposable. I'd rather have had it all disposable, to cut down on a lot of work and hot water. You'd have no breakages either then.

One thing I wanted to do was go down to Fælleskøkken – the restaurant in Christiania –and get a good drawing made of their boiler system. The heater unit they had was made of barrels and it was an amazing thing. All the old timber from the buildings got chopped up and put into it, burned in the bottom, went through an exhaust system into a higher part – it was like a heat chamber – and then the pipe came out at another angle off the back. It heated a big room that was the main mess hall of the old military barracks, so they probably used to feed a thousand soldiers in it. The room was probably thirty by twenty metres, with pillars.

Laurie wanted to go to Christiania anyway, so we were going to go over there on Monday. I'd told her all about it. On Sunday we had an easy day, so when we'd finished up I offered to show her around the city centre.

"This is the famous pedestrian street, Strøget. Up there is the town hall; Hans Christian Andersen is the statue there, and just up the road a bit is the Tivoli Gardens. If we take a right here, we'll end up at a famous American place called the Truck Stop. We can get something to eat there. The food's alright, it's a good sign outside – the bumper off a truck with flashing lights on it. That's actually how we found out about it first.

"A lot of Americans here would have skipped out of going to

Vietnam – conscientious objectors. Some have a hard enough time, some have convenience marriages. They'd all be decent lads, every one of them … couldn't see the sense, there is no sense in it – and it'll be a long war too."

We just took a long walk, got a beer or two and then we headed back. It was a nice city. I wouldn't have stayed anywhere else at the time.

Laurie came back to my room, one thing led to another and we decided she'd move in with me the next day.

Monday morning at ten, I had to meet the Hare Krishnas who'd be using the kitchen. It was only a small chat about how I wanted the kitchen left when they finished up and when they needed to be gone.

Myself and Laurie headed off to Christiania for the afternoon. You'd see rows of stalls up each side as you walked in: you could buy hashish, grass, whatever you wanted along there. There were plenty of jewellery and perfume stalls. The big building was Fælleskøkken – the big dining hall with a big kitchen in the back, and a load of guys running it. The food was cheap there – not as cheap as in our place but they all had to make a living there. They made rice dishes and pizzas; it seated about a hundred and fifty. Down around the corner was a place called Electric Ladyland, which was a club on the first floor. The river ran by the side, down to the sea to where the Burmeister and Wain shipyard was. I showed her the bicycle shop, with bicycles built out of bed ends, upside-down frames on some of them and you'd nearly need a ladder to get up on them. The proprietor was well known for riding around the city on one. We saw the candle shop, with a couple of people working in it and a huge rail full of candles, and there was the stove shop where they renovated the *kakkelovns*. Some of them were very fancy and quite tall, with a second exhaust system on the top. The middle section had two doors, like an oven, so you could bake bread and cook your stews in there. As far as I know, they used to export quite a few to Canada.

I explained to Laurie why I was called Moon. I got the name when I was about seventeen: I used to do stock car racing and it was around the time the Apollo space missions were regularly in the news. I called my stock car the Moonship, and my regular car had big orange moons painted on the doors. That's how I got the name and it just stuck.

I used to hang out in Brumelby quite a lot as well, with Butch and American Morten and Mike. One evening in May I headed over there, and we were all sitting around having a few beers outside. Suddenly, Butch comes flying out the door and says, "Hey, Moon, Dublin's been bombed!"

I went tearing into the house and couldn't believe what I saw on the black and white television – wrecks of cars and people … unbelievable! The lads said not to be worrying, but later that evening the news was back on and I found out what had happened. Bombs had gone off in Dublin and Monaghan and a good few people were killed. It was scary looking at the news, to see it getting so close to home. You'd wonder what was happening. There was a lot of trouble in Belfast at that time, but Dublin was another story. I got in touch with Clob later on and told him. He said he hadn't heard about it, but it was just one of those things when there's trouble in the country. Of course, there was trouble on the Continent too, with the Baader Meinhof gang in Germany. I had a few more beers anyway and everyone was cool, but when I got home quite late that evening I was still a little shaken.

Back to work the next day, talking to people, they said there seemed to be quite a lot of trouble going on in Ireland at that time, that it must be every single day there was a bomb going off in Belfast. But we just kept on working anyhow. I got a letter from my mother and she said it was quite a serious explosion. There was a young paperboy killed, a young pregnant woman and lots of other people, including some Italians. One of the Italian fellas had a chipper in Bray, and I actually knew his family a bit from being in the shop. But we have to get over these things and carry on.

It's a small world. I had been down in Huset a few weeks before with a few of the lads when I saw a mop of hair at the end of the bar, and I recognised a guy from Kilmacanogue, where I went to school, Julian Vignoles. I couldn't believe it!

"What has you here?"

"I came over a couple of weeks ago."

"I've been here on and off for the last couple of years, summertimes. How's Kilmacanogue?" I said to him.

"Ah, same as ever, nothing much happening."

I met him once or twice again after that.

Later on in the week, myself and Laurie took a trip to see the famous Little Mermaid and to have a look down around the shipyards. The big shipyard, Burmeister and Wain, was just across from the Mermaid; it was an interesting place. Everyone said it was a small little mermaid, but she's not that small! It's hard to tell as she's sitting down, but I suppose if she stood up on the end of her tail she'd be about five foot four! At that time of year there was always a crowd around it, so you had to wait to get a few photos. It had been a very good summer so far weather wise. Claus said that the usual amount of people were staying in the sleep-ins. You'd know by the restaurant – you could almost guess how many meals you'd have to make, so there was very little waste. If there was leftover veg that was no problem, we'd cook it up ourselves later. Sometimes I'd cook for Jack and Claus in evenings and we'd sit around and listen to a bit of music, have a few beers and a joint.

The old van was sounding a bit creaky; I'd have to give it a clean, clean the plugs and check it over some day. It was a great van and had kept us going for the last two years. Besides the regular vegetable market runs, there were often eight people in that van, going down to Amsterdam or Barcelona. We'd give them a ride and share the petrol. On any long trips we always took riders.

Down in Huset later on, there was a good crowd – Reinhardt and Morten, myself and Laurie, Birgitte. I needed a night out after all the work for the previous couple of days. I was saying to Laurie that I was definitely going to the concert in Fælledpark on the coming Sunday. I wanted to sell more perfume and get rid of the jewellery that I'd brought back from Pakistan. There would be a load of stalls there and two or three bands playing, though the only one I really knew was Burnin' Red Ivanhoe. There'd be a lot of interest in the stalls, and probably some sort of protest about something that was happening in the world as well. There were always protests at these things! But that was for Sunday, tonight was for drinking.

It would be a long time before most of the Americans could go home; Reinhart too – he couldn't go back to Germany. Clob and I were lucky there was no military service in Ireland, they still had it all over Europe. At least you could opt out in Denmark and do social work. I decided to head off early enough but Laurie said she'd stay on for a while. I didn't have to get up early but still, I wouldn't get to bed till about half two or three.

I wanted to get about a hundred bottles of perfume labelled and ready for Sunday. Laurie said she'd give me a hand with that. I'd get rid of more rings and stones as well. The sleep-in would be closing in a few weeks and I didn't think I'd keep the restaurant going any longer than that either.

I cycled into town the following morning and bought a box of labels and some markers. We wrote them up when I got back: Patchouli, Musk oil, Jasmine. They looked fine and I would have no trouble selling on Sunday.

I saw a good few trucks in Fælledpark, where the stage was being erected. There would be a lot of stalls, including a guy making jewellery out of horseshoe nails that I'd seen often on the pedestrian street. There was a fella selling Jews Harps who'd been around for a long time. I used to be able to play it a bit – had a small one and a large one. I expected there'd be a few guys selling leather there as well: saddles and belts and stuff. There was always someone selling pipes, chillums and other pipes and chebangs.

We got about eighty bottles filled on Friday evening, so we headed out for some food and a walk around. After we'd eaten, we walked down past Tivoli and sat on the pedestrian street for a while. There were lots of Canadians in town, some Americans and lots of Swedes there for the weekend – over from Malmo. It was quite strange sitting on the street watching everyone, hearing the different languages – you'd get the odd one you could fully understand. The buskers had gone silent, night-time was drawing in, the pedestrian street had slowed down now. We decided we'd go home – it was too expensive drinking out: five times the price of a supermarket. We would make an early night out of it. I needed a good hug and a cuddle – I was just a bit pissed off in general. I told Laurie I'd hit Ireland before the end of the year. It had been a long time now. I lived beside two small mountains, and I missed them.

Laurie said she'd like to go to Odense, when the restaurant finished up in two weeks' time. I said we'd leave on the Saturday evening after we finished, and then we'd have Sunday and Monday. I'd make sure there was gas in the van for cooking, enough fuel in the tank. We'd fill the water tank, get a bit of food in and off we'd go.

Everything went according to plan that Saturday. Laurie had her day off, so I was busy. There was a big crowd in, as usual. When I finished cooking, I got out of there. The kitchen was spotlessly clean. I was going over to Erik's house for the evening. I had all the stuff ready for the park on Sunday.

Erik had the most interesting hedge in his garden: they looked like evergreens, but they were marijuana plants. He kept them trimmed – clipped them every two or three weeks. "Hey, Moon," he greeted me, offering a pipe.

I smoked a pipe with him and put a few beers in the fridge. It was nice sitting out in the garden there – you'd think you were a hundred miles from Copenhagen, but you were only two or three. The old bikes were handy there, but you had to put the lights on at night-time. It was a good pipe, from his own clippings – very nice. I told him about my plans for a stall at the park the next day. I wanted to get a few bob together. The restaurant had been doing well, but I'd been having a good time too, so was spending a good bit. You'd make some money in the restaurant, but sometimes you'd spend a bit extra to make nice meals. I wasn't in it to make a lot of money, just enough to keep me going. Erik made me a lovely cup of coffee before I left on my bike and sent me off with a bag of clippings. I cycled home through the quiet city, in a warmish breeze – lovely!

It was a good Sunday for the park. We got packed up and ready to go; it was only ten minutes away on a bicycle. I got to the end of the stalls and found a nice spot, not too close to the stage or you wouldn't hear a thing when they were playing. Johan was there with his stall, selling big velvet curtains. We got in beside other jewellery stalls. There was a fella demonstrating woodwork as well, and the horseshoe nail man. It'd be a perfect spot. I put the bike against the tree, locked it and took the box off. I got the little table set up and it was an ideal place, as there were plenty of food wagons there as well.

We had everything priced at ten kroner, which was very cheap for pure perfume oils. The stones and rings were priced the same. There was a good crowd there and we were selling well throughout the afternoon, so by the time the bands were going on stage we had only five rings and a few bottles of perfume left.

Burnin' Red Ivanhoe were up next. The crowd were all moving towards the stage area. They were an amazing band: they always put on a good show – really got the crowd moving. They'd be on till five or half five, so I pulled a beer out of the bag. It was nice and cool. I was glad we'd brought a bit of food with us – you wouldn't get near the food wagons or the hot dog stand.

Next onto the stage was Povl Dissing. Everything went very quiet now for a while. He was one of the best there was in Denmark – sounded wonderful that day, anyhow. We had a great day selling and it looked like we'd have nothing left by day's end. That night, we'd head down to Huset for some food and beers. It had been a wonderful afternoon. My arms got sunburned – it was roasting hot and we didn't get that heat at home in Ireland. Just as well we were beside the trees, or it'd have been worse! As we were leaving it looked like a mini-Woodstock with the flowers and loads of debris around the place.

I dumped the bike when we got back, had a nice shower and a cup of coffee and rolled a joint to take down to Huset with me! We had made about £125, which was just lovely! I hadn't much left to sell now – just a bit of perfume. Jack was saying there had been about 120 in the restaurant over three hours, which was pretty good for that day. I'd say there would have been a lot more only for the park.

We had a good chat and few beers in Huset, talking about taking the van over to Odense for a few days. We could leave after the meals on the following Saturday. Jack would do Sunday for me again – he didn't mind stepping in now and again. We'd be back on Monday evening. It would be a bit of craic going there. The van still had the cooker and the fold-down beds – it was still a camper, so it'd be alright. Laurie would be going back to Canada in three weeks, and I only had another four or five weeks in the restaurant. I liked doing it, but it would be closed in the wintertime so I was planning to move out of Copenhagen.

It was an hour and a half drive across Sjælland on Saturday evening, then the ferry to the island of Funen. In Odense we parked up, went for a hot dog and sat in the square for a while. They made a beer there called Train beer – there was a train on the label. There was one in Jutland called Top: the Danish fellas had a joke about it, that they're all farmers – *Bornekale*, like culchies – over there, and they called it Top beer so they'd know which end to open. It's a bit like any country, I suppose, with jokes about country people. There were a good few bars around. The beer was alright, but there was a hell of a difference from Carlsberg or Tuborg. There was a dark one we tried. We'd be down later on to try another one or two. We were about ten minutes' walk from where the van was parked. I'd been told that they built super tankers in the shipyard in Odense, so I would go down and have a look before we headed back to Copenhagen. I had worked on a ship for a while, going from Belfast to Scotland, moving timber, but I wouldn't be mad about staying at sea – a day or two was long enough.

It was nice to get out of the city for a few days. We took a walk along the shore then went back to the van to make dinner. Looking through the tapes for some music, some of the cassettes had been there for ages: an old Van Morrison tape; another Irish one – Rory Gallagher; Crosby, Stills, Nash and Young; Dylan … some of them were a bit wrecked. After we'd eaten, I stepped out to get some milk for the coffee from a little grocery on the corner, and had a look around. When I got back I banged on the door, nearly causing Laurie to jump out of her skin because it was so quiet there. I'd spotted a club down the road that might be open that night. We decided to go down around ten or ten thirty. There was a big student residence near there, so there were lots of students around.

When we got down there, there were a good few hanging round outside the club so we reckoned it should be okay. It was quite a big club and the music was good, so we'd have a dance anyhow. I asked the DJ to play the Rolling Stones and he put on "Satisfaction". I got two Carlsbergs, but it was expensive for beer in there! That's why there weren't many at the bar. One beer each would have to do, then back to the van to our own bar. We'd have a joint as well. They were all smokin' down the road! I'd say half the population of Denmark smoked joints or chillums. It wasn't a big deal over there.

It was great having the whole weekend off. Whooo – it was a pretty strong joint, only smoked half of it. The Train beer tasted a bit weird, more ale than lager.

Clob was supposed to be back the next Tuesday, so we'd head back Monday evening. Laurie still had another nine days in Copenhagen. Summer wouldn't be long going, though – it was late summer now.

Sunday morning, I made coffee about ten thirty and I had a makeshift toaster – a bit of mesh put on the gas ring. Loads of people used them in the flats in Copenhagen, so, coffee and toast for breakfast.

Clob would want the van when we got back for at least a week. I would just use it early Tuesday morning and then he could have it. If I needed it I'd get it on Friday.

We locked up the van and headed down to the beach. It was warm and it was a nice sandy beach. The tide was out. There was an ice cream stall, so we got a couple and walked on. It was about a mile down to the shipyard. There were nice houses around there, and it was clean too.

Laurie was going back to college when she went back. I told her I was going to stay on in Copenhagen for a while. I had no particular plans but Clob had been going on about a tea room, and maybe he'd build it this time. He had a small site over in Christiania, near the river. He'd probably get it together – he took his time about things but generally did them right. We reached the shipyard but, being Sunday, it wasn't open. It was a good bit bigger than the one in Copenhagen. We found a little cafe on the corner, got a coffee and sat down for an hour.

I said I might hit Ireland around Christmas or a week or so before it. Now and again I missed the brothers and sisters and my mother and father. I probably wrote once or twice a year. I'd given a few people the address and said to call in, and was curious to find out if they had.

Back in the van, after dinner, I tried to cheer Laurie up. She was thinking of the next week, I suppose. I told her not to worry about it and make the best of the time we had. We decided to lock up and head off out for the night. We'd had a good summer together, and she'd learned to ride a bicycle! I'd met lots of people who couldn't ride bicycles. I'd met people who said they could, but they actually couldn't. It depended on what part of a town or a big city you were from, whether you could ride a bicycle. Down the country it was nearly a necessity when you're a young lad. Most places in the country in Ireland only had public transport about once a week! Even on the outskirts of towns, there was only one bus in the morning and one in the evening.

We walked up further and found a bar with a few people in it and music being played. It wasn't bad – there was a Danish band playing on the radio. We bumped into Paul from the sleep-in, and Birgitte, who were over for the weekend as well, so we sat down with them. He was from Odense originally and they were both at college. He used to be a fisherman but said with rough seas and no money in it, he wanted to qualify for something better. I was telling him that when Clob and I first came to Denmark, we could only stay for three months. It was the same in Germany and elsewhere, but now that Ireland was in the EEC it would give us more freedom in Europe. We could live in Denmark and work there; he could do the same in Ireland or England.

Back in Copenhagen, I was looking forward to meeting Clob again; I hadn't seen him for a few months. I put the van round the back of the sleep-in and Jack said that Clob had been in earlier – that he'd come back yesterday and said he'd be around that evening.

It was great to catch up with Clob and he was full of plans for building the tea house. He hoped to have it open in a few weeks. I agreed to meet him the next day around lunchtime. I'd have done my trip to the market and unloaded my supplies by then. I'd only need it twice a week for the following few weeks. I assured him there'd be a few lads from the sleep-in who could give him a hand.

"The whole front and one side will be glass," he explained. "The back wall will be timber for shelving, cookers, and storage for glasses and cups."

A couple of weeks later I had a few things to organise. Laurie's leaving party was set for the Saturday – I wanted to go down and talk to the chef in Huset about that. She had a few days left before she went back to Toronto.

First, I was going over to Christiania for an hour or two. Clob's place was starting to look well.

"Hey, Moon, it's all coming together! I have a water main there, three sinks should do me okay. I have the bottled gas too. The communal toilets are just twenty yards away – they're okay. I've a couple of long stools and tables – there's a big enough seating area inside anyway and a half dozen bar stools along the edge."

"There's two boxes of cups over in my place. I'll bring them over to you. You won't have room to do food here, just the teas. People can buy a sandwich and sit down and eat it here with the tea. The stove's good inside – well fitted; the fire drum outside's handy as well."

You wouldn't know what the winter was going to be like there: it could be okay, or there could be heavy snow.

"You want to put a layer of tar and asphalt on the roof, Clob – you'll be fucked otherwise! Sabine's friend – she's Irish-English – she's opening a small restaurant across the way. They asked could I give them a hand but sure I told them they need a canopy. They'll have to organise one: they want to cook and it's a low enough ceiling. Don't forget there's a party on in Huset on Saturday – Laurie's leaving on Tuesday. I'm going to get the lads to do a big Moroccan lamb dish. It won't be anything like the chicken we had out there, Clob. I didn't know what to do that night, washed and cooked in the same water!"

"That's a long time ago," he laughed.

"I'm okay without the van, anyway," I said. "I'll use the other one. The bike is good enough for getting around on."

"I should be open Friday or Saturday morning. The weekend should be a good time to open."

"We'll be busy during the day, but if I finish up early enough on

Saturday evening, I'll come over. The party's at about half eight, nine o'clock. Be a busy weekend! Nah, I'm not havin' a pipe now. I'll see you later on."

I wanted to call over and see your woman who was opening the restaurant and that young fella that she was with about the canopy. I didn't know which of them had less of a clue! The little place they had was decorated fairly well, but I wasn't sure about their menu. I told them to get a bottle of whiskey and serve Irish coffee – it's easily made.

I called over and they had the canopies up and the fan looked alright. If they were going to be doing a lot of cooking, there'd be a lot of steam as it was a low ceiling. They just needed a decent preparation table and a dishwashing sink. They were mainly going to make stews – chicken curries and stuff like that. They were in a good spot there, only three hundred yards from the main gate.

Back in the flat I just made a small joint and put on a bit of Pink Floyd. We'd go to Christiania a round nine.

"Wasn't a bad day. I'll miss you too. Let's enjoy the last few days anyway. You might as well have a toke out of that – it's only a small joint, not much in it."

We got the bus down to Huset and had a few beers and a chat down there. I talked to the chef about the food … like a big lamb stew, spicy and tasty, nice crispy white bread, roast potatoes, no skins, couple of bowls of couscous, bowls of salad. It would all be laid on, cheap enough. We were going to have a kitty, and if anyone wanted to throw money in at the end of the night they could. If everyone threw in ten kroner we'd be laughing – I might have to add fifty. I didn't mind that. I wanted to give her a few bob to get herself something in London, on the way home.

Laurie had worked hard all summer. It was a wonderful place to be in, the sort of restaurant that serves an international crowd every day – Europeans, Americans, Canadians, Australians … everybody came in and out of there, trying foods they'd never had before. Fried bread freaked everybody out! But we all learned things: I hadn't eaten crisps for about two years, I went around with a pocket full of crackling, crispy pig skin – delicious! You'd get it in the butcher's on the corner. You'd normally drink four bottles of beer in the afternoon, then a few more in the evenings. Danes like their beer, man! Everywhere you went, beer. They made a kind of dark Carlsberg – it wouldn't be like Guinness, more of a dark ale.

For the party we had two big tables pushed together, big bowls of salad, bread, nice spicy lamb stew, crispy fried potatoes and lots of beer …

"Cheers to Laurie and thank her for helping us through the summer! Enjoy yourselves tonight. Good music … beer … great session. There's a three-foot almond cake coming out later, specially made, almond and custard … lovely!"

Somewhere around this time Butch's girlfriend, Merete, moved in to Brumleby to live with him, so she offered me her flat on Fiskegade to take up when I wanted. She would still be registered there, but I could live there, paying the rent and utilities. I didn't move in straight away, but it would be useful to have later on.

20

A COUPLE OF WEEKS LATER I HAD a surprise visitor.

"Well, Päivi, I'm amazed to see you tonight. Glad you called and you're staying. I'm going to have a beer anyway, do you want one?"

"Sure, thanks, Moon. I said I'd call in and sort your broken heart out!"

"What's that you say? Ha ha! Not that broken hearted, no no."

"Oh, really?"

"Yes! I'm glad you're going to stay. Yeah, I like you a lot, must be a year and a half ago when I met you first with Sabine. How is she by the way? You're all living in Espergærde still, yeah? How're the kids – Zoe and Mia?"

"They're all fine."

"Wonderful, I'd like to see them again."

"You should come up and see us. You know you're welcome."

"I'll go to bed in a minute, I'm still just thinking … Okay, I'll forget about thinking. It's a lovely night. … Yeah, I've been wanting to see you for a long time now, but I'm glad you made the first move with me. Cuddle up and go asleep, you're not leaving early in the morning?"

"No, no."

"Okay, goodnight."

At nine in the morning she had to get back to Espergærde. I promised I'd call up in a day or two. That had been a surprise and a half! I was back to work in the kitchen now and I'd see her on Tuesday or Wednesday.

The menu signs were okay – not as good as they used to be, but they'd do. I didn't want to keep it going as the numbers were down. There weren't that many Americans around now – still a good few French, Dutch, German and English. I had decided to close at the same time as the sleep-in. I had made a right few bob and still had money from the perfumes as well.

There was a girl from Belgium helping in the kitchen now. She was only there for four or five days, but she spoke a good bit of English. The other lad was English. The students were all heading back shortly. In another week or two there'd only be Danes living there again.

I was chatting with Jack and Claus and they were slagging me about Päivi. They knew I'd had a thing about her before. I was telling them I was going up to Espergærde on Tuesday or Wednesday. I was going to spend Monday cleaning up the flat. I was also cutting back on drink. It wasn't great, going to bed completely fucked and waking up bolloxed – I didn't want it to become a habit. You get into a mess, and there had to be more to life than that. An odd smoke and an odd beer was good – a bit of craic.

I told Jack I was thinking of pulling out of the restaurant altogether in about a week's time – sure the whole place would be closing in a week or so. I headed for Christiania later, to see how Clob was getting on with the tea house. I told him I was packing in the restaurant at the weekend – time for something new.

I'd go up in the morning to the green market with the van – it'd be my second last run up there. There was a bit of rain and it wasn't as warm as it had been. The summertime was the best buzz of all time in the city; it'd be quiet in the winter. I was going to move up to Espergærde for a while, see what happened. It depended how things worked out with myself and Päivi. I told Clob I might see him later in Huset, or I'd see him in the morning. The Copenhagen summer was winding down – the following Sunday would be the last concert in the park. If I was around and doing nothing else, I might go.

In Huset with Erik, he was asking if I was staying around or moving on.

"No, I don't know where I'll be in the winter – haven't a clue! I

219

might hit Ireland, haven't been there for a while. I send a few cards home now and again alright."

Here came the lads, Mike and Morten. They could get their own beer. You'd need a bank loan to buy a round in Copenhagen. That's why the off licences are packed out! Ireland's just full of pubs – everyone goes out to socialise. In Denmark, you visit friends and bring your own beer.

After breakfast the next morning, I had to put petrol in the van if I was going to use it that evening. It was about half an hour's drive up the coastline to Espergærde. I hadn't lived really close to the sea that much.

Päivi and Sabine and their little girls Mia and Zoe were there. She showed me to my room and said she'd known I was after her for a long time. They didn't wear clothes in the house … I didn't mind! I could move in on the weekend, so that was settled. I had met them a few years before, protesting in Copenhagen about houses being torn down. Sabine had worked in Greencamp.

Here we were, walking on the beach, holding hands, laughing and joking. It was amazing up there, but renting or buying was expensive. They'd a nice kitchen and they'd made dinner. The sun had gone down, so we headed back as it was getting dark. The girls had gone to bed. I called goodnight to them and opened the bottle of wine that I had brought.

I was enjoying my few days there and was glad to be moving up at the weekend. I had never been in a house where you don't wear clothes if you didn't want to before. It was a bit strange at first, but you get used to everything! I suppose it was handy if you were going to the beach, just put a towel on and off you go!

I drove back to Copenhagen on Thursday as everybody agreed the best time to close the restaurant was Friday night. The sleep-in was closing too, so there'd be nobody around. I left the van back with Clob. I would be travelling by bicycle.

We were going to finish up with bubble and squeak on the Friday. After we closed we'd put on a few good steaks for the people working there and a few extra beers. One of the lads was coming over to collect the stuff from my room to go into storage until I came back.

It was time for a change, to do a bit of cycling and walking. Saturday morning the bike was packed and off I went, headed for Espergærde. Traffic was light, there was no wind and the sea looked very calm. I'd be there in about an hour.

"Hi Päivi … Mia … Sabine. Good to see you, Zoe. No panic, I'll get a coffee in a minute after I take the bag and box off the bike."

"You don't have much."

"I don't need much. Lighter the better. Most important is the little waistcoat with all the stuff in the pockets. Should've got a camera though – the other one broke. Hi, Päivi, give me a little hug … no messing! I'll cook the dinner this evening."

There was an amazing view there … deep blue sea, worth waiting for it. Sabine babysat, while Päivi and I went out for a while. Sabine could go to Copenhagen tomorrow, no problem.

"Good to be here. The two of us are mad anyhow, so it doesn't matter!"

We went for a few drinks, had a bit of a chat. "I've known you for about two years, always had a crush on you … anyhow, we're together now. Cheers!"

I was half lost for words. We just held hands and walked home slowly.

"Good morning, Päivi. Think I'll make some coffee, have some breakfast and go for a walk on the beach … don't start tickling again please, it freaks me out! Yes, we'll make love before we get up. Yes, I like your body. Sometimes words miss what I should be saying."

Mia and Zoe were up already, running around. "Hi, Sabine. Coffee? I'll take the kids on to the beach for a while, if you want. I don't mind. Of course I'll watch them! Come on, girls, put your hats on – it's a sunny day. We'll only be an hour or so, okay. See you when I get back."

There were little sailing boats out there and we watched them for a while – big cargo ships out there too. It felt good to be out of Copenhagen now, to spend a few weeks relaxing. We said hello to the people on the beach. There'd be a lot of people there in the afternoon.

"Mia, don't go too far in the water!"

221

You'd need eyes in the back of your head with these two! They were a little over two and a half, flying around.

"I'll give you a hand with that, Zoe. You fill the bucket, bang it down, turn it upside down and you have a castle! You want one as well? There you go – a castle each for the girls. We're going back in half an hour … sure we can come over any time, it's only five minutes from the house."

"Moon! Moon!"

"What is it, Zoe? Oh, the castle broke? We can fix the castle, but you can't sit on it! Now we have two each. When we come back, we'll bring a flag."

"Yeah, they were very good. We've to go back today or tomorrow and build more castles, and we need little flags."

It was nice and quiet there. If you went that far out of Dublin city, you'd be in the mountains somewhere. That's one thing they don't have there – hills and mountains. There were pine trees around alright.

Moon with Zoe and Mia.

"We might go into Copenhagen on Saturday night then, take you out for the evening, get a night bus back," I said to Päivi.

We sat out on the lawn for a while, had a cool beer. "They say that that sea was frozen in 1947 right to Sweden and back! Must've been like a mini ice age."

Päivi said, "Mother used to tell me it was like giant ice cubes in the sea – must've been hard to do anything."

"Still, tough enough in the winter in Denmark – cold, snow. Don't mind once you get summers like this. I could squeeze you forever. I haven't smoked a joint for a week – don't miss it either. Yes, Päivi, you're a good influence. You wear me out!"

Well, it was morning again. I was feeling a bit wrecked – must've been being out with the kids so much the previous day. I wasn't going to do much anyhow, just ramble around – take the bike and bring a packed lunch. I just wanted to go off and think for a while. There was a lot going on in my head over what to do next. The whole area was flat. I was thinking of riding the bike back to Ireland: it was an old single-speed high nelly, but it was fairly reliable.

I could see forestry huts. Apart from that, it was just miles of trees: ash and pine – that was it. There wasn't much in the woods, a few squirrels and things. There were seating areas with picnic tables, but I wouldn't be mad about walking around there too long. The valleys and the hills were missing. I headed back around four, pulled into a coffee shop on the way and sat down to think things over. It had been a great summer – a great year. It would take four or five days to cycle home to Ireland, but I didn't have much to bring on the bike. I would tell Päivi that evening that I'd be moving on in a few weeks. She wouldn't mind.

Back down to Espergærde. "Hello, girls, how are you? Hi, Sabine. I just spent a few hours in the woods, no hills and valleys, it's alright. Yous can cook dinner yourselves, surprise me!"

The kids were freaking out. I was trying to explain that I wasn't leaving yet – not for a couple of weeks. I didn't want the evenings to get any shorter. It was late enough in the year as it was, getting cool in the evenings.

Getting nearer the end of my time there, Päivi and I went out for a few drinks one evening. "Now you know and I know, we're having a great time. We said we wouldn't make things complicated and we're not. Let's just enjoy one another while we can, not make a mess of it. You knew I was going back to Ireland. You said yourself, you don't want to be tied down. Sure, we've plenty of time together. Cheers. Enjoy the evening out now. Not too many mad Finns here – only yourself, Päivi. Don't start messing! I'll throw you into a field on the way home if you're not careful. I would! Not too many in the bar tonight … give up the messing, for fuck's sake! Will you wait till we're going home, yeah, yeah, yeah …"

"Did you know the Troggs? I used to be very fond of that band. That's why I said I'd throw you into a field of grass, there was a song, 'A Night in the Long Grass'."

"Ah, I know that one!" she squealed.

"You heard of it? Well, I'm going to throw you in the long grass tonight for messing. Not that chilly – you won't be long warming up."

"You're half mad, Moon! You'll have to carry me."

"Better off to be half mad – so are you! And I won't be able to carry you. You're lucky it's only twenty minutes' walk. Probably take us an hour. There you are now, here's a field. Lie down there now!"

"Okay. I'm going to go to sleep here!"

"No, we can't stay here, its half one in the morning! Yes, it was fantastic. I can hardly walk never mind carry you. I'll try. Might carry you ten paces, that'd be it."

Sabine had been talking about going into Copenhagen for a few days. I said I didn't mind being with the kids – they were great fun.

"Oh yes, Päivi, you are too! I won't forget tonight, you won't either. Special."

Well, we were home now. I wanted a coffee. Päivi fell into bed.

I slept like a log that night – didn't know what day it was when I woke up. I hadn't drunk so much in a long time.

"How are you, Päivi? How's the head?"

"Oh, don't talk to me! I'm not used to drinking so much. It was a mad night anyway."

When Sabine came back, I said, "I'm going into Copenhagen for the night to see Clob, cos I'll be leaving in four or five days.

Yeah, well, the bike's just about together anyway. I won't take much with me – a few clothes, my sleeping bag, the little toolbox – and away I go. I'll leave on Friday, Saturday, Sunday – doesn't really matter. Take a few days to get across Denmark. No, I don't want any breakfast thanks. Coffee is enough, then a shower. Fuck! Wonderful evening!"

I got the bus into Copenhagen, walked across by Huset then got another bus, three or four stops to Christiania. I called around to the tea house to see Clob and tell him I was heading back to the Wicklow hills for a while, taking a mad trip on a bicycle.

"I'll head across to Esbjerg and get the ferry to Newcastle, then head to Liverpool. Yeah, I'll have a cup of chai. Got wrecked last night on a drinking session! If I see Pat, I'll tell him you'll probably be home for Christmas. If you see Johan, tell him I'm heading off and I'll see him. Saw Erik a while ago and told him I was going."

"How are Sabine and Päivi and the girls?" asked Clob.

"Sabine's in great form, Päivi's as mad as ever and the little ones are great."

"Cool. Listen, will you call out to see the ma when you're home – let her know I'm fine?"

"Okay, Clob. Take care of yourself. Yeah, of course I'll call out to your ma's house. I'll get some form of transport when I get home. Yeah, I will mind the road. I heard that too – it's not nice riding a bike in England. See you in a couple of months."

I had a couple of bottles of Carlsberg with my dinner, it's true what they say – it is a good cure! I wandered over to Huset around nine o'clock, as I reckoned some of the lads would be there by then. I had a beer with Jack, told him I was heading off in a few days, but I'd be back in the new year.

When I got back to Espergærde, Päivi asked if I would mind the girls the next day as she and Sabine were going into the city.

"Now, girls, Päivi and Sabine are going away and we're going to be left here. So, we'll tidy up the house and I'll pack some of my stuff in the bag and we'll take a trip to the beach. I'm not going away forever. No, I'll be back, no, no. You get your sand buckets and spades, and we'll head to the beach in about an hour."

On the beach we were building sandcastles and a wall for the

225

castles. "Not too close to the sea or it will get washed away …
very good, Mia." There were quite a few people around. We spent
about an hour there, then packed the bag. Zoe was digging away
there, all the castles looked good. Sabine and Päivi would be back
at five or six o'clock. They'd just gone to Copenhagen to do some
shopping. I was having a beer, orange for the girls and cheese
sandwiches. We said hello to a big dog. It was getting a bit breezy,
so we headed back, with our buckets and spades and the bag. We
left the sandcastles where they were; someone else would play with
them.

I packed my clothes in the bag, tools, puncture outfit and my
tape machine. It was sad getting ready to leave, but … moving on.
I put on a big tray of potatoes for roasting, a big tray of *frikadeller*
and a nice salad, ready for dinner when Päivi and Sabine got back.

"I'll miss you and you'll miss me – we'll miss one another for a
while. Yes, I did have a wonderful time here, I wouldn't change it
… I'll miss your big boobies and your smile!"

Friday morning, the kids were up, fresh coffee made and I'd be
off soon. It wasn't bad out, not as sunny as it had been, it would do
well enough. The evenings had gone a good bit shorter too.

"That's right, Mia, I'm going today. Ah, I'll see yous again. That's
tied on safely now. Well Päivi, I'm going in about two minutes.
Thanks for having me – I enjoyed myself here. Yes, I will mind
myself. I'll return. Take care of the girls. Bye, Mia, Zoe." A big hug
from Sabine. "Okay, Päivi, that's true, I did. I loved you too, to a
certain extent. Doesn't last forever. Bye, Päivi. Yeah, I have your
photo, you have mine."

21

I WAS PEDALLING DOWN THE ROAD NOW. The bike was psychedelic – pink with purple spots – quite cool! It had a flashy looking saddle too! I didn't want to go on the big roads for a while. I went through a few small towns on the way. It was fairly flat. In a couple of hours I'd be out of Sjælland, on to the ferry – roll on, roll off. You'd always meet people on bicycles up there – a lot of pedal power in Denmark. I'd been riding now for a couple of hours. I pulled up at the next bench to take a break and have a drink of apple juice. It tasted good.

At last, I got on the boat to Odense. At the other side I followed the few buses and cars, trucks and a few more bicycles. It was just about getting dark and I was starving. I stopped to ask a young couple what time the club on the corner opened, hoping it served food. "In about half an hour … we only live down the road from here. Don't do anything yet, we can find a room for you."

"Cool! I was going to stay at the youth hostel. I'm going to get the ferry to Newcastle."

The club opened as we were chatting, so we went in for a beer. They were students. I explained that I'd been travelling, and I'd been in Denmark on and off for a year or two, that I had just come from Espergærde, that I wasn't a student, but a qualified sheet metal worker and welder.

I stayed in their place that night. In the morning there was a cup of coffee for the Irish boy.

"Thanks – and thanks for the bed … thank you and farewell."

I knew if I left early enough, I should make the ferry. A few hours in the saddle and at last Esbjerg came into view. The ferry didn't leave until eight, so I had plenty of time. The temperature wasn't bad – sixteen or seventeen degrees – and there was a light breeze off the sea. On to the ferry and I was on the way to England.

Moon leaving Espergærde.

I had a grand dinner, a nice pint and another one, then I went looking for a place to lie down. It would be a good long haul. I had a pain in my back and my legs: I wasn't used to cycling that far. I'd probably die on a hill tomorrow. The North Sea was great fishing waters, full of fishing boats … but it can be rough. It would be dark for most of the sailing anyhow. This time of year, there was hardly anyone on the boat.

I slept alright. Once I was back on land, I had to remember to cycle on the left-hand side of the road. There were signs everywhere – keep to the left. The last time I had been on the left side of the road was in Pakistan, which was a maniac country for driving. I didn't think I'd last two days on the bike in England, though. It must have rained the day before – the roads were wet and there wasn't much sun around either, but I should be in Liverpool by the following evening.

I hadn't got much of a clue as to where I was going. I knew I had to head straight across the middle. I had never paid much attention to what was in between – I hoped a big enough town, so I could find a B and B. I needed a place to sleep ... this would kill anyone. I would make me mind up in the morning whether I'd get a train to Liverpool. It would be insane to stay out there, getting blown off the road.

Struggling through the dark, I saw lots of lights ahead – The ... something ... Inn. Looked half civilised and, most importantly, it looked like I'd get a meal and a bed. Yes! They did food – and rooms. I was finished after that ten hours of hardship. The shower was across the hallway. I'd have a shower and be back down for dinner. It was three pounds for the room, breakfast was extra. Not bad, and not a bad pint of ale either. It was a good bed too ... probably any bed would have been good! I put on a pair of old corduroy trousers, clean underpants and a T-shirt. The jacket was okay. I had my money in a wallet around my neck, key in my pocket. It was funny how, even still, I'd got in the habit of locking up and carrying anything I had with me. Thank God I had only been robbed once and that was in London – a toilet in Piccadilly Circus in 1971. It scared the shit out of me – knife point, what are you going to do? They didn't take everything – not that I had much, back then – I always kept my money in my sock. One step ahead of the posse, always.

By morning it was decided. I would definitely not be riding the bike to Liverpool from there. I was going to find the nearest station when I'd had my breakfast. Leeds wasn't that far from where I was – I think about fifteen miles. There was a railway there, anyhow, so I'd get a train. I packed up the bits and pieces I'd taken out in the room and paid for the night. I got the first big breakfast I'd had in a long time. I didn't eat half of it: sausages, eggs, rashers, beans, toast and a pot of tea. The coffee didn't look great – it was probably instant.

The boat wouldn't leave Liverpool till all hours, anyhow. I think it used to get into Dublin at half six, or seven in the morning, so it'd be an all-night sailing. It was a nightmare on a bike getting to Leeds: it was raining and I had to keep in really tight, with too many vans and trucks, passing too close. It wasn't a bit bicycle friendly. Thankfully, it took less than an hour to get to Leeds. It was a big station. Yes, there was a train at ten o'clock to Manchester and Liverpool, and I could put my bike on as well, although I had to pay extra for it. I'd be on the boat that night. The cattle boat, they called it, shipping out cattle from Dublin to Liverpool. It smelled like a giant cowshed. Liverpool was a massive shipping port. I got off the train, got my bag and the bike and decided I'd get a pint somewhere. I locked the bike to the pole outside, unclipped the box and my bag, and sat in the pub for an hour or two. I hadn't a clue what time they would be loading at. It would depend on what time the boat coming from Ireland docked.

When I got down to the boat, there were a few cars outside and a few motorbikes; mine was the only bicycle so far. The boat was in, but it would be an hour and a half before you could get on. I was just thinking, I hadn't been home for a long time. My father had a strange thing about people who lie on in the morning – after a week he wouldn't believe you were ever going to get up early again. Still, it would be nice to be home. I'd get on to this boat now shortly and find a place to lie down, sleep most of the way over. I got a one-way ticket and they didn't charge anything for the bicycle. I pushed it down to the car deck and tied it up.

At last, leaving Liverpool! The next morning I'd be in Ireland. I found a long seat to lie down. There weren't many on the boat. I rolled out the sleeping bag and hopped into it. Up and down, up and down and the pounding of the engines until I got to sleep.

Early in the morning I was awake but still quite wrecked. I sat up for the next while and I could almost see Ireland from there. It wouldn't be long till we'd be there. I could see lights all over: that was Dublin. We'd be heading up the Liffey in less than an hour. They were serving breakfast, so I had scrambled egg and toast and a cup of tea.

It didn't look like a bad morning. They were starting to call out people with cars and trucks to please make it down to the deck. That meant I had to go down. We would be disembarking in about twenty minutes.

Leaving the boat, I got stuck behind a couple of cars. A few lads were shouting, "Get up on yer bike!" I was definitely back in Dublin! I had to remember to keep to the left again, just like England. I'd soon get used to it – keeping well in as well. There were no bicycle lanes here at that time. Ah well, I had ridden bicycles from Dublin to Bray a few times. I was thinking there'd probably be no one in the house when I got there: my sisters would be in school, brothers would be working, the father would be working, the mother would be shopping. It was a hobby the mother had – shopping in the morning! I was heading through Loughlinstown now, only five or six miles to go. Not much traffic compared to the English roads. I didn't really know what to expect. There were neighbours there beside my mother's called Rooney. If my mother wasn't there, I'd be called in there right away, and so I was.

It's a private little park, very friendly people, but I never liked it. I'd rather live on the small Sugarloaf area, where I spent my first years. I had only been home a couple of times since 1971 – a few weeks here and there. When I got to the mother's house there was no key in the door.

"Hello, Mrs Rooney! How are you?"

"God, Tony, you're back!"

"For a while anyhow. I expect the ma will be back in a while."

"Come on in and have a cup of tea. Where have you been?"

"Cheers, thanks very much. I've been living most of the time in Denmark, travelled out east quite a lot. I'll be home for a while anyhow. I rode a bike back for a bit of fun – something different. It started off as a joke then I took it up. Any word from David?"

"We get the odd letter. He's still in England."

"Ah there's the mother, coming round the corner now. Hello, Ma, how are you?"

"God, Tony, you're back!"

"Keeping well, how's everybody?

"Ah, sure, we're all grand!"

"Great! I'll give you a hand with the shopping. Thanks very much, Mrs Rooney."

"Why didn't you tell me you were coming?" the ma demanded.

"Sure, I'd no way of telling you. I just arrived. Don't worry about it, it's alright. I was just talking to Mrs Rooney for a while."

"Good," she said. "I got a few messages off people that called in."

"That's good, yeah."

"That Canadian fella, Jack, he stayed with us for a week – nice fella. Is your man Clob back too?"

"No, Clob isn't with me, he's still living in Denmark. How's all the brothers and how's the father?"

"All great. The girls are at school, your brothers and your father are working." Then nothing had changed that much. "More tea?"

"Okay, yeah, and I'll have some cheese and tomatoes. Where was I? Ah, I was in a lot of places."

"Jack said you were in Afghanistan and Kabul."

"That's true, yeah, and Pakistan. That's a while back now. I've been selling jewellery and perfume, making a few bob. Had a restaurant in Denmark for a while."

"Your brothers are working for themselves down in Bray."

"I heard that, alright. Good idea if they can make it."

The girls wouldn't be home for another couple of hours. Time didn't mean anything anymore. I didn't even have a clue what day it was. I took a walk down to Bray. I wanted to call in to the workshop, if my brothers were there. Nothing had changed in Bray – Frank Duff's, Lenihan's, the Ardmore Bar, Tormey's, Scullion's, O'Regan's, Myrtle's Boutique. That was the top of the town and there was the Town Hall. One taxi service as well, Pratt's taxis.

I passed the Central garage, then across the road and down the lane to where the family business, Flood Engineering, was. I greeted my brothers, "Hey Gregg … Austin. Where's Billy?"

"He's out at the moment. We're all working away, doing a bit."

"Good, good. I just came in from Denmark, rode in on a bicycle – came through Newcastle then Liverpool to Dublin. Yeah, I had a great time … out east for a good while."

"We were out with that fella, Jack, from Canada – said he met you in Kabul."

"Yeah, he gave me twenty dollars. He said he was coming to Ireland, so I told him to call in to Ma's."

"Nice fella, yeah."

"Ah sure, we'll have a drink this evening. I'll meet yous all back at Avondale! See yous later, right."

I walked back to the mother's house. I'd have dinner there that evening and have a good chat. I hadn't seen my sisters yet, nor the younger brother. I thought I might stay around for a few weeks anyhow. In the morning I'd go and see an old friend of mine, Kevin Meade – he'd give me a motorbike for a few weeks. I wanted to get back up into the Wicklow hills. It was strange round there too, there seemed to be a lot of building going on – quite a lot of haystacks had turned into housestacks. We were very close to Ardmore Studios, a very famous film studios. I remember they were making great films there when I was a young boy, like *The Viking Queen*, *The Blue Max* and *The Spy Who Came in From the Cold* – to name a few. They are still making films, of course.

My youngest brother was there when I got in. "Ah, Godfrey, how are you … yeah, good travels, rode the bike back – bit of craic on it. The east was wonderful, I was amazed with Afghanistan, genuinely felt like going back a thousand years or more. And Pakistan … a bit of English there alright. I didn't bring back much – perfume and jewellery, I sold nearly all of it. I still have me old jacket and helmet and goggles. I'm going to get a bike off Kevin Meade, do a bit of touring around. Go and see a few friends out in Kilmac." I only realised how small those houses were, when I saw all of us back in one room together, having our dinner. Things had to change. "God, Elaine, you're getting big … Colette, hah, very good." I'd stay there for a few days, then I might find another place to stay. I'd go and see Pat Kehoe, Clob's brother, see what he was up to. He had the butcher's shop in Bray.

We talked about the news, that things were still bad up in the North. "You must see it every day on the TV, do you? Fuckin' hell, it's crazy. I've seen bits of it in Denmark, seems to be non-stop, rows of houses burning. There were quite a few people who thought it was all over Ireland – I met quite a few people who thought the whole of Ireland was under English rule."

I was in the Ardmore Bar relaxing over a pint of Smithwicks. The usual group of auld fellas was over in corner there – they must've been screwed to those chairs, sat there every night! They were a bus conductor, postman and railwayman. They all looked similar with the uniforms – strange when you think about it, blue, blue and blue. You only notice these things when you've been away for a while. I drank the Smithwicks but I wouldn't get another. I should've asked for lager.

"How ya doin', Mick?"

"Ah, Jaysus, Tony, how're you doin'? When d'you get back?"

"Not bad. I only came home this morning. It's quite fuckin' strange being back home."

"I was talking to your da, Gus, about half an hour ago. He's down in Hollands."

"No, I won't go down. I'll leave it and see him when I go home. Oh, Jaysus, Mick, don't get me a Smithwicks, get me a Harp will you – lager. Thanks! MacDonnell still workin' out in Sweeney's, yeah?"

"Sure is, and Kelly's still fuckin' around with the trucks. Nothing changes except the fields are disappearing. Oh, fuckin' planning permission all around us. New estates going up."

"You're still up in Ballywaltrim?"

"Oh, yeah, I'm not planning on going anywhere!"

"I'm headin' off, Mick. I'll catch you during the week. I left a pint on the counter for you, okay?"

Father wouldn't say much anyway, so I'd just say hello when he came in, tell him on the weekend where I'd been. I was too knackered by the time he got home. There was no way I could stay in the house more than a couple of days, too confusing there. Nothing but noise in the morning, from six o'clock on, between work or going to school. I'd find a place in Greystones.

Early next morning, I dropped into Kevin Meade's motorbike shop. "How are you, Kevin, old boy?"

"Jaysus, Gaddafi, how are you?"

Kevin always called me Gaddafi. I asked if there was any chance of a loan of a bike to use while I was home.

"Yeah, there's a nice 250 Honda there – it's one of mine. You can take that for a while."

"You don't mind if I don't hang around today, Kevin? I'll give you a hand during the week."

"No bother! It doesn't need anything done: all the lights are working, good tyres, oil. It just needs petrol."

"Cheers. It's a good while since I had a helmet and goggles on."

Kevin lent me a pair of his gloves and a jacket. The old leather boots I had would do me. Down to Castle Street to fill it up. That was it then, Kilmacanogue here I come. It had changed a bit there too but not too much. I headed on up through Calary, thinking I'd stop at the old Calary filling station, but it had closed down altogether. You could have ridden a bike up to the top of Sugarloaf a couple of years before, but now it was fenced off. I cut across down the Red Lane, into Glen of the Downs, through Delgany into Greystones. There was loads of Clob's stuff there in his little house, so I was going to ask Pat if I could stay there for a week or two. I carried on into Bray, called down to the shop to see Pat.

"Hiya, Moon, how's things?"

"Not bad. Clob said to say hello, said he'd be home soon, home before Christmas. Not far off it anyhow. I just wondered could I bunk up in Greystones for a few weeks? Yeah, keep the house aired out for Clob coming back. I'm on me own."

"Yeah, no bother! See you in the Burnaby this evening then … you can pick the key up there for the house."

"Cheers, that's brilliant."

I wouldn't have to buy anything except a bit of food. Moving in there that evening. I had got a place to stay – far out!

I collected my stuff from Avondale Park, said goodbye to the mother, got the key off Pat and headed straight down. It was in the centre of Greystones, facing the LaTouche hotel. It was a good safe, quiet place, in off the road – and that's the way I wanted it.

The open fire wasn't bad, but he used to have a stove in it. I stuck the kettle on. There was a gas cooker – cool! I had a cup of coffee, then discovered there were no firelighters! I'd have to get a few small sticks to start it. There was a good axe there, so I got the fire going to warm the place up a bit. It was just as well I had me little tape machine, as the radio wasn't great. I was only two hundred yards from the beach there, maybe less. The harbour was about a hundred yards. I had spent a lot of time in Greystones; it's a nice town. The bars were okay: the Beach House and the Burnaby. When I had the fire going well and the fire guard up I went down to the Beach House for an hour. It was only a five-minute walk. I knew they probably wouldn't have draught Carlsberg – bottles maybe. Otherwise it would be Harp, Smithwicks or Guinness. It was nearly nine o'clock, very dark out too and a little bit windy. The bar hadn't changed much. I ordered a bottle of Carlsberg. "Hey Sean, how you doin'? What are yous up to?"

"Still fuckin' round driving lorries. How about yourself, what've you been at? Heard you were out foreign?"

"I've been living in Copenhagen, running a vegetarian restaurant. Earlier in the year I was out in Afghanistan. Yeah, it's mad out there, bit of craic!"

"When d'you get back?"

"Couple of days ago. I was in the mother's for a day or two. Couldn't live like that anymore, I need me own place. I'm just staying in Pat Kehoe's place up the road. I've got a loan of a motorbike as well. The craic on the bikes round here years ago!"

"Ah yeah, what's your man's name – Bradley – he's still around. Have you been over to Kilmac yet?"

"Nah, just passed through it. I'll have to go over to Sweeney's, see what the craic is! Probably see ya later, Sean. I'll stay around for another couple of bottles, bound to meet someone."

I got another bottle of Carlsberg. The money was a bit confusing – I still wasn't really used to the hundred pence in the pound. We used to have 240 pence to a pound, but then decimal currency had come in when we joined the EEC, a year or two before. No one else I knew came into the bar, so I got a couple of bottles to take out.

You'd need a coat on alright! The old chipper was still there anyway. Fish and chips and a beer, grand job! The fire was still going well. If I fiddled around with the radio I might pick up Radio Caroline – a pirate radio station on a ship out in the sea, that had started a good few years before. It had been started by an Irishman, Ronan O'Rahilly, and played good music at a time when Radio Eireann and BBC radio hardly played any – not any that the average teen wanted to listen to anyway. It was an era of having your little transistor radio under your pillow, listening to Caroline or Fab 208 Radio Luxembourg, well into the night. The fact that they were pirates, that is broadcasting without a licence, just added spice to it!

The bedroom was warm enough. I finished up the last beer. I'd get up sometime tomorrow and drop in to Bray, probably in the afternoon, see Kevin. There was a stainless-steel works, called Walsh's, in Shankill that I used to do a lot of work in. I'd have to tell him I was home, in case he had any work for me. A good trade is always handy to have. Two or three days a week, cash in the hand, would be lovely! It was only about six miles away.

Oh, Jesus! I couldn't believe it – quarter to twelve. I must have needed that sleep – it had been a long time since I'd slept for thirteen hours. There was a grand little shower and my hair and beard needed a good wash. Everyone passes comment when you've a beard – when you're moving around a lot it doesn't matter.

There was a little shop down beside the Ormonde Cinema, sold pretty much everything. I collected two bales of briquettes, firelighters, soap, shampoo, toothpaste and a toothbrush, dropped it back up to the cottage and headed off to Bray. Kevin didn't have any work for me so I drove on out to Shankill, to Walsh's.

"Hi, Mr Walsh, how are ya?"

"Ah, Tony, where've you been?"

"Everywhere! Travelling. I'm home for a while."

"I can give you a few days a week if you want to come in, no problem."

"Great! I'll see you on Monday morning then – tables and a few sinks'll be no bother. Martin's still in there? I'll call in to him on the way out."

"We could always do with another fella for a few days, same old routine. See you Monday then."

"See you later, man."

On the way through Bray, I got the few groceries then headed for Greystones.

Back home now, I got the fire going and put on the steak and onions, few spuds and carrots and had it with a bottle of beer.

After I'd eaten, I went for a walk on the beach. I was planning to doss around for the weekend: take the bike, cut across the Red Lane into Calary, up to Roundwood and hang around there for a while. I'd come back by the old house where we used to live, near Kilmacanogue. It had changed a bit there too. I might drop into Sweeney's on the way. One of the lads I went to school with used to be the barman there. The Red Lane is some hill – it goes right up the back of Sugarloaf – that's big Sugarloaf. I was born and raised on small Sugarloaf. In the village of Kilmacanogue, as you come in from the north, small Sugarloaf is on your left and big Sugarloaf is on your right. It's a nice little village, where I went to school. The strange thing about school is I only really began to learn when I got out of it! I had learned more in the three or four years since I'd left Ireland. The world has to be travelled! Books are good introductions, but travel – seeing, meeting, sitting talking to people about their cultures, their food and learning about their lives – is where you really learn. When I was sitting on a bike at the back of Sugarloaf, what was I doing there? Well, I knew for a fact that I was really just home in Ireland visiting people. I wasn't settled yet – I still had a lot to learn from travelling.

Saturday morning, I took a trip up to Roundwood and Laragh and on up to Glendalough, hoping to spend an hour wandering around up there. It was a nice day for a spin. There was really nobody around Glendalough that day. St Kevin's Bed is on the far side of the lake; there's a round tower and a small church on the near side. The round tower was supposed to be built way back when the Vikings were here, as a place for storing valuables, but the early churches had already been there a few hundred years by then. It's a part of Wicklow that's fairly famous for its scenery: you have Glendalough and you have the Powerscourt waterfall. The mountains are amazing round these parts: it's one thing I love about Wicklow – hills and valleys. Most people have the illusion that Ireland is a small little island. It's not that small. The population was small, even for the size of the country. Things would change in Ireland anyhow, everything changes in time. I headed down to Kilmacanogue: I'd get a bottle or two in Sweeney's – or maybe a pint – then go back over the hill to Greystones. I pulled in at Sweeney's pub. The old school was at the back … I nearly got beat to death in that place! It was a bit insane – you weren't allowed to be left-handed back then. You were afraid not to go to school and afraid to go to school. Weird!

"Hello, Ollie!"

"Young Flood! What are you doing here?"

"Ah, home for a while. Benny still working here? Well, give us a pint of Smithwicks. No, you wouldn't have anyone in at this time. I'm just passing through anyhow. Good luck." It was surprising, nobody was in the bar.

I drove on over small Sugarloaf, a place called Borhilla, and down by the fairy bush, down to our old house. I was born and raised up beside the fairy bush in a big old granite house: nothing overly fancy, but a nice life. We used to get all the milk and butter from Sutton's farm nearby, water from a well. Of course, everyone was in that situation in the fifties, growing their own food.

I got back down to Greystones, got the fire going, put on some Bob Dylan music and had some dinner and a bottle of beer. This was a new habit, a bottle of beer with my dinner. I left the washing up till later on.

I wandered down along the beach before it got dark, met a few people out with a dog or two. It's not a great sandy beach but it's alright – just under the railway bridge and you're on to it, a mixture of sand and stone. The sea wasn't very rough, just a wave or two: a nice evening. Clob's parents lived at the far end of the town. I would have to call down and say hello some day soon.

I couldn't wait till Monday morning, when I'd have something different to do. It had been a while since I'd been doing stainless-steel fabrication. The last big welding job I'd done was putting an upper deck on on the barge in Holland. There was a girl that had been on my mind for a while, that I'd gone out with several times. She might be home or she could be away. She lived near where my mother lived. I used to hang around with her when I lived there and we got on really well. I hadn't seen her for a long time. Her name was Roisín Connolly and, years before, her brother Jim used to hang around with my brother Austin.

Back at the house, I checked the fire, made coffee, then headed out to the Burnaby. I told myself I'd call down to Rois's tomorrow, hoping she was at home. There were a few in the Burnaby anyhow; I met a fella I knew called Birdy and it was great to see him and catch up over a couple of pints on what people were up to. I'd probably see most of them over Christmas anyway. I finished my pint and headed back to the cottage. It was a lot more comfortable now, having had the fire lighting that evening and the day before. It could rain tonight if it wanted to, not tomorrow.

I checked everything on the bike the next morning and headed into Bray. There were always kids in Avondale Park, playing at the gate outside. You'd have to warn them, "Mind the exhausts – they're hot on that bike. No, you can't sit on it! Just don't go near it, please! It's dangerous – the engine's hot and the exhausts are hot."

I went inside and said hello to the mother and sisters, Elaine and Colette. While my mother was making tea, I told her I had the job in Shankill.

"Ah that's great, Tony," she said. "When are you starting?"

"Monday morning, so more or less straight away. Mr Walsh would always find something for me."

"Isn't it great to have it. Your da'll be delighted."

"Yeah, I'll catch up with him later. I'm goin' over to see is Roisín home."

"Oh, she is home. I was talking to her only last week."

"Good, good. I'll see you later. Thanks for the tea!"

In Oldcourt Park, I parked in the driveway. "Hi Rois, how are you?"

"Hi, Moon. Yeah, come in. I've been home for a while. Good to see you."

"Good to see you too. It hasn't changed much here round the place. Afghanistan was amazing, scary at times, like biblical times, y'know. Nice people. Even in Iran they're cool enough, I didn't like the cities though. So, what've you been doin'?"

"I left London, got fed up with city life, I moved up north – to Staffordshire, and as you probably heard, I have a little one on the way."

"I heard that all right."

"I'm on my own now though. Just didn't work out, so here I am. We should meet up later on for a proper catch-up."

"Yeah, I can call back later. We'll walk down the town, we'll have a good chat. Yeah, I missed you too. See you later."

It would be good to talk to someone who understood where my head was at. We'd been friends for years, meeting up whenever we were both home. I wanted to have a good talk and find out what had been happening in Ireland. I went home to Greystones for a while, made a bit of dinner. I was quite happy Roisín was at home.

I didn't think I'd be staying too long in Ireland. Clob was supposed to arrive on Wednesday or Thursday. I didn't light the fire 'cause I was going back out. If it was my place, I'd have put a stove in it, but I would only be there for a while. I learned a lot about stoves in Denmark. It's the most efficient way of heating – you get eighty percent of the heat, instead of most of it going up a chimney.

I got on the bike and headed back towards Bray. I put the bike in Rois's driveway, and we walked the fifteen or twenty minutes down to Bray. "Yeah, I had a great time, a bit bothered since I came back, the usual. They're fuckin' building all over the place anyhow, all the fields are disappearing."

"They're building behind us, already built in front of us. The bog is gone, no more short cuts through that field either – full of houses."

"The last farms around Bray have been moved – fuckin' housing estates! Anyway, how's your mother and Rob?"

"They're great. Both working in that Becton and Dickson place: Ma's in the factory section and Rob's in the office – computer programmer. It's a bit of a change from horticulture but it pays well, and he seems to like it."

"I heard you were in London for a while alright. I'll be going back to Copenhagen, but we should keep in touch."

"You can always write. You know me address!"

"I know. Fuckin' useless at writing! Want to go into the Ardmore or what?"

"Ah sure, we'll have one or two here."

"Two bottles of Carlsberg, please. I'm working in Walsh's on Monday and Tuesday during the week. Yeah, it's been alright since I got home, have a lend of a motorbike and a loan of a house. He doesn't rent that place out, I don't think. I just keep the place clean for him. Plenty of good jobs in Copenhagen, you should come over. It's no problem. Qualified workers get treated really well. I have a nice apartment over there at the moment, there's a fella staying in it while I'm away … kitchen, bedroom, sitting room. It's only three or four stops on the bus from the square in the centre. No, well, at the moment I'm really happy living in Copenhagen – nice city; Danes are pretty good people."

"Well, I'll think about it. Remember the last time I was supposed to go, we were to meet in Lime Street Station in Liverpool and get the train to Newcastle? I came up from London the day before and waited for hours on the platform, turned out you were there but on a different platform! That definitely wasn't meant to happen, so we'll see."

"I'll keep in touch when I get back to Copenhagen. In the meanwhile, we can hang out together while I'm home. Yes, I will write. I'll give you my address before I leave, same one. Ah, sure, we've been walkin' and sittin' and talkin' for hours so we'll head back to the main street."

"Every time I see your da, he asks if I've heard from you, and when are you going to take the cars out of the garden!"

"Tony Kelly's chipper! I worked in there when I was a young fella – myself and Fergus Crab, washing dishes and peeling potatoes, making the chips. Friday evening and Saturday."

"Your uncle Joe still parks the pony and cart across the road there sometimes, outside the pub. That pony definitely knows its way home."

"We'll walk on up to your place, have a cup of tea, then I'll hit the road."

That was a great evening. I was really very fond of Rois, always a good friend. I'd go home and turn on the radio, have a bottle of beer, take it easy on Sunday, back to work on Monday.

So, Monday morning arrived, off to work. Martin still worked there, and a fella called John. I started with two tables, which was no bother as none of the machines had been changed since the last time I had worked there. I remembered, a couple of years back, getting my hair caught in the guillotine button! Two five-foot tables, wall and centre: I would have them finished that day. It was good money, so I didn't mind.

Tuesday, I had two sinks to do: tricky enough but no big problem. They would take a while. There was a guy there for polishing, so I wouldn't have to do that, though he was a moaner as well. If a weld wasn't filled in right, he'd moan, put too much on he'd moan. I worked late that day because I wouldn't be in for the rest of the week. I'd call in on Friday to get paid.

In the meantime, I bought an old Commer van; it would be handy for getting around.

I called over to Rois a few days later, said we'd go out some evening when Clob got home.

"What I said is true, I'll be goin' back in a few weeks, but I'll write to you. I think we have a lot in common: your ideas and my ideas aren't too far apart."

Thursday morning was a nice bright day but it got dark very early. Strange – it didn't seem to get dark as much in the city. Once you're out on a country road, it's pitch dark!

Another two or three weeks and I'd be heading back to Denmark. It was one of those things – you think you're coming home, but a couple of weeks here was long enough. I missed Wicklow a lot but there wasn't enough to keep me here. I still had a lot of things to do. I was looking forward to meeting Clob again.

"Clob, how you doin', man? You got back okay?"

"Howya, Moon? You just missed the mother and father."

"Ah sure, I'll see them later on. You're stayin' up in the cottage too? Cool! We better get a bit of food in, a couple of bales of briquettes, bags of logs to keep the heating in. Fuckin' great to see you! I'm goin' back in a few weeks. Yeah, Rois is comin' out this evening."

"Cool, well, let's go and get the provisions in."

"Right, okay Clob, we're off to the shops. Briquettes, logs, plenty of cheese, we'll get a bit of meat in Pat's."

"I have some good smoke."

"Well, I have the big Afghan waterpipe."

There was plenty of Carlsberg in the fridge and we'd get some more.

Clob had left the Transit behind. It would be too expensive to bring it home all the time. When we got back, Clob lit the fire while I made some dinner, which we had with a couple of beers. We headed out in the Commer and called in for Rois.

We had good craic in the pub in Bray. Clob wasn't planning on hanging around at home any longer than I was. When the pub closed, we dropped Rois home and headed back to the house in Greystones. Back at the house, we had a couple more beers and I got out a big pipe that I'd bought in Mazar-e Sharif. There was a pretty powerful hit off it and Clob ended up flat on his back in the garden! I had to bring him in to go to bed before he froze.

I left Clob to have a lie-on in the morning. I put the coffee on and checked all was in order with the van. I needed a good cup of coffee or two, then into Walsh's to collect my money. He was saying he wanted a job fitted, so I told him I'd be available Tuesday, Wednesday and Thursday. There were a couple of canopies and a bit of sheeting to be fitted and fans to put in. I'd take the apprentice with me. The job was outside Kilkenny, so I'd drive my own van and bring my tools. Mr Walsh would pay the expenses, hotel and petrol. We'd head down early on Tuesday morning. We'd probably only get five hours done on Tuesday, put in a long day on Wednesday and a good day on Thursday.

Back in Greystones, I got the bushman out and cut a few sticks up for the fire. After dinner we walked down to the beach. The sea was nice and calm, there was always someone walking around there. I had a good chat with Clob and we talked through our plans. I had a few things on my mind alright. I still had a few pounds from the jewellery and perfumes and the restaurant, and the bit of work in Shankill would help. I had registered in Denmark so I had the papers, my person number – which is the ID card – and I'd change the driving licence for a Danish one.

We had a couple of drinks in the pub and then back at the house I got Clob to roll a joint – the pipe would have been a bit much two days in a row!

Next morning was a busy day for a Saturday. I shouted in to Clob that I was heading down to the mother's and that there was coffee in the pot. I said hello to the mother and sisters. Mother wanted to talk to me over a cup of tea about the five cars I'd left there. Two of them were old racing cars and none of them were going. Dad wanted the place cleaned up, so I told her they could dump the whole lot. The old silver Jag could go as well. I wouldn't be coming back to Avondale Park. My box of tools would be alright left in the shed: I did use them. Austin had been using the old shed, doing a bit of work there. The neighbours would always moan about something – the noise of a machine or a grinder. If you weren't making noise, they'd have nothing to moan about! It was the same when I had the bikes and the cars there. All they were interested in was football, horses, cigarettes and drink! That wasn't going to be my life … I did my own thing. I stayed for dinner, and to see the father when he got in. Yeah, the back was a mess, I realised, looking at it. Scrap metal! I told the father he could clear it all away.

I hung around Greystones on Sunday, thinking about the job in Kilkenny, going through what I'd need to bring in my head. The van was going alright, so I didn't have to worry about it. It was rattly, but it was okay.

"What are you up to, Clob?"

"Fuck all, Moon! You spend a day or two trying to get back here and then you wonder why."

"Well, you said you're hanging on for a while, but I'm not. If there's someone looking after your tea shop, it should be okay – if not it'll just be taken over."

The Kilkenny job went smoothly enough. Mr Walsh was happy and I got paid straight away. I booked a flight to Amsterdam for the following Monday, I was planning to spend a couple of days there and then go on to Copenhagen.

I spent the weekend saying goodbye to the mother and father, brothers and sisters. I promised Rois I'd write – that'd be a first! I felt sad and shitty but I knew I was doing what I had to do.

Sunday night, I had a beer and a joint with Clob, checked my bag, passport, money, driving licence. All was good to go.

Monday morning Clob drove me to the airport in his father's car. I did get a couple of days' work with Jaak in Amsterdam, then caught the train to Copenhagen. I passed the journey thinking about what I might do next, what kind of work to look for. I wanted something different – no more restaurant work for me.

When I had been back a few days, Butch suggested I try the shipyard. They had an office, so if I called in they would tell me if there was any work going. I decided I'd cycle over there in the morning. I stayed for a few beers in Brumleby, with the American guys, Butch, Mike and Morten. Mike was a great man for making the home brew, it'd kill a horse though!

I still had to write to Rois too, to tell her I got there okay. I wasn't the greatest man at writing letters. I don't know whether being dyslexic has more advantages or disadvantages. You can bluff a lot, get someone to answer a question they don't even know you've asked!

In the morning I got up on the bike and went around through Christiania, heading to the shipyard. It was far enough away. It was such a big yard with cranes everywhere and ships. It was my first time near a shipyard that size. I went into the office and asked about work. They were taking on some welders and they told me to come in on Monday at nine o'clock for a test.

A test! I had welded JCBs and oil tankers so I thought I would have a chance. There were thousands of workers in there and it would be something else to get a job there. I stopped off in Christiania on the way back home. I passed Clob's tea shop but it didn't look open – he wasn't back yet, but I thought there was a guy minding it. I went in to Fælleskoken and got a coffee and a roll.

I got back home and decided to scrub the flat: the kitchen needed a hell of a cleaning. I checked the oven and it didn't work right – it probably hadn't been cleaned since I'd left. I took everything out of the kitchen, cleaned everything down, got a paintbrush and paint and gave it a coat of paint. I didn't mind cooking, but I hated cleaning. All the oven and cooker needed was cleaning: it was working perfectly. I had to clean the *kakkelovn* and get a wick – it ran on paraffin. They used to run on solid fuel, but they converted them all. One of my favourite colours is light blue, so the kitchen and the small bedroom were going to be light blue – if I had enough paint!

The welding tests took most of Monday morning. I had to take two 20mm thick steel plates, tack them up and stand them up vertically in the vice. It was hot in there. I had to use low hydrogen filler rods and I'd never used them before, so I was scared shitless doing that test! I was in there for more than two and a half hours.

I was given a ticket for the canteen, told to eat and to come back in one hour. There was one Dane doing the test, me, and a fella from somewhere else.

I passed the test, so I got a note go to Søren Petersen's office and he'd give me the starting date ... I had a job! I would get my work number on the Thursday, and I would have to join the union too. I'd go there on Thursday as well.

There were three thousand workers in the shipyard. I was going to be welding ships ... one of the highest paid jobs in Copenhagen. The canteen was massive, there were showers, saunas, beer on tap – all subsidised by the shipyard. I couldn't wait for Thursday!

The days flew by and on Thursday morning I arrived at the shipyard and went to talk to Søren Petersen, the boss of the building dock area. I would start work on Friday, at 6.15 am in the building dock, work number 20347. I was to go next door and they would give me overalls, a helmet, gloves and boots. My locker number was 3275, I was to keep all these in my locker, and they gave me my key. I found my way around the locker room, then spent the afternoon getting my union card. I was given a big canvas shoulder bag, with BV stamped all over it. There was a day shift, evening shift and night shift. I was hoping I could stay on the day shift, start at 6.30 am, finish at 3 pm, don't get paid for lunch hour.

I left all my details with the union; my card would be posted out to me.

Friday morning, I headed into the changing room. You needed an amazing amount of gear: earplugs, goggles, leather apron, welding gloves, helmet, wire brush, chipping hammer. The overalls were deep purple! I put it all in the bag and went over to the canteen. There were tractors and trailers to bring everyone down to the building dock, one leaving every two minutes for the start of the shift. It was probably five or six hundred metres down to the dock. The first thing you heard was "G'morn, camarade." I realised the whole shipyard were comrades, all hands were one hand. The shipyard had its own newspaper – a Communist paper.

Arriving at the ship I was awestruck. The ships were monsters, fuckin' huge! They were bulk carriers, seven or eight hundred feet long. I got down off the trailer.

"You're Anthony? I'm Sven, the overseer on this part of the ship. This man, Erik, speaks good English and he will look after you. You're on this team: shipbuilder, two welders, and an assistant."

"I only have a little Danish."

"Don't worry, Anthony, it'll be alright. Get your rods and start the welding where you're told. There'll be quite a bit of vertical welding – they do it in different stages. When you're here long enough you'll be moved from one place to another. You get used to cranes moving around and noise all over the place. Stick by me and you'll be fine. The little office over there is where they hand out the rods; the grinder for sharpening your chisels or chipping hammer is all there beside the toilet area. The main hall is huge, they build sections in there and bring them out on a platform with two hundred wheels. These are sixty- to eighty-thousand ton bulk carriers. The two we're working on at the moment are for Canadian Pacific Shipping."

There was a luxury liner in the other dock – I think it was for the Cunard line. There were six of those bulk carriers being built. The canteen was big too. You could get anything you wanted in there and it was all subsidised, only cost you a couple of kroner and your beer was the same. I had never worked in a job where you could drink beer! There was no problem there, you could get a glass of schnapps with your lunch if you wanted … maybe! That was an interesting day. Finishing at three o'clock was strange too, but I supposed I'd fall over by nine or ten. Ah well, I had the weekend off now. I'd get in touch with Päivi and Sabine and tell them about my new job. I had never worked with so many people; it would take me a few weeks to settle in.

When I got back to the flat, I put on a bit of music, got a beer and wrote a short letter to Rois.

Moon C/O Rosen
Fiskegade 7th
2200 København N
10/07/1975

Hi Rois

I'm back in København and all is okay. I got a job last week in the shipyard – it's a fucking good one! I get £6.50 an hour after tax – over £100.00 a week. My flat only costs £6 a month. It's good too – it has a few rooms and I found all the things for it.

So, if you want to come it's all well with me. You should come over to see what it's all about. You can write back and if you need some money, I can send some. All is cool here.

So write back soon

Love Moon xx

See you soon okay.

I put a stamp on the letter and stuck it in the post box on the corner. I went for a cycle over to Brumleby, to get some air. I was fairly tired: it was hot, heavy work, welding in the shipyard. I saw the old bird cage was still in the flat. I used to have a cockatoo. I thought I might get a small bird to put into it. I'd get up late tomorrow anyhow – it had been a long day. I was looking forward to Monday, to meeting a lot of people and learning a bit more about the Danes. There were a few other foreign workers there, including some Polish. There was a huge shipyard in Malmo as well and you could see the cranes moving across the Sound from Copenhagen. Next day I'd go to a few shops, might look for a bird and go to Huset.

Saturday night, I headed down to Huset for a few beers. There was always a possibility some of the lads would be there. It was only nine thirty so someone was bound to come in. I hadn't seen much of Jack since I got back. Erik came in after a while, so we had a few beers and a chat. I told him I'd started in the shipyard, so I wouldn't be around on the weeknights, since I'd be getting up at the crack of dawn for the early shift.

In the morning I cleaned up the kitchen. I went out then to get some food in and called over to Butch and Mike in Brumleby for a beer. I headed back early as I would need to be in bed by half eight or nine. I had to get up at quarter past five in the morning.

Monday morning, I had a quick cup of coffee and on the bike, then got the boat that took the workers across to the shipyard. Into the changing room, put on the overalls and grab the bag, helmet, gloves, up onto the trailer: "G'morn, camarade!" Down to the dock. Sharpen up the chipping hammers, pick up my box of welding rods.

There was a lot of noise: super massive cranes and machinery, and there must have been nearly fifty welders working around me. We all had our ear muffs, goggles, helmets and leather aprons – the amount of equipment you had to put on, but it was cool, everything you had was good quality. We got a break of about ten minutes to sit down and drink a bottle of orange – I wasn't on the beer in the morning – yet! I liked the food in the canteen, but it was a bit early for dinner. I was still surprised at the amount of beer they drank. The lunch hour went by quickly. Time would fly in the shipyard when you were working.

It was hard to believe the time of day I was finished working. I was home at twenty past three. I'd plenty of time to get to the shops for a few beers, potatoes, veg, couple of pork chops and some food, then to the bakery for fresh bread and yoghurt. I put the stuff in the fridge and went for a walk. There were one or two second-hand shops nearby, and a pet shop, so I thought I'd have a look around. They'd no talking birds there but they said you could teach the cockatoo to talk. I'd have to think about it. Parrots are big and I didn't really want a parrot, or a mynah bird. I didn't really know one from the other anyway.

I soon got used to living and working with the Danes, though I'd only been talking to a few in the shipyard. Paul and Erik were two that I was working with. So far, I'd been working on the vertical welding on the outside of the ship. You could be anywhere on them. The foreman's name was Ole and he was a nice man. Erik was sound. After a month there I was well into a routine and I had a lot of money in the bank account. I met a young fella from Ireland who had started in the shipyard: he was a welder too, but I couldn't see him staying too long. They were talking about getting teams together in a month or so: two welders and shipbuilders and a helper. They had really strange welding equipment on the decks: it was like a robot that travelled along tracks. After the runs were done by hand, they'd use the automatic welder. The decks were the size of a football field, with two sets of toilets – one at each end. I couldn't believe the size of the engines – they were three floors high.

My foreman said he was very happy with my work and Søren Petersen was very happy with my time-keeping, so I was in for a raise. The days were getting longer now, but it was still cool enough. I was invited over to Erik's apartment one day to have a drink with him – lovely family. It was strange walking down the street and meeting fellas that you worked with rather than other foreigners you hung around with. I was getting really used to the place now and I usually got a beer with my lunch. Sometimes I'd take one or two back to the boat in the afternoon. Life revolved around the job now. They were a very communist socialist gang in the shipyard. They were like one huge unit – it was amazing the way everybody looked after every one else. I could feel myself getting into their system and the political ideology. It was a very productive shipyard. There were more people working in the shipyard than there would be in a small town in Ireland. The only thing I didn't like was the alarm clock in the morning, but that's life.

At night I dropped off as soon as I went to bed – I was really knackered. It was a good job but it was heavy work. In August I went on nights for a week. I was writing to Rois about only getting two hours' sleep in the day because it was too hot. I couldn't wait to get back to the day shift and getting a good night's sleep. I was still hoping she would come over, but I hadn't heard from her for a while. Her little boy would have been around six months old now, so I guessed that was keeping her busy.

Once I was back working daytime, I looked forward to Monday mornings again. There was something very positive about the shipyard – the way it was organised and the comradeship: very deep and strong. It was a great feeling in the morning, with everyone – maybe up to a thousand men – saying "G'morn, camarade." You could feel part of something – the whole yard with the one voice. It was strange, but it was a wonderfully powerful feeling. There was a definite togetherness, you were never alone on the job. One for all, all for one. I was never very political, but I think they understood about Connolly and Joe Hill. The power is in the hands of the people. If the people are together they have power. It's the voice of the people. If you haven't got a voice, you don't have the power. I could see myself being affected by the great feeling in the yard. I was hoping for this new team to come. At that stage I was doing tough enough welding jobs: we were doing T-junctions, working overhead and on the top. All of those joints were X-rayed. If there was any porosity or slag, they blew them out – it was called a bomber. The gouger man would come in, and all the weld had to come out and it would have to be done again.

I wasn't too bad – I hadn't had any blown out yet. There was a poor Israeli guy working near us and, to be honest, he shouldn't have been near the welding plant. He just couldn't hack it! He'd be moved soon enough. He was holding up our line. He'd take two to three days to do a junction and then it got taken out again, so it would be another two or three days. Sven operated the little mobile welder on tracks that did the flat decks. He'd fill a hopper full of flux and there was a big roll of wire; he'd press the button and it would weld all day on its own; he just had to keep the flux filled, change the wire and move the tracks. It was a boring piece of shit but that's the technical revolution: automation in 1975.

The new teams were put together: myself, Eric, Sven and a shipbuilder – two full-time welders, one automatic operator and a shipbuilder. It was a good team. I got a big box together, with my work number, *tyve tusind tre hundrede syv og fyrre*, written across the top: twenty thousand three hundred and forty-seven. I was using a big 600-amp MIG welder, using porcelain placed in a steel track and held up from the underneath with magnetic pieces. I was welding from the top down through. It's a very interesting process. The porcelain burns away slightly from each side, so you get a perfect weld underneath. It was so big, I had to use a very dark glass with a mirror for deflection. It wouldn't be good to get a flash from that. I loved the shipyard and when I'd been almost four months in it I got a hell of a good pay rise, so I was on top dollar now. I was very glad I wasn't welding in the tanks – it was hot noisy work inside there. It was brilliant when they put the main decks in: I loved working high up on a deck.

I got word that Clob was back in Christiania. I would have to drop over on a Sunday, or give him a shout some evening going home from work. There were all these meetings going in the shipyard, which I didn't really understand until I had it explained to me that they were looking for a thirty-five-hour week, which basically meant you didn't work on Friday afternoons. They had been organising protests, which would be starting in a month or two, marching into Copenhagen town hall, bringing our placards and banners. I heard that the Royal Copenhagen Porcelain workers were planning the same. That would be some rally – I reckoned there'd be over four thousand there, between the two of them. It was something to look forward to!

The shipyard was my life now anyhow, apart from a few things. Sometimes I'd get a bit depressed in the apartment on me own: I hadn't lived that long on my own for a long time. I was planning to get Rois and the baby over in the next couple of months anyhow. Like I said, most of my friends were shipyard workers now, apart from a couple of guys I'd known for a long time. All four of us were happy on the team, because we knew we'd be working together for a good while and we worked well together. It was handy with that big box there, all our tools went into it, including the welding shields.

I called over to Mike in Brumleby one evening. He was thinking of heading back to the States.

Erik had an allotment where he grew tomatoes and onions and veg, and he had invited me to come and visit him there. I'd bring a few beers with me and call over on the weekend, it was about an hour's distance. One Saturday morning I got a bag of fresh rolls – that's all I needed to bring with the few beers. I'd stay off the schnapps! Erik was a whore on the schnapps. There's the old saying, "one for the road", but beJaysus he'd have one for every sentence! I headed out towards the airport. There were quite a few allotments, but I found him soon enough.

"Hi, Erik. Wow, it's cool – not a bad spot at all! You've got quite a bit of stuff growing. I'd say in a week or two your tomatoes'll be perfect. I brought a few beers and a bag of rolls."

"Hey, Moon, welcome! Come and have a look around. Here's the lean-to shed, and have a look in here – the greenhouse."

"Wow, I've never grown anything under glass. The cucumbers look nice, the courgettes are doing well outside – it all looks great. Anyhow, I came to give you a hand with the weeding. So, you get the barbeque going and I'll work away here doing a few of these beds for you."

It was all well under control anyhow. He had cucumbers, lettuce, scallions, tomatoes and courgettes – it was great. It was all hand weeding as he didn't believe in using chemicals. He threw a couple of steakburgers and one or two pork chops on the barbeque – cool! I'd soon worked up an appetite, so it would go down a treat.

"Easy on the schnapps! I'll toast one with you." Time flies when you're having fun. "Ah, no, lay off the schnapps, I've had two beers and two schnapps. I'll get one of them pork chops though. I'll have a roll with it and a small bowl of salad. Yeah, that new team we're on, it's cool, Erik, isn't it?"

"Fuckin' right, Moon! Great job – worked out well."

"Yeah, it works out easier on the lot of us. It's easier to pace off your teammates than to pace off someone else. Cheers to the gardening."

"One for the road?"

"Nah, I've got to ride a bike back – I've had enough!"

"Haha, okay, farewell! See you Monday."

Aw, that had been enough alcohol. I wasn't too bad. I'd kept the hat on as it was fairly hot and sunny.

After a good weekend, we were back to work on Monday morning. I hopped on the bike, and there was always a bit of traffic but there were cycle lanes there anyhow. It was getting a bit cooler in the mornings. There would be a lot happening that day. Two big cranes were going together and large sections of the ship were coming out of the hall. We had to stand well away when the alarm bells sounded and all the smaller cranes were turned out of the way.

When they linked both cranes together, they could lift a thousand tons. The section they were bringing out was a side piece, weighing about five hundred tons. They'd be the whole day setting this one up. I think one of the propellers weighed forty tons on its own. There was lots of noise and we were all working down near the wheelhouse. There was a big bowie coming out of the building hall that looked like it had hundreds and hundreds of wheels under it. It was driven from the front and the back. All the safety precautions were in force that day. There was a lot of precision work there, lining up top deck plates that were only about 30mm thick. I'd only seen individual parts before, I hadn't been there when they were putting sections together. It was like a huge Meccano set. The big boss was out there that day.

The hooter for lunch sounded and everything came to a standstill. It all went very quiet.

When we got back after lunch the crane bells were still ringing and lights flashing. In a couple of hours that section would be secured, then they'd do the other side. Off went the wires and all the shackles were loosened. We'd only got a bit done that day and we'd all be flat out the next day. I heard someone say it was a sixty- to seventy-thousand-ton bulk carrier. I had never worked on anything that big. The wheelhouse was like a medium-sized hotel. The accommodation was massive. The engine was about eighteen feet high, in a massive engine room. There were eight 500mm diameter pistons.

Monday was always a hard day, but that had been a really interesting day.

I was writing to Rois a lot that September, still hoping she'd make it over. There was still a lot of talk about the thirty-five-hour week. They were supposed to be starting a new protest shortly: all hands out, march to the town hall. The Copenhagen porcelain workers would also be involved. The comradeship in the unions was very strong – three thousand men made one strong unit in the shipyard. I didn't know how many were in the Porcelain, probably a couple of thousand as well … It was a big ask – a thirty-five-hour week. A lot of places in Ireland were still working a forty-four-hour week: five and a half days.

My welding had come on a hundred percent since I'd been in the shipyard. I had been terrified for a while at the start, but by this time I was on the high rate of pay and I was doing a lot of awkward spot weldings and junctions, and was using the big 600-amp CO^2 machine with porcelain backing. That was a cool machine. I'd used smaller versions before, not 600 amp though. We were a good team now. The lads were joking about the winter, shovelling snow off the deck before you weld. I wasn't looking forward to that, but that's what it would be like: minus eighteen Celsius!

I liked having my own place – my own door key. I picked up an old black and white telly as well. I only had Danish stations: they had English programmes sometimes with Danish subtitles, but the ads were the best – fuckin' crazy! Ads for the TV licence, ads for condoms, milk, beers. I used to watch the speedway. There were no more concerts in the park now; it was too late in the year. They had the odd band playing in Huset. I would meet the lads the odd weekend and go out for a few beers. They say, all work and no play … but I needed it like that at the time, and I didn't mind it. I had an awful lot of good friends that I worked with in the shipyard. There weren't too many of the lads I worked with that were fully qualified. I'm a qualified sheet metal worker and coppersmith, and sheet metal workers always did welding as well.

That week had been very interesting. Putting on the large sections was like working with army ants: everybody knew what they had to do. There were elevators now on the front section of the boat, which would bring you up to the top or let you down to the bottom of the building dock. I was there watching the other guys doing the overhead welding. It was a tough job – sitting in a chair with your head back and your arms up all day. It was always cooler down there.

By the end of September I was getting homesick, writing to Rois that I would like to sit on a mountain top for a few days and clear my head of all the noise. I was planning to get back to Ireland for a few weeks in November, as soon as the ship was finished. Most of my friends had left already. Copenhagen would be empty, cold and wet in the winter, and I didn't want to be there for that.

A couple of years before, myself and Clob had got stuck in Germany in nearly a metre of snow. Crazy! We'd pulled into an area to sleep in the camper and woke up in the morning to find we were nearly buried. We'd been heading to Amsterdam.

I was still meeting Big Erik and Sven now and again, down in Huset. We were talking about the nuclear power plant they were supposed to be building in Malmo.

"Sure I think they're trying to get workers from the shipyard to work on the building of it – welders, fabricators, fitters."

"Would you go? I bet the money would be good."

"It wouldn't be my cup of tea, no. I turned down jobs years ago in South Africa, same fuckin' reasons, don't believe in it. It's not always about how much I make or what the money is. I like building ships anyhow – and the money is good and working with the lads is great."

"I hear it's good there alright."

"Yeah, there's showers, a massive canteen, the food's all top class. I've a good few Danish friends there now. Great lads, funny thing is there's a namesake of yourself there, Erik, good friend in the shipyard. He has an allotment; he's always giving me tomatoes, scallions, lettuce; it's great though."

"One for the road?"

"Okay, thanks! No, I'm a single man at the moment. Yeah, it's a bit strange but it's okay. I can clean up when I want and cook when I want. I'm on the third alarm clock! I freak out sometimes, fuck the clock at the wall, then I have to buy a new one! Anyhow, I'm off. Farewell, see yous around."

"Yeah, see you, Moon. Take it easy."

I spent a day checking out the old *kakkelovn* stove in the corner of my living room and made sure it was working properly. They're beautiful stoves: about a metre high, with double baffles. They used to burn "duck eggs" – a kind of anthracite – in them, but now they were converted to oil – kerosene burners. They gave out great heat. They were cheap stoves to run with no cleaning out. They were all over the city. I would bring a couple of them back to Ireland whenever I moved back there full time.

I got a letter from Rois. She was delighted that I'd be coming back. I wrote back telling her about the demonstration that was coming up at the end of the month. I had been involved in one small strike in Ireland, when I'd been working in Blackrock Engineering. It would've been 1968 I think – a freezing cold winter and no heating. The boss didn't get the tank filled for the hot blowers, so we went on strike for three days. He got the oil in then alright.

After a great weekend, I was heading off to work on a Monday morning. I'd be having a word with Søren Petersen by Friday, booking a few weeks off. I had a few things to do in Ireland so hoped I'd be able to get extended leave. At the shipyard I got all yoked up with the welding gear. I didn't like working in the tanks that much, as we had to use breathing gear with air pipes, but it was only for a week or two. I was using the big 600-amp welder and the porcelain. We'd put down about five metres at a time and then check it. Sometimes you'd have to warn the guys that it wasn't a great idea looking through a welding glass without a shield. You could be blinded and it would nearly lift the skin off your face, never mind welding flashes.

Erik was saying that there were two more of those ships to be built, but they weren't going to take on any more workers. The last of the upper deck on this one would be put on that week. We'd been welding on them for a couple of months. The lead on that welder would pull the arm out of you, but I got used to it. Ole was using the powder machine – it has a big hopper, you lay your tracks along, feed it and just press a button, weld to finish off the top of the deck. Move the tracks and continue in straight lines. The welder I was using took a bit of concentration, but I was beginning to like it.

After lunch I went to see Søren Petersen.

"Good day, Søren."

"Hi, Anthony."

"Em, I have a little thing to do in Ireland, take a couple of weeks … just a family thing, you know. I want to get time off and keep the job."

"Yes, Anthony. Take as long as you need. Your job will be held for you."

"Thank you very much."

"Yes, your job will be here. *Farwel og tak.* See you, Anthony."

That was one big weight off – I still had a job and I had time off. Walking back down by the main hall, I was reminded yet again that it was huge. You always had to be very careful, always had to have your helmet with you; we even took them up to the canteen and back down. You had to watch everything there: cranes, moving platforms. They were some machines in the building hall!

I told Erik that I'd got the okay to take some time off. I'd have to go over and tell Butch, and make sure I saw Clob. I could stop in on the way home. As I approached the tea house, smoke was rising so the fire was lighting – the tea house was open anyhow. I told Clob about my plans for a trip home. He'd been back in Copenhagen two or three weeks. He said business was slowing down in the tea house but they didn't need that much to keep it going. He was still living in the van and the tea house was still standing, despite some concerns we had that it was too close to the water. I said I was planning on leaving the following Thursday and that I'd call in before I went.

259

I went round to Huset that night, got a bit of food and a few beers and met some of the lads, but before that I cycled home and got changed. The old clog boots were handy – I didn't wear them all the time, but if it got snowy I would. I headed off to Huset. I took a few bob with me, locked the door properly, and made sure the cooker was off. I'd have to get oil for the stove the next day – it was nearly empty. Living on your own, you have to think of everything. If there's nothing there, it's your own fault.

I had a good catch-up with the lads in Huset and told them about my trip home. I was saying that I hadn't seen Päivi or Sabine for about three months. Sabine had gone to Canada but Päivi was still up in Espergærde, as far as I knew. I headed home after four or five beers – couldn't stay awake much later after the early mornings.

I always woke up too early on Saturdays. I went back to sleep for a while then put on a pot of coffee and had a nice bit of cheese on a roll. The back wheel of the bike was flat. I hated fixing punctures. I had a spare tube. There were already a half dozen patches on the tube in the back wheel, so I put the new one in. Fælledpark reminded me a little bit of the Phoenix Park as I was riding through it. It was well maintained. I called into Butch and family for a coffee and filled them in on my plans too.

Next morning, I went down to the travel agency and booked a train and a boat to Harwich for Thursday. I could organise a train in England from Harwich. I'd get that lad to take my flat again while I was away. I went back to the flat to pack a bit of gear. I already wished I was going the next day.

Eventually the last day came. On Wednesday at the shipyard, I said my goodbyes to Sven and Erik. I told them I'd be back once I'd sorted out a few things in Ireland. We had a drink at lunchtime. I was mostly staying off the schnapps – a bottle of Carlsberg and maybe one schnapps.

"Skol! Jaysus, that stuff'd kill you! No, I'm only having one. Yeah, see yous all in about two months. Right lads, see you later."

Shipyard cranes, 1975.

The robotic welder, 1975.

One of the big cranes, 1975.

Big propeller for a big ship, 1975.

Moon welding, 1975.

Pre-wedding nerves.

Rois and Moon's wedding day.

 On Thursday I got the train to Esbjerg, then the ferry to Harwich. It didn't look great out in the sea – very choppy. Thank God I had a cabin – it was an all-night trip. We would get into port about nine in the morning. You could never predict what time these boats would get in at. I had a couple of pints of Carlsberg then went to the cabin; I wanted to get to sleep early. I might be home Friday night. It was always annoying if you missed the Dun Laoghaire ferry – you'd be sitting in Holyhead for hours. At two in the morning, I woke up and it felt like the ship was jumping out of the water. I rolled over and tried to go back to sleep. By a quarter to seven it was a good bit calmer, so I lay there for an hour. Only a couple of hours left anyhow. It had been a rough enough night. I'd never take a long ferry without a cabin. It was pissing rain outside as well.

One thing about travelling on your own is you've no one to argue with at any time. If it goes wrong, it's wrong; if it goes right, it's right. I'd been travelling the best part of two years now on my own. An odd time I'd get pissed off, most of the time it was good, and I met a lot of interesting people.

Once we were docked, we unloaded and I went through customs and passport control.

"I'm going to Ireland. Nothing in the bags, clothes. Only a wash bag, toothbrush, soap, stuff like that. No, I'm not carrying anything. Yes, I live in Copenhagen. Okay. Thank you."

The usual. Probably just as well he hadn't seen all the stamps, just looked at the photo page and that was it!

I got the London train, thinking it would be the quickest. The Holyhead express train from London should get there an hour before the boat left, so I should be in Dun Laoghaire by nine or ten o'clock that night. It was always a good bit quicker by train. I'd done the coaches a few times and you'd get a pain in your face – too many stops: pull over for something to eat, pull over to use the toilets. It was a bit dearer on the train but well worth it. I'd have tea and a sandwich on the train and I could get dinner on the ferry.

We got into Holyhead a few hours later. I was getting tired at this stage. I bought a ticket – it was only a couple of quid. In a few hours, I'd be back in Ireland. It'd take about half an hour to get from Dun Laoghaire to Bray. Being a Friday night now, the father'd be in some pub in Bray. He always had a couple of beers. I wouldn't have known where the brothers were.

Then I was back in Ireland: misty mountains, hills, and the winding roads. It felt strange sitting on the bus and the conductors getting the money off you. They had a ticket machine that they would wind, then they gave you a bit of paper and your change out of a little leather bag they carried. They didn't have bus conductors in Denmark: one-man buses and an hourly ticket.

I was standing on the main street in Bray. Should I walk up the town and get a pint or walk home? Only fifteen or twenty minutes. Ah, I'd head on home, sure. It was late enough. No key so I knocked on the door.

"Howya, Ma! How are you keeping?"

"God, Tony, I'm glad to see you. I thought you were never coming back!"

"The girls are here? Rest of them's out? No, I'm not hungry. Hi, Elaine, Colette. Cup of tea and we'll have a bit of a chat. Ah, I'm fairly worn out – been travelling since Thursday morning: trains and ferries for two days. Everyone keeping well?"

Up in the morning for breakfast with the ma and da.

"Hi, Dad, how are you keeping?"

"Jaysus, you're home?"

"For a while anyhow. I'm working in a shipyard in Denmark at the moment – Burmeister and Wain – a pretty big one. Yeah, I like it. I'm around for a while anyhow."

Travel with Moon

*

Hanging out with Rois for the next couple of weeks, we agreed that we loved each other and we really should get married. So, there it was. That thing that I had to come home to sort out … Yes!

Myself and Rois went back a long way. I'd met her first when she was about fourteen. I was messing about on motorbikes and she used to come over then and polish the bikes. I never took her out on a bike, though, for years. I used to have some Japanese motorbikes and got on to a few English bikes – BSAs and Velocettes. I think the only time in my life that I hadn't had a motorbike was when I went to Denmark. We had gone our separate ways – me travelling, she to work in England. We both went out with other people, but whenever we were both home at the same time, we always met up and hung out together. We missed each other when we were apart.

We set about arranging the wedding without any delay. We told Rois's mother and my mother first. Both of them were delighted. Telling my father was funny. He was having a shave, getting ready to go out.

"Hey, Da, I've something to tell ya: we're getting married."

Rois was standing beside me in the hall.

"Wha'? Who are you getting married to?"

Rois put her hand up. "Er, me!"

"Ah, Jaysus, that's great! Congratulations! When?"

"As soon as we can arrange it. I've a job to go back to in Denmark, so we won't hang around."

Her father invited us for a drink so he could meet me, then asked her mother if I was a chancer! We got a good laugh out of our fathers' reactions anyway.

We called on the local parish priest – a Franciscan, Father John Bosco – who said the soonest we could do it would be six weeks. Letters of freedom had to be got from every place we'd ever lived, confirming neither of us was already married. The banns had to be put up in the church and birth and baptism certs had to be found – lots of paperwork! We thought it would be much simpler. Anyhow, the date was set for December twentieth, and he organised for us to use the neighbouring parish church as his was a newly created parish and only had a temporary Nissen hut for services. In fact, I

263

think ours was the first wedding in his new parish. We only invited family and a few close friends. Clob would be best man and Rois's friend Winifred would come over from London to be bridesmaid. Neither of us wanted a big fuss, so Rois's mother and brother, Gretta and Rob, were happy to have the reception back at their house. Mrs Rynhart – the mother of one of Rois's close friends – said she'd make the cake and do the food as a wedding present, and my brother Gregg and a couple of his mates from his band would play for us. Another brother, Godfrey, and his friend John would do the photography. All we needed now was to organise our clothes and for me to get the ring.

I got a few days a week working in Walsh's in Shankill again. Mr Walsh was talking about a job in Killala, over in County Mayo. I said I'd do it because I'd be properly paid for it. There was money in the account in Copenhagen still, though I'd brought a good bit with me. I'd get a good bit of cash out of Walsh's. No one else would go down to Killala anyway.

The job involved fitting two canopies and barrier rails, starting in about a week or so.

"I'm getting married on the twentieth of December, so if it's all done before that, all well and good," I said. I told him my van wasn't great, so he said he'd send everything down and then we would follow.

He said, "It's for the Asahi plant in Killala. You'll be booked into the hotel there. It's a big union site."

He would leave the drawings ready for me to start in the morning. Cool, that was organised: two or three weeks, cash in the hand.

In the meantime, there was wedding stuff to organise. I bought a wide nine carat gold band, which was what Rois asked for. I didn't need one. You couldn't wear a ring in my line of work – you'd risk losing a finger if it got caught in anything. I went to Allen's clothes shop to have a look around. I didn't care what colour. I spotted a safari suit, it had a nice cut on the jacket, medium wide legs, snow white and in my size. It was cool, and I even got him to knock the price down. "It's the middle of winter. Who else is going to buy a safari suit?" Little did I know – my brother Gregg turned up at the wedding wearing an identical suit!

I had the clothes now. Gregg had a nice brown shirt – I'd borrow that – and I'd polish me clog boots. Clob would be there on time, all the rest would just fall into place. That's what weddings are about anyhow – friends and family, don't need ten tons of bullshit. A couple of weeks after that we'd be in Denmark.

The van sounded a bit funny. I'd have to look at it, but I didn't want to spend money on it. I'd just check the plugs and the points. It had a couple of dodgy tyres but I'd get away with it. I gave the points a little bit of a clean and cleaned up the old cylinder cap as well. It was starting okay, it'd be alright.

Driving through Blacklion, near Greystones, I saw a man waving at the bus stop, looking for a lift. I pulled over. "Yeh goin' to Bray?"

"Yeah, sure."

"Would you bring something?"

"What? A fuckin' bed and a wardrobe? To where?"

"Near Ardmore."

"I'm goin' that way alright. So you're hitchhiking with a bed and a wardrobe, to Bray? Jaysus! All right, shove them in the back there and hop in. I'll bring you."

Unbelievable! Hitchhiking to Killarney Park, with a single bed and a wardrobe!

"Right, okay. Ah. Jaysus, thanks! A pound!"

I called in to Rois. "You have your passport organised anyway. That's cool. Yeah, you'll have it in a couple of weeks. I heard that the laws were changed alright: drink driving and helmets on bikes, I hear. That's the EEC. Ah, I'll come in for a cup of tea or coffee. It'll be alright in Denmark, I'm guaranteed a job there and I have the apartment. Rupert'll have a good time when he gets there. I have his room all painted up. I have friends with kids there too."

We rented a little place out in Greystones, for us to live in before we left for Denmark. Walsh was paying me well enough – four days one week, three or four the next week and three or four the following week, and that'd be it. I wouldn't have to touch any of my savings.

Monday morning, I went in about half eight, to see was there something to do in the workshop before I left for Mayo. We'd be leaving at six o'clock on Tuesday morning. Sure enough, it turned out that a crucial part – the blowcap – hadn't been made in time to be sent down with the rest of the material. We got that made during the day and loaded into Mr Walsh's Volvo with all the rest of the gear we'd need to bring down with us.

Early next morning, we were off to Killala. It would be a long drive. We were told that it was all regulations and union rules. Sometimes the regulations could be sticky and hold you up for a day. I wouldn't be having that this time. We dropped the bags at the hotel and went up to the site. I'd heard that they were going to build a factory and there'd be lots of jobs in the Asahi plant. There was a large prefab that was the canteen area for the construction workers and that's where we'd be putting the canopies.

We went back to get our dinner in the hotel. I had the young apprentice with me. "You're happy now, Sean. I'll have the steak and I'll have a glass of Smithwicks, get the young lad an orange juice. What are you smiling at, Sean? See how you get on: if you can work I'll let you drink."

By the time we were leaving at two o'clock on Thursday afternoon we'd got a lot of the work done. I had got Sean to ring Peter Walsh in the yard and order a few bits we'd need to finish it off the following week.

Early Monday morning I was outside the yard in Shankill; the gates were locked, no one was there yet. I had to pick up three boxes of stuff that were inside the doorway. When they arrived, we got loaded up quickly and headed off to Killala.

On the site in the morning, I met the foreman and told him I wanted a 430mm hole in the roof where I'd marked it. Union rules said that only a carpenter could work on that. He said he'd have the carpenter over at nine o'clock.

"Hey, Sean, I think this is our carpenter coming up now. I know – he's carrying Our Lord's fuckin' tools with him! A bit and brace, Jesus Christ!"

Nearly an hour later he headed off for a tea break. "Get up and have a look, Sean."

"There's two holes here and a little crack cut with a hacksaw blade."

"Fuck this, get the big grinder up here. Your man's like a fuckin' woodpecker. Here we go, I'll have this out of there in fifteen minutes. Belt of the hammer there'll bang it out. That's it!"

There was smoke everywhere but it'd go away; it cleaned up really well. At twenty-five past ten the woodpecker came back. There'd be trouble now.

The foreman arrived up. "What's that? I sent you a carpenter!"

"You didn't send a carpenter to me," I said. "I wanted a hole out in an hour. It's been two hours now. You sent a fuckin' woodpecker over – the fuckin' tools he has … are you codding me? Well, the hole's in the roof now; there's nothing more we can do about it. We'll be gone by tomorrow. You can have a site meeting if you want to, we'll work away." I wasn't going to worry about it. That job had to be done. "I'm getting married in a few days. I can't be hanging around down here." We kept going, got everything ready, then we were going to have to ask for about four big men to lift the canopy up to the ceiling.

When we were all done, I got Sean to collect up all the bits of cut aluminium and put them into boxes, not to leave them on the floor, and to make sure all the hand tools were in the right boxes. We'd be out of there next day around two or three o'clock.

I rang Mr Walsh from the hotel. "Seamus, how you doin'? Tony here. Ah, it's going well. There was a row here this morning on site alright. They sent over a carpenter to put a hole in the roof. In an hour he had two holes drilled with a hand drill, then he went off at ten to ten and came back about half ten. We'd the holes cut out by then. The foreman said they were having a row on the site over it because of union rules, carpenters do this or that. More like a woodpecker than a carpenter! Ah, don't worry about it. I said we're on site to do a job, can't lose half a day waiting for a hole in the roof. We should be finished around two or three tomorrow."

Luckily he was still in the workshop, looking at drawings; he'd be there till eight o'clock sometimes. Sometimes I thought he slept there!

In the morning we finished the job off, packed up the van and I spoke to the site foreman. I showed him everything we'd done and told him we were heading off.

We set out for the long drive back to Shankill. I dropped Sean off and headed for Greystones, hoping Clob would be there. Thankfully he was, so I parked the van up and we walked down to the Burnaby – our last chance for a few pints before Saturday.

I asked him how things were going in Copenhagen.

"The usual – good. The lads all send good wishes."

"Great! I think I've everything arranged, just left a few small things to be settled Saturday morning. Rois and I have to go out to the airport tomorrow evening to collect Winifred. She's flying in from London to be bridesmaid. Two years ago, I never dreamt I'd get married at all. Things change though."

"So, you're moving back to Copenhagen after? Have you still got a job?"

"At the shipyard, yeah. I should have a job when I go back. I took a compassionate leave type yoke, he said 'no worries'. Yeah, we found a little place down in Greystones to stay in for a while. We just have to get a few things organised before we head back to Copenhagen. Ah, it should be good craic now. The reception's in Rois's house. Of all the priests that's marrying us, do you remember in … was it Austria? Remember the Franciscan guys over there, with the brown robes and the sandals? They gave us a few bob and that … Well, they're the ones that's marrying us in the new Ballywaltrim parish. We're getting a lend of the church in the Vevay. Ah, they're cool guys. A lot of bullshit papers to organise, you know, birth certificates, baptism certificates … you've to go all round the place. Good to have you back for the best man anyhow."

We finished up and walked back up to the cottage, chatting about some of the trips we had taken. Clob said he was thinking of selling the Transit. We'd had some adventures in that yoke! Pisa had been a long time ago. We'd been very lucky that time.

"I'll have a little small pipe with you – don't want to go too mad."

"I'll chance a coffee, you put the kettle on then."

"I'll make that, you make the pipe and don't kill me with it. No, you light it. That'd blow your head off, man. There's enough in that alright!"

"You'll sleep like a log," he laughed.

"Wow, that pipe's after finishing me off, going to hit the sack. See you in the morning."

"See you, Moon."

I called over to Avondale Park in the morning. I was going to stay there that night. Then out to Greystones the following night. The place we had rented was a tiny summer house beside the railway tracks, with the grand name of Laburnum Lodge. Honeymoon in Greystones! Nah, we'd only be there for a few weeks, then we'd be off to Copenhagen.

Friday evening, we picked Winifred up and I dropped her and Rois back in Old Court Park, then headed into Bray for a few drinks with the brothers and the father – who was already down there. We had a good laugh and a few drinks, then I said, "I'm goin' after this. You get in the front of the van, Daddy. No, I wasn't. I only had a few pints. Won't speed in this anyhow."

In with the lads through the side door, sat on the old bed I had in it.

"No, we're not goin' that quick."

It was like sitting up in the windscreen in those yokes. We got home anyhow, had a sandwich, cup of tea and off to bed.

Saturday morning, we were blessed with the weather – the temperature was up and there was bright sunshine. God, panic – I had to take the heels off the clog boots! My father had good cobbler's tools, so I took out the nails. It was only a piece of car tyre anyhow. I nailed the new heels on and I was trimming them off. Trimming round the edges, I cut me leg with the Stanley knife! It wasn't much, but it was sore. I got out a plaster and antiseptic; it was only a small nick. I was lucky I didn't stab myself altogether, as it was only three inches away from me *liathróidí*! I thought I might sneak down to the Ardmore for a pint. Clob had arrived and was sitting on the wall talking to one of the lads. Avondale was a small park; they weren't nosy people, they were just friendly and inquisitive. They'd all be standing at their front doors when I walked out later. There'd be a good few over at the church too.

By three o'clock, I was all dressed and ready to go. "Right, Clob, we're off. I'm drivin' over to the church; you can take it afterwards."

We stood over at the church door to wait. What do they say? The bride is always late! Good crowd there so far. Well, everyone was there now except Rois. There she was now with her dad and Winifred. All sitting down inside now. Few photos, the vows, the blessings, the ring, and a piece of silver. It's traditionally a coin, but for a joke I gave her a piece of silver paper; even the priest was laughing.

"You may now kiss the bride!"

Big cheer. Back up now and sign the register. So we were married now. Strange. Does that mean you own me, and I own you, or we both own each other, for evermore?

Outside the weather was great so there were plenty of photos taken, with Bray Head in the background. Then we all headed back to Rois's mother's house. Mrs Rynhart had laid on a fantastic buffet, there was plenty of food and drink.

Speech from the best man: he wasn't going to say too much anyhow apart from, "You're all welcome! Have a good day, eat and drink plenty and the best of luck to Moon and Rois."

Later on, we had another collection for more beer. Rois's granny looked like she was having a good time, and Gretta and my mother. My father, Gus, was singing duets with Mary Fields, including "Are You Lonesome Tonight?" Everyone was dancing and having a good time. I noticed a lot of the lads were missing for a while. What were they up to now? I hoped they hadn't been at the van.

"We'll be leaving shortly, Rois. They can carry on as long as they want. Gregg's upside down, your granny is falling over, my mother can't stand up; Gretta's in some state and my father's speaking Chinese. Think the band's pissed as well. Right, everyone, we're off."

They all bundled outside to cheer us off.

Oh, shit! Someone had been at the van: they'd written "Just Married" all over the sides in pink lipstick. We got in and I started it up, but there was an awful rattle. There was a metal bucket tied underneath! I got a hand to take it off – you couldn't drive with that. They were all still laughing when we took off, there was still a lot of noise! We drove out to Greystones, rattling the whole way. We parked up outside Laburnum Lodge. What a great day! Everyone had enjoyed themselves, a great day for everyone.

You wouldn't run up that stairs anyhow. It was quare small in there alright! It was clean, but tiny – all the chair legs had been cut down and we never figured out why. It was a bit like a doll's house! But it had a decent enough stove and the bedroom furniture was the normal size. It was only for a couple of weeks.

Next day we picked Rupert up from Rois's friend Marion who had looked after him for the day. It would be Christmas in a couple of days, so we had to do a bit of shopping for that. We were going to spend it with Gretta and Rob.

I had figured out a handy way of getting back to Copenhagen. The easiest would be for us to fly to Amsterdam, then get the train up to Copenhagen. We'd leave a couple of weeks into January. I'd leave the van up with Harry Rynhart, the dad of Rois's friend.

We spent a quiet few weeks at Laburnum Lodge. We didn't go out much but friends would call in, stay for dinner and a few beers, so it was a nice time. We were getting to know each other properly, getting used to our little family.

24

Finally, the day came and we were on the plane. We had three seats together, so Rupert had the window seat. At that time they still served a breakfast on short morning flights, so that was a distraction for a while. We landed in Schiphol and made our way to the train station where we had to wait for the afternoon train to Copenhagen. It was cold – it had been snowing in Amsterdam.

It would be a long train journey, a night-time journey up through Germany. When we got to the German border the train stopped for passport checks. There were armed soldiers on the platforms and someone being led away at gunpoint. Sometime in the middle of the night Rois went to get some food heated for Rupert, but was refused. She was told she wasn't allowed to leave the carriage we were in and was turned back by an armed guard. It seemed quite a hostile place. At the top of Germany the train went on to the ferry, then into Denmark and on to Copenhagen in the early morning.

Here we were in Copenhagen at last. We got a taxi to Fiskegade and carried everything up the three flights of stairs and fell into bed, exhausted.

We would need to get a few things for the kitchen. There was a shop just around the corner that had new and second-hand stuff. There was a three-ring hob and a small oven. The fridge was okay and had a small freezer part. The apartment belonged to Copenhagen Council. I couldn't put it in my name because there was another one in my name across town, a bigger two-bedroom apartment. This one was in Merete's name – Butch's partner. They said every second row of these buildings was to be taken down within two years, so the rent was very cheap.

My old bike was still out the back, with flat tyres. If I pumped it up and squirted oil on it, it would be alright. It was only a fifteen- or twenty-minute walk from there to the town hall anyhow.

There were a good few people around with kids around Rupert's age: Pat and Jytte, who had little Johan, then there was Merete, Butch and their kid, Joel, and Reinhart and Marilyn with Ena, who lived upstairs, and Kirsty who also had a little girl.

Over the next week or so we met up with Reinhart and Marilyn and Ena, and Butch and Merete and Joel. Merete took Rois out to sort out her residency papers and identity papers for herself and Rupert. It would be pretty cold for a while there. It didn't really warm up till round the end of May. There could still be a good bit of snow. Rupert would need some warm clothes.

I went over to the shipyard to see Søren Petersen, and he said I could start on Monday morning; my job was still there. It was back to the early starts though – I'd have to get up around five o'clock in the morning, go to bed around ten or half ten. I'd soon get used to it again. I decided I'd look out for a *knallert* – that's what they call a moped. I'd use the bike for a while, and the bus.

The people in the shops around our area were all very helpful; none of them had much English but they would tell you the Danish word for whatever you were pointing at. They were little independent shops like the bakery and the kiosk on the corner, and the "Ostman" who sold wonky fruit and vegetables, and cheese so ripe it ran down the window on a hot day. They would all give Rupert little treats whenever he was with us in the shop.

Monday morning, I got up early, starting work in the shipyard that morning. I had a quick cup of coffee, said goodbye to Rois and Rupert, and cycled from one side of the city to the other, along the shortcut through Christiania. Nothing much had changed at the shipyard – it had only been three months since I'd been working there. I hoped I'd be back with the same lads. It'd be strange to see them all back in the yard. I went up to Søren Petersen's office. I had the same work number, so just had to hand in the certificate and get my tools. I got my stuff and went down to the building dock. I saw one or two of the lads.

"Hi, Erik. Hi, Ole. Yeah, I'm back, back to stay now – have my wife and the baby with me."

"Cool! You are working with us again?"

"Yeah, well Søren said to me I'd be back in the building dock. I prefer it here anyhow. Still pretty cold and shitty alright. Wasn't that great in Ireland either. Yeah, I got married just before Christmas."

"Oh yeah, you did say you'd be back. See you at lunchtime."

I was put working on the upper deck, back on the vertical welding for a while. I'd sit on the edge of the scaffold all day and weld. It was good to see the lads again. They were moving something out of the main hall: you could hear the bells, the cranes moving. Looking over towards Malmo, the boats were going back and forward all day. It looked like they were up on a set of skis. I'd take Rois and Rupert over some day: I think it took about half an hour or less on the flyboat … There went the hooter, lunchtime. They'd be like ants coming out of the tanks and off the boat, over to the row of tractors and trailers, then off we went up to the big canteen.

"Hi, Erik, you still got the allotment going?"

"Yeah, I started back in it only a week ago. So, you got married?"

"I did! We had a great day for the wedding, nearly twenty degrees. It was an amazing day actually – wouldn't get a better one in the summer. Just had family, a few friends, right craic! Yeah, you would have enjoyed it, plenty of beer, wine, spirits. No, no schnapps! We're Irish – plenty of whiskey! Yeah, sure, when we all get settled in we'll drop over."

They were still on about the thirty-five-hour week. The marching would all start in a month or two. I would definitely be into it. Three o'clock in the afternoon, the first day was over and it had been alright. Bit cool but not raining.

We'd be settling there for a year or two anyway, seeing how it went. I've worked in a good few places in Europe, but I'll tell you one thing, I've never worked with such nice guys as in the shipyard. The Danes are good people – they like a beer, they've a great sense of humour. I'd never get the hang of the language, but I had enough to get by. I used to know more. The older guys in the shipyard didn't speak English but that was okay, I still got on with them. The younger people had a certain amount of it. Lads around forty or that wouldn't have had it then, but now they all learn it in school. In the summertime the population of Copenhagen doubles with tourists. It's a nice city. I'd rather have it any day than London – easier going. Amsterdam's a bit too hectic as well. I've said it before, but I'll say it again, we made our first trip to Denmark in 1972 by accident. We'd left Bray and were heading up through Germany when we saw a sign for Copenhagen, so many kilometres, so we kept driving, got a boat to what I now know as Sjealand, ended up in Copenhagen, and found our way to Greencamp sleep-in. At that time we couldn't stay in Denmark because Ireland hadn't joined the EEC, but that changed in '73 and I'd been going back there for a couple of years and now I was living and working there with one of the best jobs you could get.

I picked a good moped. Once it had pedals you could go in the cycle lane. The insurance was fifty kroner a year and I didn't need anything else – that was only about a fiver in our money. A fill a week would do and it only held about five litres, so it'd only cost about two kroner a week to run. I had a helmet, leather jacket and gloves – that's all I would need.

I would have to go to the tax office some day in the next week. There were a load of forms to fill out, to send money to Ireland. Rois's mother would have to fill them out in the bank in Bray. We could send between sixty and eighty pounds a week, tax free. It had to be to an adult dependant who was not a relation of mine. Butch had explained it all to me. Gretta could keep some for herself and transfer the rest into our account. We'd be able to save a good bit that way and save on my tax. The Danish tax was pretty high. I didn't know anything about the social welfare system there, as I never was out of work. I didn't know anything about it in Ireland either.

I wouldn't have a car in Copenhagen; I had a Danish driving licence alright, and I could borrow a car if I needed it. Cars were insured in Denmark, not the drivers. They weren't cheap either – cars or insurance. Big Johan had said he'd give me a lend of his

Citroën Dyane anytime. The old camper van was still in Christiania anyway. Clob was talking about selling it, but it was fairly worn out by now anyhow. It had a lot of miles on it.

It was the start of a new week and my first day out on the moped; the weather was pretty good, but it was still quite dark in the mornings. The journey would be a lot quicker – fifteen or twenty minutes, as I could use the cycle path. The road out to the shipyard wasn't too bad. I wouldn't be going through Christiania on the moped. In work that day, all talk was about the thirty-five-hour week we were looking for. Time flew there when you were welding, and we were welding for at least six hours out of the eight. You could be on your knees, you could be standing up or you could be down in a tank. There was a good difference between the shipbuilders and the welders though we could both do quite a bit of each other's job. I was welding the main floor sections on the upper decks: you'd hammer them in places, get them even – there were tons of wedges and plates.

Rois and Rupert had settled in well. The odd day, they would go over to Butch and Merete's, so he could play with Joel – they were more or less the same age. Other days Rois would put him in the baby backpack and either walk or get a bus and go exploring the city. The evenings were getting longer and it was a bit warmer. "You could have a good summer here," I told her. "Couple of years we had great summers. Ah, sure, we're only fifteen minutes from the centre. Yeah, I'll take Rupert down to the park. He's walking now anyhow, not very quick, but he's walking. I'll take the pushchair out. He's wrapped up alright. There are always people out here walking dogs and kids."

I was putting away a good bit of money. In three weeks' time we were going to have that first march, on a Friday afternoon. Copenhagen Porcelain were coming in on it. They'd a big strike there too. We all raised money for it. They were in the square nearly every day painting paper plates, and people were buying them to support the strike. It got very political in the yard. Everything was fine there – conditions, pay, the whole thing was fairly well organised. When I got back to the shipyard after my trip to Ireland, there had been money there that I hadn't taken from the previous holiday time, and there was a fairly big bonus system on the ships if we got them finished on time.

Rois and I would go out sometimes on the weekends. Reinhart or Big Johan would mind Rupert for a few hours. We'd go down to Huset or ramble around the pedestrian street. Sometimes we went for food in the Truck Stop. We'd go over on Saturdays to Christiania and take a walk around. There were hundreds of people there now; it had been open for nearly five years. There were a lot of good places: stove repairing, old cars, couple of good restaurants, candle-making workshops, tie dying; there were record shops, clothes stalls, you could buy hash and grass. You could probably get other things too.

The day of the march came: we carried banners and posters about the thirty-five-hour week and we had the flags flying. It was a good walk from the shipyard. It was a right crowd – you wouldn't be long getting fifteen hundred together from both sides: porcelain and shipyard workers. There was very little police presence there, but no trouble was expected. We were only asking for a shorter working week. It might never happen, but you get nowhere without trying. There were one or two more of those marches planned for different times in the summer. It wasn't that loud: just a few people shouting, waving the banners, drinking beer. We'd all be gone in an hour and a half anyhow.

Summer came with a heatwave and soaring temperatures across Europe. A shortage of insects brought a plague of ladybirds to Denmark: they arrived in their millions, descending on the ship's deck as we were welding. We couldn't avoid burning them. Rois and Rupert were on a bus out to the beach at Charlottenlund and the driver had to turn on the windscreen wipers so he could see where he was going. They were so hungry, they would nip you if they landed on you. The ground was covered in dead ladybirds, it was so strange. There were free concerts in the park almost every weekend – great atmosphere, families with little kids running around playing. Everybody half naked – except for us: we're Irish, never see that kind of sun!

Work carried on, but it was tough in that heat because you

couldn't take your overalls off, or any of the other gear – hard hats, ear muffs, goggles, gloves, boots. The overalls were very dark purple; everyone wore the same. They were talking about changing the shifts around, so you could work in the evening if you didn't want to work on the hot days. I never got used to it though. I tried it once on a night shift, but I switched back after two days. I couldn't do it. We got salt tablets on the hot days, one or two extra beers as well. There was already extra Carlsberg and Tuborg coming into the canteen. Back in Ireland, eight months before in Walsh's, they wouldn't believe me, that you could drink on the job in Denmark. I wouldn't drink that much, but some fellas would. We also made tea on the deck. There was a gas ring in the big box we had – great for soup in the winter. Our boss didn't mind, once the work was done.

The whole idea with the team was to keep ahead, so when they came to fill in the rows of weld after us, we weren't in their way, we'd be gone. The decks were hundreds of metres long, made of close to 30mm thick plate, with seven large hatches. Hundreds of men came down in the morning but if you looked around you'd only see four or five, until the lunch break hooter blew. Then they came out of all the holds in the boat and all the sections – at least two hundred men standing on the side of the building dock. Safety is safety, everything had to be right. They had a terrible accident one night; one of the women crane drivers was killed. They had two tower cranes on rails, which were meant to be turned facing the big building hall when the big crane came. She hadn't moved out of the way quickly enough. There were very few accidents, but it did happen.

I was still driving the moped to work. One thing you wouldn't do there is go through a red light – the speed of the cars in the centre: make a mistake and you'd be flattened! I got knocked off the bike one evening and had a big bruise on my hip. A woman drove straight out in front of me, I slid along the ground, wallop! I didn't ride the bike for a day after that. I rang them up at work and told them I had a bad back. I suppose your hip's not far off your back anyway. I had only taken one or two sick days. I was black and blue for a week, but the old clog boot saved my foot, even if it cracked at the heel. They've a fleece-lined leather boot top and a wooden sole on them. They're a great yoke in the bad weather. I wore them on the bike all the time. Some eejits go around with T-shirts on and only runners on their feet. If you hit the ground at forty or fifty kilometres an hour, you'd know all about it.

Things were changing in Denmark. Quite a few people were moving in because of the common market, the EEC. The Irish got on well in the shipyard: there were a few of us there by that summer. About a year before I had worked in a stainless-steel place, on one of the industrial estates. It was quite good but the money wasn't near what I was getting in Burmeister and Wain. It was a different type of work though.

It was a couple of weeks now to our holidays. I was looking forward to getting out of there for a week. Rois's brother Rob was due to arrive a day or two before we went on holidays. He was coming for about ten days. Johan said we could have the car, all we'd have to do was check the oil and put petrol in it. It was air cooled. We were planning a nice camping trip on Jutland. The weather wouldn't change – it was red hot.

Sometimes I took Rupert a round in the backpack on the moped. No one said anything – not if you were driving safely – just go a bit slower. We'd go over to Butch and Merete's so he could play with Joel. Marilyn and Ena had gone back to Canada so there was only Joel and little Johan still around for him to play with.

Earlier, we had spent a weekend in the countryside with Butch, Merete and Joel. Her aunt had a house out near a forest. When we were driving up there we passed lots of gateways with fruit and vegetables for sale. Whatever you grew in your garden, you weighed it up and calculated what it was worth and sent it in to the government. It would be deducted out of sick pay or a pension. I thought it was a joke at first but some people do it! Quite a strange one – how do you make up the time and the seeds and the work? It was a mad idea. We went for long walks in the forest, a lovely area but quite flat – not a decent hill in sight!

Another time, Butch, Merete and Joel went on holidays to Czechoslovakia, so we spent the week or so house sitting their place in Brumleby. It was cool having a bigger place with a garden. The weather was so good we set up a table outside for our meals – it was nearly like being on holiday, except I still had to go into work.

Rob was flying in on the Friday, so we had plenty of beers in the fridge and there'd be a bit of craic for the weekend. We'd probably head over to Jutland on Saturday. It would only be a couple of hours' drive and a ferry. Johan said he'd leave the car round on Saturday morning.

On Friday Rois went out to the airport to meet Rob while I finished up at work. At three o'clock I was off now for a week – deadly! If I went through Christiania they always moaned about the moped so I stuck to the road. I pulled up and got a hot dog and sat in the square for half an hour. It was pretty busy, more tourists there than Danes now. The pedestrian street was always packed. I was thinking about the first year I arrived there, 1972, the time I attempted Irish dancing on the street! A Turkish/Irish guy I had met would play a silver flute and I would dance … we did it more for a dare than anything. Ah, we collected a few bob, then got chased by the police – busking wasn't allowed. Anyway, with that daydream the hotdog was finished, so I went on home. Rois, Rupert and Rob came in soon after.

Next morning Johan brought the car around and we packed up: water container, sleeping bags, tents, a few clothes – we'd keep the hats on. I was going to be fully dressed on the beach – if I wore shorts, I'd get the legs burned off me! We'd use the sea for a fridge for the beer, in a bag. Early Sunday morning, we were packed and ready to go. There was a quarter tank of fuel: enough to get out of Copenhagen. I'd pop another fifteen litres in it then. I had to remember what side to drive on: stick to the right – roundabouts were confusing! In fifty minutes we were at Funen, then onto the ferry. There was another shipyard down there. They built oil tankers – supertankers. It was the biggest one in Denmark.

Jutland was nicer up the top end. We spotted a nice piece of beach, drove down to a nice green spot and parked up. The sun was still shining. We pitched the tents and shoved the gear and sleeping bags inside. We got the beers and put them in the water. The fire was going well. We put a bit of mesh over the rocks, put a bit of oil and paprika on the ribs and rolled the sausage in it too.

With a couple of beers, lettuce and tomatoes, it was a good meal. You can't have a barbeque without smoke but there were some people looking at us a bit suspiciously. A couple of Germans came over to say there was too much smoke from the fire, but it'd be gone out in an hour.

We had days on the beach, paddling and building sandcastles with Rupert, then driving around exploring the countryside. It was mostly farmland; in one place we came across a big field of hemp, which was quite unusual for that time. Rob and I checked it out, but it wasn't the kind you could smoke! Long sunny days, warm nights, good food and beer – great holiday! When I was back at work Rob and Rois would bring Rupert to the Tivoli Gardens and different parks around the city. Eventually he had to go home but he promised to come back in the winter.

We did a bit of work around the apartment: painting, cleaning the oven and servicing the *kakkelovn*. The kitchen was looking a bit better now, everything was blue. I thought the fridge was wonky, but it was okay. It only had a small freezer section in it and one big fish I had filled it up – a big cod. I brought it home from work on the bus, in my canvas bag – its head sticking out one end, its tail out the other. I got some looks!

Erik from work had a party for his fortieth birthday, so we got the bus up to his apartment with Rupert. We got over to Erik's about six and spent a few hours there. There was a good crowd there and it was a nice big apartment. There was a huge buffet spread out, so we all sat round the table, helping ourselves to whatever we wanted. There were several types of fish: smoked eels, herrings, prawns; there was chicken and meatballs and salads from his allotment. It was a fantastic spread. I recognised a good few people there – nearly all the welding team from the shipyard. In between each course we had to toast the birthday boy, with schnapps of course! *"Skol!"* and knock it back. There was no shortage of beer. By nine o'clock we were ready to leave – had to get Rupert home to bed. We got out into the fresh air and couldn't find the bus stop! We had to get a taxi. Great party though.

Gretta came to visit in September. Rupert was delighted; he hadn't seen her for almost ten months but he hadn't forgotten his granny. Johan drove them up to Helsingør one day, to Hamlet's Castle, then they called into Päivi on the way back. That must have been some session, Gretta teaching Päivi how to make Irish coffee! Seems it took several goes, so they were a little worse for wear by the time they arrived home. I had to be up early for work so was not impressed with all the racket!

Another evening was a bit more cultured – Rois took Gretta to the Royal Danish ballet to see Swan Lake. We went to the geological museum where they had a piece of rock brought back from the moon. Amazing when you thought about where it came from – it didn't look like anything special.

Gretta went home and then we were into the real winter, getting chillier in the evenings and the days starting to get shorter. Once you got into October that would be it. By the middle of October rumours were flying in the shipyard about loads of guys getting let off, but I got a good rise in my wages so you wouldn't know what was going on. We still had three ships left to build, which meant only about seven or eight months' work unless they got new orders. We had nothing planned yet other than I would be working there for the next year anyhow. The long hot summer was just over, so we'd see what the autumn brought – darkness anyhow.

The children's allowance was paid quarterly at the beginning of each season, so we went out and got Rupert kitted out with quilted ski suits and warm clothes and a pair of little fleece-lined leather boots, getting ready for winter. I got the stove working right too. They were a bit tricky to light but worked really well.

It was getting tough in the shipyard. On the colder days we made soup on the two-ring cooker, to keep the chill away. Our boss in the building dock was sound. He'd only say to enjoy it. It was all go at that time: they were pushing it to get that ship together. There was the one that was nearly finished, this one was half done and there was one more after that. There were rumours around that there were no more orders coming in, and that it wasn't only our shipyard.

Rois and I would often get Big Johan to babysit and we'd head out to the cinema. Most English and American films were subtitled rather than dubbed so it wasn't a problem. There was also an arthouse cinema in Huset. Butch told us they were showing a movie about Joe

Hill, the union organiser, so we all went to see that one: what a great story!

Our friend Pat called over. He and Jytte and Little Johan were going to spend Christmas with his family in Wales and they wanted us to mind their apartment for a few weeks. It would mean taking on their caretaking jobs, but we didn't mind. It was a couple of weeks in December and the snow would be down. It was a tough enough place to maintain: we'd have to wash the stairs back and front, over four or five storeys, and keep the footpath along the front of the building clean and clear of snow. It was a nice apartment though, near the park – handy for walking with Rupert.

We were waiting to hear what was happening with the shipyard. The latest rumours were they would be laying off at least a thousand in the next six months. There was a cold spell coming in and the older guys in the yard said it was going to be tough enough. But the Danes were well used to clearing the streets – as soon as the snow started the snow blowers would be out, so it never got a chance to build up on the roads. Every building had someone responsible for keeping the pathways salted and clear of snow and ice. Wear the right gear and it would be fine.

Christmas was only a few weeks away, so I started building an F1 racing car – a blue Ferrari – for Rupert. I did it on the weekends. It was all wood: plywood reinforced with a timber frame. We could pull it along with a rope. It was coming along well and was nearly all saved timber. I got a sheet of plywood for nothing – it was split – and a man in Christiania had loads of damaged timber that he'd give to you for a few kroner. I'd glue it and screw it. It was the same colour blue as the cot.

By the end of November, a regular thing at work in the morning was to scrape the snow off the deck. They had heaters in for drying up where you were welding. You had a little hut over you but, beJaysus, it was cold! Steel gets very cold. We were using about fifty amps higher than in the summer. At least the lockers had a bit of heating in them, so we'd have dry clothes the next day – overalls, boots, hats and extra socks. You wouldn't last too long without them. Down in the shipyard with the sea beside you, you got any breeze going and you'd think you were going to die from the cold!

They wanted to get this ship out of the dock by the middle of January. It would be around the far side of the harbour for about six months, being finished. The next one would be the last of the six. As far as I knew, there were still no orders in.

We were looking forward to Christmas anyhow. Rob was coming back over for the new year. Rupert's racing car was just about finished. The whole city was starting to light up for Christmas – shop windows, streets, everywhere. I had only spent one other Christmas there and I'd been on my own, more or less – just a few friends. We'd make an effort this year. Christmas this year would be for Rupert. I'd be off from the twenty-second, for nine days. I'd do a bit of shopping. I reckoned I'd get a big duck from the butcher's and a nice lump of ham, a crate of beer and a few bottles of wine.

By the time we moved into Pat and Jytte's apartment, the snow was lying a couple of inches deep in the mornings. I had to scrape the snow off the path before I left for work, spread the salt and put the shovel and brush back in the storeroom in the yard. Then I'd get in to work and get into the good boots, good socks, heavily padded trousers, overalls and a fur-lined jacket – everything you needed was provided. I'd shovel more snow off the deck and use an air hose to clean off the block for welding. The rain could be worse than snow, but there was a little mobile hut over you, so you weren't outside that much. It had little wheels on it and you pulled it along as you were welding.

The racing car was nearly finished. I had it all undercoated and had found a nice steering wheel. All the wheels were the same size – I'd got pram type-wheels. It looked good. I'd paint it up in the next few days. We stored it in Reinhart's. It was a tough situation, as he was on his own – Marilyn had gone back to Canada with the baby. It was tough for him.

We'd been trying for a while to have another baby and it worked. Rois was pregnant, due around the end of June. We were over the moon now and making a few plans again. We got word we'd have to be out of our flat around the end of January. They sent out designs for the upgrade they were planning for the area. It looked alright: one section of each block would be taken down and the courtyards would be planted with green areas and flowers. The side we were on, Fiskegade, was to be demolished. We arranged with Big Johan to stay at his place as he would be back in Amsterdam so we could house sit for him. He lived on the next street down – Jagtvej.

Christmas Day was freezing. After dinner we took Rupert out for a walk in the park with his new racing car, but it was minus fourteen degrees Celsius, so we didn't stay long! There was a phone in that apartment, so we made a few phone calls home and Clob's mother phoned us, just checking he was okay, so I promised to keep an eye on him. Rob came over for a week in the new year and had fun playing with Rupert in the snow. Holidays over and back to work – frost in the shipyard every morning now, sometimes snow.

As word spread that they were laying off more than a thousand from the shipyard, people came over from Malmo looking to recruit workers for the nuclear power plant they were building, offering all kinds of jobs, and money. But no, I'd rather stay where I was. There was another company that made machines that had something to do with breweries in Denmark and then brought them over to Brazil to put together. It was only in the ship-building area that there wasn't much work – it was happening all over. There was to be a huge meeting in the shipyard in the union hall one Friday. At the beginning of the year they always had one. I had missed the last one, but I wouldn't miss this one.

I'd made a lot of good friends in the shipyard – a very good friend in Erik. It was a bit of a job now shovelling snow off the deck before you started welding – it was minus fourteen most days, sometimes as low as minus eighteen Celcius. It was quite strange welding a boat right beside the Baltic, but that's where we were. In the morning coming in to work, it was pitch dark. You could see the lights of the shipyard in Malmo. I was working with nearly all Danes, the odd Pole, a few from somewhere else. The six on our team were all Danes and we got on very well together, all *camarades*, a lot of solidarity between everyone. The old men who'd been there all their working lives were talking about 1947, talking about people riding bicycles and driving cars across to Sweden, across the frozen sea. Mad! I remember my mother in Ireland talking about '47 – the sea around Greystones froze round the edges, you couldn't go outside, and there would be only a fire for heating the house, and no electricity. Things had come on a lot by 1977. This was my second winter in the shipyard too. I was still riding the moped in and out, just taking it easy – especially in the mornings. It was cold at six in the morning alright – fuckin' freezing! We'd to be out of the apartment the day after the big union meeting. It wasn't too bad as we were just moving to the next street, to Johan's apartment, but we had made our minds up that we would go back to Ireland in March.

Friday morning, the meeting was starting at twelve, just after lunch. We'd get something to eat then go up to the hall. We needn't have bothered though, because the union had laid on more food than you could eat, free beer, schnapps. Oh no – not too much of that! After an hour everyone looked like they were wrecked, shouting about the world's best shipbuilders and welders. Holy Jaysus! I was tanked myself.

"You all right, Erik?"

"You don't look too good, Tony."

"Ah, I'll make it home. Another schnapps, yeah, one more beer. Enough prawns, no more, fuckin' kill ya!"

That was enough of that. Another beer or two. Well, no one knew what was coming in the post. Lot of fellas getting rowdy in there too, including me …

"What d'you say, Erik?"

"You're not riding the fuckin' bike home."

"Yeah, I am."

"No, you're not! Get a fuckin' taxi, man!"

There were lads bangin' the tables, broken glasses. They said by the next week we'd all have got a letter. Three thousand men! There were more rumours about Copenhagen porcelain. Things were changing.

"Ah, Erik! I know I'm rowdy, shouldn't have kicked you in the leg either. Fuck!"

They put me in a taxi anyhow. Every time I moved in the back of the taxi the driver went faster. I think it cost about 150 kroner less, he went so fast in places. Never seen a taxi driver so happy to get rid of a customer! With a helmet in me hand, I got into the house and fell down the stairs into the basement. I was down there for hours. I eventually made my way up to our apartment, knocked on the door and fell in. Rois said I was grey. Rupert ran and hid! She put me in his bed with a basin beside my head. We were supposed to be moving out in the morning, but I couldn't do anything. I was very sick – dying! Don't know how I found the door. I swore I'd never drink schnapps again. Poisoned with alcohol!

An Irish guy we had gotten to know – Mark StClair, nice fella – came around on the Saturday and he and Rois carried all our stuff round to Johan's, while I nursed the toilet bowl.

I was convinced that was it, I would be told my job was gone on Monday, along with the other rowdy heads. I wasn't even sure if I'd make it in … I couldn't stand up as it was!

But on Monday morning I went to work, convinced I'd have my walking papers that evening. Instead, when I got there I was greeted with shouts of "G'mor'n, Cassius Clay"! It seems I had put the fists up and offered to take them all on one at a time if they didn't let me ride my moped home! I wasn't the worst though. Apparently there was war after I left. The hall was wrecked. Jesus Christ, they gave out too much schnapps – everyone was completely wrecked! It looked like a bomb had hit the hall. Fellas fell over, broken arms, fingers, cuts – it was mental! But as I was apologising to Erik again for the bruised leg he told me there'd be nothing about it because the union hall was our hall, not the shipyard's so it was all off site, nothing had happened in the shipyard. That was a relief!

"Erik, man, I love Denmark! Copenhagen's a great city. Yous are great people to work with and yous are whores to drink as well. Ah, Ireland's different, well, you know we live up in the mountains when I'm at home. Which you don't have any. I think the biggest rock you have is the one the mermaid's sitting on."

I drove the moped home that evening, it was very quiet in the yard. All heads down working away. A lot of people expecting the worst. Not to mention the savage hangovers being nursed!

The following Saturday night was Rois's birthday party. Rupert and Little Johan were going to stay with Jytte's parents for the night.

287

We all piled in to Big Johan's Dyane and headed for Christiania to Electric Ladyland. There were a good few people around, Rois – being pregnant – wasn't drinking so we all made up for her. Dancing on the tables, even the dogs were dancing! Great music and the craic was mighty! We crawled home around six in the morning, passing the bars closed for the hour for cleaning up, the hard-core drinkers sitting outside with a crate of beer, waiting patiently for them to re-open at seven.

The Monday after that it was very quiet in the canteen in the morning, the odd one having coffee. Night shifts having a beer before going home – couple of hundred on the night shift. The shipyard operated round the clock but the biggest shift was in the daytime, the night shifts were smaller.

The letter from the shipyard finally arrived.

"Dear Comrade, happy to inform you that you are not one of the workers being let go. In the next year we are laying off at least half the workforce (about 1500)."

That was the gist of it. Wow! That was something, to go in to work the next day and every second person you met would have the letter to say they were finished. I sat back and thought about that. I was actually amazed, but then our team was one of the best, I suppose. Would the whole team be left? There were always one or two guys working behind or in front of us. Erik was on the tanks with me, I was up on the top though. A lot of our work had to undergo ultrasonic sound tests, and we very seldom got any of them wrong – another reason I was still there. Still there was loads of shit going on in my head about it. I still hadn't figured out what I was going to do. I was twenty-seven that year and Rois was twenty-three.

The next day I went straight into the canteen. There were a good few of the lads sitting around.

"Hi Erik, get your letter?"

"Yeah, I'm being laid off."

"Fuck!"

"It says another three or four months though."

"Mine said I'm staying."

"Very good. There's two of our team going."

We went down to work for a while. There wouldn't be much done that day; there was more than a cold breeze in the yard now. Half the main hall were going to go, half the finishing dock, half the building dock – fuckin' hell! Phased out over a year. We met a lot of unhappy men that day, lots of them that I thought would be safe. When you talk to nearly a hundred men and half them had a tough letter, it was rough, even when I didn't know most of them personally, just knew them from working.

When we headed back to Ireland in the spring, I'd be due a lot of money out of the shipyard – holiday money and such. It was a percentage of your wages. I had a good bit in the bank there, and in Ireland. There was a bonus scheme on the ships if they were finished on time, but if it wasn't finished by the time I left, they'd send it on.

I went to see Søren Petersen the day after I got the letter to give notice that I was leaving the shipyard in March. I thought maybe someone else could have my job, but he told me it didn't work like that.

I would miss the yard, the comradeship, the craic in the canteen. I liked the job, but it's not all life. I had fully intended to go back to the Wicklow hills and having a second baby on the way made my mind up. We'd find a place somewhere. We had a small party for Rupert's birthday: himself and Joel, little Johan, and Kirsten came with her little girl. Pat and Jytte made him a little jacket with some of Big Johan's velvet. There were more presents and a cake with two candles.

For our journey home, I had arranged with Big Johan to get a lift to Amsterdam in the Dyane. We would stay with his family for the weekend. I wanted to buy a Citroën, so he would help me find a good one. At first I was a bit pissed off about everything, but now I was looking forward to it – the trip, the next big adventure. We'd spend a couple of days in Amsterdam and a few days in Paris.

I didn't expect to be working in a place like the shipyard again. I'd miss all the lads, all the close friends I had made there. I had a few drinks with them in the canteen on the Thursday evening before we left. I said goodbye to Søren Petersen. We were all packed ready to go.

It was a good drive to Amsterdam but Johan said the Dyane would be well able for it. It was usually laden to the ground with piles of velvet. I dont think he'd put that much in it before. There was just about enough room for Rois and Rupert in the back, so we told Johan he could keep anything we left behind. All we were taking was personal belongings. We headed for the border, got the boat over to Germany, then a full day's drive to Amsterdam.

We stayed in Johan's for a night or two, met some of his brothers and one of his sisters. He and I went looking for a car and we found a red 2CV4, less than three years old. It had been damaged but repaired properly. I took it for a drive and bought it for 950 guilders. I got the insurance sorted at the same time, so everything was ready. We packed it up in the morning early. It had plenty of space in the boot area. I drove around the block a few times in it to get used to it. It had a four-speed gearbox. We thanked Johan for everything, promised to keep in touch and we would have him come over when we were settled.

25

I HAD NEVER DRIVEN IN PARIS. IT'D be alright though, Rois was a good navigator. We went through Belgium and on to Paris. It was cold, but not as bad as Denmark. We went round the ring road in Paris till we found a way in, then into Montmartre. We stayed at the Roma Hotel, close to Sacré Coeur Cathedral. The hotel didn't do food but there was a Moroccan restaurant next door that was very welcoming, especially to Rupert. I think they were both run by the same family. We spent a few days there – a kind of honeymoon.

I had been in Paris before, but I had never looked at much. My French is useless. We went to the Louvre to see the Mona Lisa; there weren't huge crowds so we didn't have to queue. At the Eiffel Tower we could only go halfway up; the top section was closed. It was high enough though – it was very misty but you could still see quite a lot from there. People were tiny when you looked down, cars as well. We had a picnic in the Tuileries Gardens and visited Notre Dame Cathedral. I had never noticed the heads up there before – angels and devils – or heard the story of the hunchback of Notre Dame. What an amazing building!

It was a nice few days with a lot to see, but eventually we had to pack the bags. I wanted to leave by ten in the morning. It would be a long crossing – about twenty-two hours – so we had booked a cabin. We had our breakfast in the restaurant next door, said our farewells and would have to find our way to Le Havre. We'd be lucky to get fifty miles per hour out of the car with the stuff we had laden on it, but we'd be there in plenty of time. There wasn't that much traffic. The car was going alright for our first decent trip in it.

We got to the port in plenty of time, paid the fare and drove onto the ferry. It was dear enough – about thirty-five pounds one way. They said the weather was going to be bad, so we were very happy we had a cabin with bunk beds and a toilet. Rois took the top bunk and Rupert and I claimed the bottom. We left the bags there, locked the cabin and went to the restaurant to have some dinner. We would be in Ireland by the next afternoon.

After a very rough twenty-four-hour crossing, we finally landed in Rosslare and were grateful to be on solid ground. We had never been so happy to reach the end of a journey. We took a breath, pointed the car north and headed for the Wicklow hills to begin the next big adventure.

Acknowledgements

I have many people to thank for their help in putting all of this together, so in no particular order:

My heartfelt thanks to all of the amazing, friendly, generous and interesting people we met while travelling, who shared companionship, food, shelter and so much more; Also to the many friends made in Greencamp and afterwards in Copenhagen who made Denmark such a welcoming place.

Thanks to my co-workers in Burmeister and Wain who showed me the meaning of true comradeship.

Most of all to my now grown-up children, Rupert, Johan, Ruth and Bosco who have listened to these stories for years and have encouraged me to get them written down, and to Rois, my very patient wife and partner in all things, for all of the hours spent transcribing, editing, prodding my memory and helping me to keep it real; my unending love and gratitude to you all.

Thanks are also due to Julian Vignoles, another Kilmacanogue native and author, for invaluable advice, encouragement and pointing me in the right direction.

Finally but by no means least, I have to acknowledge a huge debt of gratitude to Chenile Keogh and her team at Kazoo Independent Publishing Services Ltd, for excellent advice, encouragement and guidance every step of the way.